Bob + Mar...

Thanks for your support over the years. I hope this help you to eat the "Free Lunch."

Mike

JACKASS INVESTING

Don't do it. Profit from it.

by
Michael Dever

This book has also been released under the title "*Exploiting the Myths: Profiting from Wall Street's misguided beliefs*"

ISBN: 978-0-9835040-0-9

Library of Congress Catalog Number: 2011905243

Cover Design by AuthorSupport.com
Cover Photography by ThinkStock.com
Figure Graphics by Kerry Gibbons
Interior Design by Nick DeRose

For information please contact:

Ignite LLC
381 Brinton Lake Road
Thornton, PA 19373
www.IgnitePublications.com
484.356.1028

To the memory of my dad, Jim Dever, who measured wealth in the happiness he brought to his family and others, and who always made it clear to my mother, brothers, sisters and me that we were his most valuable investments.

Table of Contents

INTRODUCTION

This book should not be controversial, but it will be. That is because investing, which should be a rational pursuit, is not. I am sure this statement will raise more than a few eyebrows, especially from those in the main-stream financial media and most academics, who have spent their careers trying to prove the rationality of markets and who continue to instruct people to take unnecessary risks with their portfolios (the very definition of Jackass Investing). It is my intent for you to benefit from my experience and, after reading this book, avoid creating a "Poor-folio" – a poorly-constructed portfolio that is exposed to far greater risk than is necessary.

Experience has taught me a lot. I first witnessed the mass delusion suffered by the average individual when I set up a commodity fund in 1984. Despite the fact that the person whom I hired to manage that fund had a solid eight year audited track record that showed strong performance with low risk, just about every prospective investor was backing off. Why? ... Because the fund traded in commodities. As one potential investor told me at the time, "I would never invest in commodities. They're too risky." When I asked what he would invest in, he said "only blue-chip stocks - like IBM." This was mid-1984. IBM stock had just dropped 20% from its peak price eight months earlier. The manager of the fund I was offering had never been down more than 10% over his entire eight-year history. When I contrasted this with the fact that IBM was down more than twice that in just eight months, the only response I got was for him to reiterate "I'd never invest in commodities. They're too risky." I knew there was a story behind that irrational behavior; it just took me 25 years to finally put it down on paper. I learned a lot from that irrational investor and many others in the years since. I've seen investment decisions, based on complete misconceptions, put into play, repeated ad

1

nauseum, and cause countless portfolio failures. But I've also learned how to turn the biased and often risky behavior of others into profit for me and my investors. One goal of this book is to enable you to do the same.

Most people begin their investment process by intentionally restricting their opportunities, eliminating many excellent options before they even start, whether they even know it or not. These self-imposed constraints are not always irrational, at least not to the person making that decision. Many institutional investors, for example, face career risk with each of their decisions. If they lose money doing what their peers do, they will usually retain their jobs. But if they lose money doing something different, they risk getting fired. But what I've observed – as being much more common – is that most people's investment decisions are not based on rational facts. They're based on myths and emotions.

Exposing investors to the truth behind those myths and revealing the facts is one of the reasons I wrote *Jackass Investing*. With its anecdotes and references to popular culture, this book is designed to comfortably provide novice investors with a plan to follow to manage their money – one that they are unlikely to encounter if they are only exposed to the conventional financial wisdom. It's also intended to provide a rational alternative to the beliefs of experienced investors who may have fallen prey to the myths; written to help you to specifically exploit some of the countless opportunities that are ignored by, and very often created by, the mass of irrational investors who litter the virtual Wall Street landscape.

Each chapter of this book is devoted to one costly myth that permeates common financial wisdom. I first describe the source of each myth, as it is often based on some level of truth, and then detail why it is a myth, and not a truth. Within each myth I break out key concepts as separate italicized paragraphs and also summarize them at the end of each chapter. I also provide definitions in call-out boxes and in a glossary at the end of the book. Many of the myths also have an "Action" associated with them. Each of these Actions is a specific "how to," often an actual trading strategy, designed to enable you to exploit the trading opportunities that arise from the risky behavior of the people who follow the myth. Because of the dynamic nature of these Actions, and my interest in keeping them updated with changing opportunities, I present them in an "Action" section on the www.JackassInvesting.com website. The intent is to provide you with a book that is not just entertaining and educational, but also a useful resource you can use to make money.

Towards that end, I have been careful to include Actions that can be used by everyone; because the reality is that improving returns for those people who have smaller portfolios is at least as important as providing an extra few million to people who manage larger portfolios. In this way *Jackass Investing* levels the playing field between the haves and will-haves.

While I specifically cover 20 myths in this book, certain themes persist from beginning to end. One is that the conventional investment advice of building a portfolio of stocks, bonds, and possibly real estate, and holding those positions for the long-term, is not only risky, but is in fact the equivalent of gambling – no different than betting on Dancing Prancer in the 5th at the track. The performance of a portfolio structured that way is far too dependent on a single set of "baseline conditions" (such as rational credit markets and available financing) to be considered "safe." Another theme is what are often considered by conventional wisdom to be "risky" investments are actually essential to producing a portfolio with reduced risk; precisely because their performance is powered by "return drivers" that are completely independent of those powering stocks and bonds.

But the most important theme of them all is the fallacy of the myth that "There is No Free Lunch." In fact there is a free lunch, a veritable free three-course buffet. It's called true portfolio diversification. By that I'm specifically not referring to the standard "60% bonds – 40% stocks" song-and-dance that is offered at every strip-mall and franchise investment firm. It's also decidedly not the "stocks, bonds, real estate" mix that you hear on every golf course from San Diego to Maine. What I am referring to is a portfolio that is powered by a diversity of return drivers. A return driver is the primary underlying condition that drives the price of a market. My experience is that most people's portfolios are driven by one, or at most a few, separate return drivers. They are most definitely not diversified. If those few return drivers become invalid, the portfolio will suffer losses...potentially extensive losses. They'll end up with a "poor-folio."

Throughout this book I reveal the return drivers underlying the typical positions held in most people's portfolios. But more importantly, I introduce many new return drivers you can use to properly diversify your portfolio. By simply learning how to identify these additional return drivers, you will be able to shift from gambling your portfolio on only one of them to becoming an "investor" by diversifying across many of them. What that also means is that the simple act of selecting stocks in a portfolio should be just one small part of any portfolio, of no more significance than any other part. By making the stock component a dominant portion of one's portfolio, we are turning investing into gambling. I address the gambling paradigm throughout this book, hand in hand with the concept of return drivers.

I find it scandalous that investment magazines and periodicals and even seminars waste so much time and thought on touting "Dream Stocks at Affordable Prices" or helping you to "Get Your Money Back" (recent headlines from a popular financial magazine). Sadly, absolutely no time is spent teaching people how to turn their well-ingrained and accepted gambling habit into functional investing. (There's nothing that identifies gambling more than the headline "Get Your Money Back!") Focusing on picking a "better" stock, but leaving your portfolio vulnerable to a single baseline condition or return driver, such as economic growth or the availability of easy credit, is like putting earrings on a pig. It's a superficial adornment that can't possibly change the nature of the animal.

In contrast, "investing" is following a systematic process that results in a truly balanced diversified portfolio whose returns are derived from a multitude of return drivers. It starts with first identifying and understanding the necessary baseline conditions and return drivers that underlie the performance of each trading strategy. A trading strategy is a combination of a system that exploits a return driver (such as the concept that earnings growth leads to higher corporate value) with a market best suited to capture the returns promised by the return driver (such as common stock). Trading strategies are then combined to create a balanced and diversified investment portfolio.

The investment process:

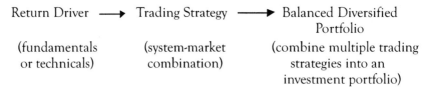

Return Driver ⟶ Trading Strategy ⟶ Balanced Diversified Portfolio

(fundamentals or technicals)   (system-market combination)   (combine multiple trading strategies into an investment portfolio)

Legions of people before us were forced to accept the myths foisted upon them. They did not have the tools available to either expose the truth or rebut the myths. Today that is unacceptable. Just as easy to find as the Blue Book price before you step onto the car lot, the facts you need to make the right decisions are readily available through the most basic forms of online research.

Databases are free or virtually free. Best yet, the tools are available that allow people to employ the results of their research and to create truly balanced diversified portfolios that earn their returns from truly differentiated return drivers. The tools are available to turn yesterday's gamblers into tomorrow's successful investors.

Finally, *Jackass Investing* is intended to put to rest the investment paradigm that has been over-preached and accepted without hesitation, despite its obvious flaws, for far too long. Moreover, my hope is that people will use the theories and practices articulated here to transform their lives and gain what every adult in the modern world dreams of and rarely achieves...financial security.

Michael Dever
Thornton, Pennsylvania
May 1, 2011

Stocks Provide
an Intrinsic Return

I t was 1923 in Berlin, Germany and after a life of work as a writer and editor;
Maximilian Bern went to the bank and withdrew more than 100,000 marks,
a lifetime of hard-earned savings. It took his entire withdrawal to buy one
single subway ticket.[1] Inflation in Germany had destroyed his entire savings. Max's
hard-luck financial story was common throughout Germany's hyper-inflationary
"Weimar Republic" period following World War I.

Walter Levy, the son of another unfortunate victim of those hard times
remembers, "My father was a lawyer and he had taken out an insurance policy in
1903, and every month he made the payments faithfully. It was a 20-year policy, and
when it came due, he cashed it in and bought a single loaf of bread."[2] In January of
1918 it took five German marks to equal one dollar, but by January 1923 the
number had risen to 18,000. But the worst was yet to come. By the end of 1923 it

---

[1] Otto Friedrich, *Before the Deluge* – A Portrait of Berlin in the 1920's (New York: Harper
& Row, 1972), 126.
[2] Adam Smith, *Paper Money* (New York: Summit Books, 1981), 57-62.

took more than four trillion marks to buy one dollar.[3] A complete debasement of the currency had taken place. Life savings were destroyed. Those German investors could never have expected that this would be the horrific result of a lifetime of work and investment.

Of course hindsight is 20/20, but if they had any idea of the disaster that was imminent, they never would have left their savings so completely exposed. But history has taught us, again and again, that when it comes to finance, the unexpected should be expected. No single

Figure 1. *Here's a definite red flag that a country is headed for a financial meltdown. A fifty million mark bank note from the Weimar Republic in 1923.*

financial system in recorded history has operated without experiencing a crisis that decimated value. It has never been a question of "if"...just a question of "when."

History repeats

It's October 2009 and Maria Adriago, a farm worker in Odzi, Zimbabwe, lays motionless in the makeshift grass house where she has lived for the past three months. The property's new owner, Mark Madiro, had evicted Maria from the farm where she had worked twelve-hour days to barely scrape by. As a result of her eviction, she was no longer able to qualify to continue receiving treatment for her breast cancer. She joins the ranks of the 100,000 other workers who also lost their jobs over the course of the previous year.[4] For the first two decades following its independence in 1980, Zimbabwe became the embodiment of social and economic success in a free African country – a shining example to the world. Its gross domestic product had seen a 5% annual growth throughout the 1980s, providing Zimbabwe's citizens with free education and relatively good access to medical care for the first time in its history. After further growth in the 1990s, this era of prosperity and high hopes came to a brutal and abrupt end in 2000 when the executive branch of the Zimbabwean government, led by President Robert Mugabe, initiated a "land reform" policy that involved the forcible taking-over

---

[3]   Costantino Bresciani-Turroni, *The Economics of Inflation* (Northampton, UK: John Dickens & Co Ltd, 1937): 335.

[4]   Tapiwa Zivira and Ndaizivei Kamoto, "Eviction a ticket to death for the sick Zimbabwean farm workers," *Citizen Journalism in Africa* (October 2, 2009).

of all white-owned commercial farms.[5] In addition to causing immediate damage to the country's newly found equilibrium, this outright theft was to cast a long-lasting financial shadow. It affected not just the wealthy commercial operators and their workers such as Maria, but the entire Zimbabwean economy. It's a great example of how a single wrong decision can destroy the wealth of an entire nation.

The commercial farmers received absolutely no compensation for their confiscated land. Of course, when they were evicted, they took with them their knowledge of farming particular to the harsh and arid conditions of Zimbabwe. In addition, the new "owners" did not receive title to the land. They were required to pay annual lease payments to the government. Because they did not hold title to the land, the new owners could not borrow from banks in order to purchase seeds or farm equipment.[6] As a result, farm production completely collapsed. More than half the vacated farms were left unused. Within two years planted acreage dropped by 75%. Farm exports, which had previously accounted for 40% of the country's exports, dropped to nearly zero. Zimbabwe was forced to rely on the generosity of other countries to prevent its people from starving. The farming industry's non-existent status led to a total collapse of the Zimbabwean industrial sector. Tractor sales, which previously had averaged 1,600 per year, fell to a pitiful eight units.[7] As lending constricted further, the banking sector was also added to the industry death toll. Banks stopped receiving payments on prior land loans and were unable to foreclose, as the government now owned the land. Zimbabwe's gross domestic product (GDP), which measures the economic output of the country, began to fall at an alarming rate. And all this was just the tip of the iceberg.

A perfect example of the "domino effect" proceeded from there. The decline in the country's farm exports, in particular its cash crops – tobacco and cotton – resulted in a collapse in the country's hard currency reserves. Deficits expanded. In an effort to finance the rapidly expanding deficits, the Reserve Bank of Zimbabwe bought millions of Zimbabwean dollars worth of government bonds. This began to fuel inflation, as there was little demand for the dollars – after all, the farmers, who no longer held title to the land they farmed, were unable to borrow to run their businesses – and the supply of dollars expanded rapidly in order to fund the purchase of the government debt. By the end of 2003 inflation was running at 500%. In order to control prices, the government instituted price controls. The result was predictable. The remaining companies that produced fertilizer stopped

---

[5]　Craig J. Richardson, "The Loss of Property Rights and the Collapse of Zimbabwe," *Cato Journal*, vol. 25, no. 3 (Fall 2005): 541.

[6]　"Zimbabwe, African Economic Outlook 2003, OECD Publishing," *OECD Development Centre and African Development Bank* (2003).

[7]　"Zimbabwe: 2003 Article IV Consultation – Staff Report," *International Monetary Fund*: pg. 26. As cited by Craig Richardson, pg 551.

their shipments, as they were obviously reluctant to sell the product at a price below their cost. This led to further reductions in farm output, resulting in increased need for food imports and increased need for new currency to purchase those imports.

The downward spiral continued in an accelerated free-fall. In order to keep up with its ever-expanding debts and lack of revenues, the Reserve Bank of Zimbabwe stepped up its currency printing. About the only constraint on printing the flood of Zimbabwean dollars was the fact that the government, lacking hard currency, was unable to import the necessary ink and special paper. They quickly adapted by printing "banknotes" instead.[8] The rampant creation of currency fueled inflation further. The Zimbabwean dollar, which was roughly equal in value to one U.S. dollar in 1983, collapsed in value. By mid-2006, inflation was running at a 1,200% annual rate and it took 500,000 Zimbabwean dollars to purchase one U.S. dollar. At the end of 2007, inflation was running at 215,000%. Shockingly, they still had yet to bottom out. Inflation continued to accelerate, reaching a whopping annual rate of 41 *million* percent in June 2008 and, by mid-November 2008, the annual inflation rate was clocked at 89 *sextillion* percent per year![9] The result was a complete collapse of the Zimbabwean economy, the end of foreign direct investment in the country, the destruction of national wealth, and a closing of the once-booming Zimbabwe Stock Exchange. It now took more than one hundred trillion Zimbabwean dollars to equal one U.S. dollar. A single government decision, the loss of property rights, resulted in the total financial destruction of an entire, once-booming, country.

Figure 2. *A one-hundred-trillion-dollar Zimbabwean banknote. Seriously! At the time of its issuance in January 2009, this note could purchase less than a dozen eggs.*

"Thank God it's them instead of you"

This section's heading echoes the anguished cry of rocker Bono singing "Do

8   S. Njanji, "No Let Up in Zimbabwe's Forex Woes as Country Fails to Even Print Bank Notes," *Agence France Presse* (May 11, 2003). As cited by Craig Richardson, pg 557.
9   Steve H. Hanke, "R.I.P. Zimbabwe Dollar," *Cato Institute*, (May 2010).

They Know It's Christmas?" Written by musician and global entrepreneur Bob Geldof, and performed by a who's who of British and Irish musicians, the goal of the song was to raise money to help stem the tide of widespread famine taking place in the African nation of Ethiopia. We watch these unfortunate human hardships take place from the "cheap seats," oceans and continents away. Any relative security we may feel is echoed in one of that song's signature lines, "thank God it's them instead of you." But the reality is that "The Zimbabwe Phenomenon" can occur anywhere and at anytime. Even an economically advanced country like the United States has tip-toed across the abyss a number of times. Richard Nixon exerted power from the White House and imposed price-controls in an effort to stop inflation in the early 1970s. Property rights were challenged when eminent domain was used to confiscate personal property for the "common good" of commercial development in the 2000s. The U.S. Federal Reserve bank purchased trillions of U.S. dollars in government debt in 2009 in order to stave off collapse of the banking system. Sound familiar? The leaders of Zimbabwe had taken the same exact course of action. But the trigger for economic collapse does not need to follow a single script. It does not need to be the confiscation of property. There are many conceivable and historic catalysts for economic collapse.

The purpose of this book is not to make predictions of economic collapse. It is to ensure that your portfolio is positioned to profit regardless of the economic environment or the performance of any individual market. If there is one theme at the heart of this book, it is the theme of portfolio diversification. Unfortunately for the private investor, it has become widely accepted that a portfolio diversified across a number of stocks will provide inherent return over time, that it is virtuous and pragmatic to buy-and-hold stocks for the long-run, and that the longer your viewpoint, the lower your investment risk. This strategy is flawed because it is dependent on a single set of baseline conditions and return drivers, and there is no guarantee that the future won't deviate substantially from the past. In fact, it's a certainty that it will.

Time is not always on your side

People generally accept that short-term stock market returns tend to be random. And, it also seems to be accepted as fact that if you buy stocks for the long run, they will provide you with an intrinsic return. The fact is that when stocks are bought "for the long run," capital destruction is virtually guaranteed. The U.S. financial system, held up as the pinnacle of stability, has existed for 200 years, but wasn't even mature enough to warrant a market index until Dow Jones released the

Dow Jones Index in 1884. Virtually every other financial system in the world has come and gone since 1884. No system can ever be assured of continuity. And the overt discontinuity that has occurred in Weimar Germany, Zimbabwe, Russia, Argentina, Peru and numerous other countries throughout recent history can literally destroy wealth. Just as savings in Germany in the early part of the 20th century and land ownership in Zimbabwe in the 21st were not assured, today no investment can provide you with a guaranteed return. This is not intended to be a depressing concept. Hopefully it will prove to be enlightening.

The performance of every trading strategy is based on one or more return drivers that are the source of the performance. By understanding the return drivers, it is possible to understand not only the probability of the performance itself continuing, but also to allow you to construct a portfolio that produces returns derived from a variety of return drivers. That way, no single event or condition can destroy the value of that portfolio.

In this myth I will show that there is no magic "intrinsic" return provided by stocks, but that stock prices are driven by specific return drivers. What then becomes clear is that the conventional wisdom – that national and international economic growth powers stock returns – is not only wrong, the direct opposite is closer to the truth. Over the long-term, it's the performance of each individual company that drives economic growth.

So what people often think of as being an intrinsic return from stocks is actually just the symptom of the aggregate performance of individual companies and the resultant performance of those companies' shares. Before I show the specifics that drive stock performance, let's look at the significance of what I call the "baseline conditions."

The necessity of favorable "baseline conditions"

At the basic, longest-term level, the "baseline conditions" are simply the conditions which must be maintained for any given trading strategy's return drivers to be effective and to produce a positive return. In the U.S. today, just as it was during Germany's Weimar Republic in the 1920s, savings held in cash and fixed-income securities require a baseline condition of a relatively stable currency, a sound, fair and consistent financial system, and full faith in the credit of the government. These conditions are neither preordained nor permanent in any society. Most countries fall short of meeting all baseline conditions. Some become outright hostile to investors. Even the U.S. has been known to spontaneously modify its baseline conditions without warning. This has created inconsistency and confusion in its financial system. On September 18, 2008, for example, the U.S. Securities and Exchange Commission (the SEC) revoked the right of most people to sell short most financial company stocks. The fact this was done with the belief it would help stem the collapse in stock prices occurring at that time is irrelevant.

What is relevant is that all investment strategies dependent on being able to sell short stocks immediately became invalid. (See *Myth #10 – Short Selling Destabilizes the Stock Market* to see why banning short selling failed to stabilize the market.) Despite its occasional transgression, the United States has been a great place to invest for more than 100 years. The population and economy have grown. Well-run companies have thrived. Over time their share prices have risen along with their profits. But it is not incomprehensible that some day people and their governments could lose faith in the ability of the United States to support its currency. *There has never been a national currency that has lasted forever.*

Again, I am not stating these facts to trigger fear, only for your rational consideration. The fact that the U.S. stock market performance is predicated on a continuation of the favorable baseline conditions that have existed for the past couple of centuries should itself serve as a reason not to depend on this as your sole return driver going forward.

....

Return drivers for the stock market

Once we're comfortable with the baseline conditions that underlie any trading strategy opportunity, we can evaluate the primary return drivers from which a given strategy's returns are derived.

We'll see that what appears to have been an intrinsic return from investing in U.S. stocks over the past 100 plus years was really just the result of two primary return drivers:

- The aggregate profit (or "earnings") growth of the companies that comprise the "market," and

- The multiple that people were willing to pay for those earnings (the "price/earnings" or "P/E" ratio)

Figure 3 displays the relative contribution to stock prices (represented by the S&P 500 Total Return Index) by each of these two return drivers. Together they account for more than 90% of the S&P 500s returns.

The "S&P 500 Total Return Index" is a measure of the aggregate performance of 500 stocks, including the reinvestment of dividends. A detailed description of the S&P 500 is contained in Myth # 4.

What the graph shows is that in any period of less than ten years, *earnings* accounted for less than 25% of the price change in the S&P 500 TR index, while *changes* in P/E accounted for more than 75% of this price change. It is only over the longest periods that earnings come to be the dominant return driver. Perhaps most importantly though, is that this shows that

What appears to be an "intrinsic" return of the "market" is simply the aggregate result of corporate earnings coupled with the enthusiasm people have for buying stocks.

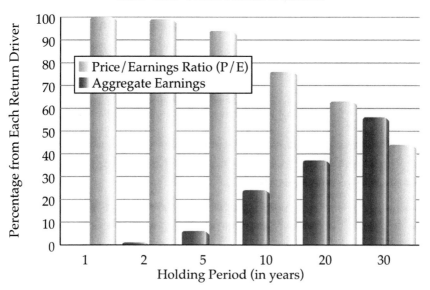

Source of Returns
S&P 500 Total Return Index

Figure 3. *A description of the methodology used to produce these results is included in the Table of Figures*

Sentiment dominates short-term stock performance

In 1999, Jack Welch was at the top of his game. He had been anointed "Manager of the Century" by *Fortune* magazine, and it was under his leadership that General Electric became widely acknowledged as one of the world's best-run corporations. GE was highly profitable, earning $1.07 per share in 1999 (accounting for a stock split in 2000). World-wide adulation for Mr. Welch and GE was reflected in the company's stock price.

At the end of 1999, GE stock closed at a split-adjusted $38.06 per share and sported a P/E multiple of 35. Eight years later, during 2007, GE earned $2.20 per share, a 105% increase over the earnings for 1999. Yet the stock price closed at just $33.06. Despite strong earnings growth over the eight-year period, the stock price actually fell 13%. The divergence is explained by the dramatic decline in the P/E ratio that people were willing to assign to the stock, which fell from more than 35 in 1999 to just 15 by the end of 2007. This is just one of many examples I could use that point out that in shorter time periods, stock prices are driven more by the psychology of people buying and selling stocks than by corporate earnings.

The myth of intrinsic returns

Widespread, face-value acceptance of what can actually be *disinformation* is how investment myths are formed and perpetrated. The classic "stocks provide an intrinsic return," just because it is widely accepted as a "truth," is not a sufficient cause to make it valid. It is only when carefully researched facts are understood that logical investment strategies can be developed and implemented. Understanding this is important for a number of reasons, as it points out that:

- *Every valid investment opportunity has one or more fundamental return drivers.* Understanding these drivers is the core tenet underlying successful investing. With respect to the stock market, it allows people to understand the true source of returns, rather than simply accepting the myth that stocks always provide an intrinsic return over time.

- *Every return driver has a relevant time period over which it is effective.* For example, a company's earnings are essentially irrelevant if a person is only prepared to hold a stock for a year or two. In that time frame, stock prices are driven far more by people's demand as measured by changes in the P/E ratio than by the company's actual earnings. It is only over the longest periods that corporate performance (earnings) becomes the more important return driver.

- *It may be possible to identify only the best stock-buying opportunities and avoid the worst.* This makes it clear that not all companies' stocks will provide an "intrinsic" positive return. This capability also enables people to identify stocks to sell short as well as buy long. The true value of this advantage will be discussed in *Myth #10 – Short Selling is Destabilizing and Risky.*

To own stocks is referred to as being "long" stocks. Being long has nothing to do with how long the position is held. You can hold a long position for mere seconds; you are still "long." When you hold no position it is called being "flat." A "short" position, which will be described in more detail later in this book, entails borrowing a stock and then selling it. The holder of a short position profits as a stock drops in price.

The myth of intrinsic returns is one of the most pervasive of all investment myths. It has been misused for years by proponents of stock investing as being the primary reason for people to buy-and-hold stocks. Like any myth, once it is understood and the truth revealed, decisions can be made that are based on facts and that provide opportunity to create profitable trading strategies.

Many successful major investors, such as Warren Buffet, Peter Lynch, and Sir John Templeton, either intuitively or through calculation, came to understand the significance of this basic concept. They were able to develop disciplined trading strategies that matched their investment time frame with the return driver they intended to capture. There is no "magic" of intrinsic returns. Understanding the primary factors that drive stock prices allows you to invest in stocks intelligently and with the conviction that over time the positions will provide returns that exceed those achieved from random stock selection or from simply buying "the market."

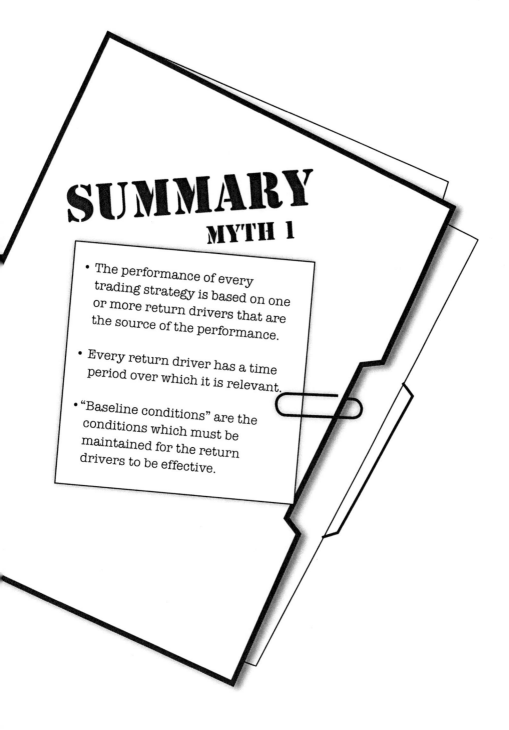

SUMMARY
MYTH 1

- The performance of every trading strategy is based on one or more return drivers that are the source of the performance.

- Every return driver has a time period over which it is relevant.

- "Baseline conditions" are the conditions which must be maintained for the return drivers to be effective.

Buy and Hold Works Well for Long Term Investors

I have a good friend who actively, and successfully, trades stocks for both himself and his clients. His general process is to research sectors that he believes will outperform other sectors and then buy (enter into "long" positions) stocks in those sectors that his analysis deems most likely to appreciate in price. (Don't confuse my friend taking "long" positions in stocks, which simply means he buys them expecting to profit from them rising in price, with holding positions for the "long-term." He's certainly not a buy-and-hold guy.) Every Halloween all the neighbors on our culdesac get together and have a party before we take the kids out for the trick-or-treating march. Halloween 2008...while the children were eating "mummy dogs" and showing off their costumes, my friend and I were talking about America's financial crisis. I'm sure we weren't alone. That same conversation was taking place in every community across the country. When I made a comment that I thought stocks would break through their recent lows, not merely test them, my friend was disturbed. Why?

The answer is that he had long positions in the market and he didn't allow himself to think about profiting from falling stock prices. Instead, he held out a somewhat perpetual (and very common) hope that "his" stocks would climb, allowing him to profit from his long stock positions. Hope is not a trading strategy. (I know. I've tried it.)

But my friend adapts quickly. I had previously made a comment to him, which he reminded me of recently. "Mike," he said, "There's something you said that I've repeated to others now at least a dozen times. 'Don't trade the market you want. Trade the market you've got.'"

What I meant by making that comment was that if the market is in a downtrend, don't fight it. Sell stocks short or at least don't hang on to long positions in the "hope" they'll go up. Face up to the fact that they're going down. In the coming chapters I'll explain why this seemingly simple concept / strategy has historically been almost impossible for the average person to follow and initiate.

When I first conceived of the need for this book in 1999, global stock markets were at the peak of an 18-year secular bull market. Buy-and-hold had become a mantra. That's no big surprise. At that time, there was no doubt that a person who had bought and held U.S. stocks over a long period would have made more money than in almost any other investment. But that belief was neither rocket science nor sound investment advice. It was merely a simple observation. Yet books, articles, and investment seminars, by the truckload, were produced that expounded on the benefits of buy-and-hold.

For many people the validity of the "buy-and-hold" myth has shriveled together with the values of their stock portfolios throughout the secular bear market that began in 2000. For many others though, the buy-and-hold approach continues to be a rallying cry and is continually touted as being a virtue and the ultimate strategy. In fact, however, buy-and-hold is not an approach at all, but merely a way to rationalize losses. Before I explain why, let's look at the historical results upon which this myth is based (using data provided by Robert J. Shiller, author of the bestselling book, *Irrational Exuberance*[10]).

---

[10]   Robert J. Shiller, *Irrational Exuberance* (Princeton: Princeton University Press, 2000, 2005, updated). Data used in Shiller book and for S&P 500 Total Return performance available at: http://www.econ.yale.edu/~shiller/data/ie_data.xls. Retrieved February 14, 2011.

Historical performance of investing in U.S. stocks

Since the start of 1900, U.S. equities produced a real average annualized return of 1.82% if dividends were spent, rather than reinvested; and a 6.27% real annualized return with dividends reinvested. The "real" return adjusts the performance for the negative effects of inflation, which reduced the returns by more than 3% per year on average. If we were to look at the "nominal" return, the amount stocks earned before adjusting for inflation, the returns jump to 4.92% if dividends were spent and 9.51% with dividends reinvested. I am showing the returns both with and without the reinvestment of dividends to stress the importance of reinvesting dividends. For various reasons, such as the fact that people are taxed on dividends and want to have the money available to pay taxes, many people do not reinvest their dividends. As the following data shows (Figure 4), over time this neglect will cost them the vast majority of their cumulative profits. On the surface, the nominal return, with dividends reinvested, seems to fit the definition of "healthy." Someone, placing $100 in U.S. equities at the start of 1900 and holding tight for the next 111 years, reinvesting all dividends, would see their portfolio grow to a stunning $2,383,810 by the end of 2010. It clearly demonstrates the power of compounding, which Albert Einstein said was one of the greatest human creations he had known.

> The "Annualized" return, also referred to as the compound annual return, accounts for the effect of compounding. This means that (in the case of a positive return) as the initial investment grows, it will earn the same return each year on an increasing investment size. For example, an initial $1,000 investment that earns a 10% annualized return will grow to $1,610 at the end of five years.

Even after adjusting for inflation, the ending value of this portfolio is $85,598. This is still an outstanding return. Taxes would reduce these returns further but are not included in these calculations due to their ever-changing nature and varying impact on each person.

What is obvious from the data, however, is that the majority of the real returns did not come from stock price appreciation, but from dividends. If rather than reinvesting the dividends a person spent them instead, the real value of the portfolio at the end of 2010 – 111 years later – would be only $744.

Returns People Achieved by
Buying and Holding U.S. Stocks Since 1900[11]

Case	Value of Initial $100 at end 2010	Annualized Return
Real Returns - w/o Reinvesting Dividends	$744	1.82%
Real Returns - Reinvesting Dividends	$85,598	6.27%
Nominal Returns - w/o Reinvesting Dividends	$20,623	4.92%
Nominal Returns - Dividends Reinvested	$2,383,810	9.51%

Figure 4. *Real Returns are returns adjusted for inflation. Nominal Returns are returns earned before reducing for inflation.*

In hindsight, the performance looks great. But as you may suspect, there were downsides hidden within this performance. Let's look at those statistics.

The downside of buy-and-hold

We can see that if a person had held stocks over the 111 year period ending December 31, 2010 and reinvested all dividends, they would have achieved a return of 9.5% before inflation. But the average person's life expectancy is in the range of 80 years. If you consider that the last 15 or so of those years are the period when they will be spending their savings, then that leaves about 45 years to accumulate and invest their earnings (from the ages of 20 to 65). So when considering implementing buy-and-hold as an investment strategy, the first important question to ask yourself is "what length of time should I plan on holding the position?" The answer is "probably much longer than most people can wait."

Figure 5 illustrates the real (inflation-adjusted) growth in an initial $100 placed into a basket of U.S. stocks at the start of 1900, assuming dividends are spent and not reinvested. The most interesting observation here is that it took until 1950 before the value of the initial $100 exceeded and stayed above that $100 value. That will undoubtedly rock the world of people who have been told, as long as they've been alive, that stocks work best in the long-run.

[11]   Shiller, *Irrational Exuberance.*

**Growth of $100 Placed into U.S. Stocks in 1990
Real Returns – Without Dividends**

Figure 5

That means that for more than 50 years any person who placed $100 into a broad basket of U.S. stocks, and who did not reinvest his or her dividends, would have suffered a loss, allowing for inflation. That really does give new meaning to the term "long run."

Perhaps most troubling though is the following fact:

> *all of the real stock market returns earned over the past 111 years can be attributed to just an 18 year period – the great bull market that began in August 1982 and ended in August 2000. Without those years the real, inflation-adjusted return of stocks, without reinvesting dividends, was negative.*

This points out the greatest risk of the buy-and-hold strategy, which is that stock market returns are extremely "lumpy."

Secular bulls and bears

Let's look at real returns without reinvesting dividends. Over the past 111 years, the U.S. stock market experienced four secular bear markets and three confirmed secular bull markets (it is not yet clear whether we are still in the bear market that began in 2000 or have entered into the fourth bull market). Each bear market averaged just less than ten years from the prior peak to the bear market low and suffered an average loss of 68%. On average it took the market 14 years to recover from each loss and the market continued to rise for another six years subsequent to recovering the ground lost in the bear market. This means that for 82 years the market was either in a bear market or recovering from one. It spent 27 years breaking into new high ground.

These figures aren't as bad as they first appear. First, they are the "real" return from stocks. So this is what your money would have grown to, even after reducing its value for inflation. Second, these figures represent only gains from the rise in stock prices and do not include the benefit of reinvesting dividends. Unfortunately though, a lot of people do not reinvest their earned dividends, or as was the case of the growth stock market of the late 1990s, do not put money into high dividend stocks. As a result they miss out on what, over time, becomes the greatest source for potential stock market returns...dividends. Finally, for people who hold stocks, recovering from a bear market is still good, it means that money is being made (although if they were also invested during the bear market they are merely recovering past losses). So the fact that, on average, 14 years was spent recovering from each bear market still means that the market was going up. If you were astute enough to miss the bear, every year of recovery would have put you into new high ground. Figure 6 lists the secular bull and bear markets since 1900.

Secular Bull and Bear Markets 1900 - 2010

Event	Start	End	Losses Recovered	Duration	Gain (Loss)
Bear	Sep 1906	Dec 1920		14 years	-70%
Bull	Dec 1920	Sep 1929	Sep 1928	9 years	415%
Bear	Sep 1929	Jun 1932		3 years	-81%
Bull	Jun 1932	Dec 1968	Nov 1958	36 years	755%
Bear	Dec 1968	Jul 1982		14 years	-63%
Bull	Jul 1982	Aug 2000	Jan 1992	18 years	666%
Bear	Aug 2000	Mar 2009 ?		9 years	-59%
Bull	Mar 2009 ?	???	???	???	???

Figure 6

The average person can easily examine stock market history and feel confident that he or she would have the discipline and perseverance to hold through significant declines of this magnitude. But over the past decade, the investing public has proven otherwise. An average secular bear market length of ten years requires a person to sustain a vigilant, faith-like adherence to the policy of buy-and-hold.

Figure 7 overlays the market P/E ratio at the time of each secular peak and trough. What is obvious from the chart is that the P/E ratio (the price people were willing to pay for earnings) peaked at each market peak and bottomed out at each market trough. What is also evident from the chart is that each of the prior three secular bear markets bottomed with the P/E ratio settling in the single digits. At the market bottom in March 2009 the P/E dropped only to as low as 13.

Growth of $100 Overlaid with P/E Ratio

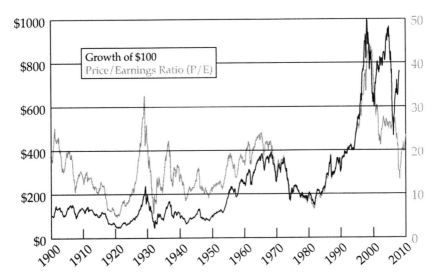

Figure 7

What does this information mean to a person committed to buy-and-hold? It means that if their timeframe is less than 20 years, they may be taking on the significant risk that their money in stocks will be worth less at the end of that period than at the beginning. And, as we learned in *Myth #1 – Stocks Provide an Intrinsic Return*, their returns over that period are more dependent on the whims of other people as reflected in the P/E ratio than on the performance of the stocks of the individual companies in which they place their money.

> *Bear markets are not caused by economic contractions,*
> *but are instead driven primarily as a result of changes in the*
> *multiple that people are willing to pay to own stocks.*

Now – why buy-and-hold is wrong

So much for history. Now I will explain why all of that is meaningless.

First, virtually every part of buy-and-hold data was created with the benefit of hindsight. I've often joked how much fun investing would be if we could invest in the "Hindsight Fund," where we decide today where we would have placed our money last week or last year and then get the credit for that. That's what all the buy-and-hold studies are. Of course, every study is based on retrospective analysis, which may have little to no bearing on real-time action or reaction. Announcing what would have or could have happened, after the fact, with any particular market pick is simply a basis for mildly interesting conversation. *It is not a revelation. It is simply an observation.*

In 1900 there were more than 100 recognized countries, or sovereign nations, existing across the globe. And, according to Steven T. Brown, William N. Goetzmann and Stephen A. Ross in "Survival," "there is historical evidence of at least thirty-six (stock) exchanges extant at the beginning of the (20th) century."[12]

How many reports have you seen issued extolling the benefits of buying-and-holding stocks for the past century in The Netherlands, Germany, Belgium, Hungary, Argentina, Egypt, Denmark, Hong Kong, Turkey, Portugal, Spain, Mexico, Russia, Brazil, Chile, Korea, Japan, Austria and Poland? The answer? ...None. And that's for one simple reason. All of those countries had stock exchanges at the beginning of the 1900s and all of them provided opportunities for people to buy stock for the long run, but all of them suffered major interruptions in their activity due to nationalizations or war. None of them outperformed the returns a person would have made if, instead, they had put their money into U.S. stocks. In fact, out of the remaining countries that did not suffer interruptions in their trading, the inflation-adjusted stock market performance of only three of them, South Africa, Australia and Sweden, outperformed the United States.[13] Investing in stocks in the U.S., South Africa, Australia and Sweden beat all those other countries during the 20th century.

Here's why: The baseline conditions in those other countries changed, sometimes multiple times, during the 20th century. Many people were wiped

---

[12] Stephen J. Brown, William N. Goetzmann and Stephen A. Ross, "Survival" *NYU Working Paper No. FIN-94-02*, (March 1995).

[13] Elroy Dimson, Paul Marsh and Michael Staunton, *Triumph of the Optimists: 101 Years of Global investment Returns*, (Princeton: Princeton University Press, 2002), 52.

out or had the money they placed in those markets substantially destroyed. In fact, as stated by Brown, Goetzmann and Ross in "Survival," "more than half (of the markets that existed in 1900) suffered at least one major hiatus in trading." The reason there aren't a multitude of books using historical performance to promote the buy-and-hold strategy in all those other countries is because it didn't work in those countries. Or at least it didn't work as well in those countries as it did in the U.S. The focus on the out-performing U.S. market is called selection bias. It is sufficiently damaging, all by itself, to be the reason not to rely on buy-and-hold as a strategy.

Think about that. All the studies showing the value of buying-and-holding U.S. stocks have one thing in common; they all had the benefit of hindsight. It did pay to buy stocks in the U.S. in 1900, when the U.S. was an emerging economy, and hold on as stocks rose in price over the past 111 years. But that's not a good reason to buy stocks *today*. Baseline conditions change. The conditions which existed in the U.S. in 1990 are different from those which exist today. Merely relying on historical repetition is not a sufficient return driver.

A recent example

Not all economic/currency failures or nation-wide destructions of wealth are the result of full-fledged revolutions. Nations, at any particular time, can shift their policies and confiscate assets with the stroke of a governmental or dictator's pen. In the last myth we saw how this happened in Zimbabwe. What happened in Venezuela provides another excellent example.

In the 1990s Venezuela was able to offer global corporations extremely attractive and lucrative investment opportunities. It had vast reserves of oil that brought in tens of billions of dollars in exploration and infrastructure improvements from companies such as Exxon, Mobil and Total.

That all changed in the 21st century however. Under the rule of socialist Hugo Chavez, Venezuela stole assets that were previously legally obtained in the country by international oil and electricity companies. In April 2006 he ordered a state takeover of several major oil operations. In January 2007 he announced plans to nationalize Venezuela's electrical and telecommunications companies, including operations owned by Virginia-based AES Corp. In May 2007 he took over 60% of four refineries owned by ConocoPhillips, Chevron, Exxon-Mobil, BP, Statoil and Total.[14]

---

[14] "FACTBOX – Venezuela's state takeovers under Chavez." *Reuters* UK (October 14, 2010). Retrieved February 14, 2011.

While some compensation was paid to those companies, their financial backers saw the future value of their capital investments in Venezuela transferred from them to Venezuela. If you or I did this it would be called theft and we would be prosecuted for our crime. When countries do it, it's called "nationalization." The point is, Venezuela, which once appeared to provide a relatively safe investment environment, with well-defined baseline conditions, changed overnight with the election of Hugo Chavez as President. In reality, stable and beneficial baseline conditions are the exception around the world, not the norm.

One-in-a-million

In the mid-1990s I began serving as the moderator of a trading strategy panel at an annual investment conference in Chicago. One year while there I sat down to observe another panel. One of the panelists presented the result of a "study" he conducted that was intended to reveal the seasonal tendencies of various commodities. In that study he discovered two dates, a buy date and a sell date, that if adhered to over the prior 30 years or so, would have produced a profit every year in the platinum market. He said he actually followed that "strategy" over the previous year, but rather than making money, as buying and selling on those dates had for each of the prior 30 years, he lost money. He wanted to know why.

It's a shame he wasted his time conducting his "study". Everyone reading this book now understands the importance of first understanding the return drivers underlying the performance of any strategy. He obviously did not. There was no sound underlying premise for why buying platinum on his one date and selling on the other should have been a profitable trade. He convinced himself that the results were significant based solely on the statistics. After all, he had 30 trades in the track record, and that is the number statisticians quote as being necessary to establish statistical significance. However, just because the results contained 30 data points does not mean the results were significant from a statistical standpoint. In fact, each year he sifted through more than 30,000 combinations to find that single combination that was profitable every year in the platinum market.[15] Worse yet, he didn't just do this for platinum. He ran this process on dozens of markets. Platinum just happened to be the only one that

---

[15]   30,000 combinations is calculated by taking the 252 platinum trading days there are on average in a year, then testing buying Januuary 2nd and selling January 3rd; buying January 2nd and selling January 4th, etc.

had a combination that proved profitable every year for the prior thirty. In all, he needed more than one million buy-sell combinations to come up with one that worked every year. Literally, a one-in-a-million long shot. Not only had his entire strategy been built without any basis of sound, logical return drivers, but his even more egregious error had been to employ an intrinsically flawed statistical analysis.

Just because something happened in the past does not mean it will reoccur in the future. We must first understand all the return drivers, and then determine whether those return drivers are still valid. Then, and only then, can you be ready to "pull the trigger" and make the right move. The process can never be abandoned or put on "auto-pilot." An evaluation of the return drivers must be ongoing, as the baseline conditions and return drivers often change.

The hindsight study of buying and holding U.S. stocks is subject to those same rules. As we saw previously, out of the 36 stock markets that existed in 1900, 32 under performed the U.S. market. This means that there was only a one-in-nine chance of selecting a market that performed at least as well as the U.S. stock market did. This isn't as bad as the one-in-a-million odds I describe in the platinum story, but the odds were still just one-in-nine. Buying-and-holding in 1900, without the benefit of the hindsight that we have today, would have been gambling.

This does not mean that the odds weren't better for some people in 1900. There were certainly some who evaluated the baseline conditions and return drivers and concluded from that analysis that putting money into U.S. stocks was the way to go. In fact, that is exactly what I'm arguing people should do now. Evaluate the return drivers and baseline conditions *today*. Don't accept a one-dimensional hindsight "study" as today's truth. Buying any market today and holding for the next 111 years is no different than it was in 1900. *Settling for odds of one-in-nine isn't investing. It's gambling.*

The second reason that the statistics displayed in this chapter are meaningless is precisely because no one bought a basket of stocks, represented by an index or otherwise, at the beginning of 1900 and held them through to today. This is telling for a number of reasons. First, as described above, there were virtually no pundits espousing buy-and-hold in 1900. But just as importantly, even if there had been; the fact is that people need to use their money in the process of living day-to-day. Nobody just puts it away and then lets it grow indefinitely. That itself says a lot. It means that you *must* operate pursuant to a *trading strategy* that provides not just for buying stocks, but also selling them. Of course, any chosen strategy should be based on maximizing your potential return. That potential is exponentially increased by incorporating well-researched timing for every investment *and* withdrawal. "Buy-and-hold," as a strategy, falls short for its inability to provide a person with any user-friendly information on when to do either.

> *This is why buy-and-hold is really not a "strategy" at all,*
> *but merely a way to rationalize losses.*

Third. The conditions that created the opportunity for buy-and-hold to have been successful in the U.S. since 1900 are an economic anomaly. They have no chance of being repeated in our times. The U.S. started the last century with a GDP of just over $20 billion. At that point, we fit the definition of an "emerging" economy. Today the GDP of the United States is over $14 trillion,[16] more than 500 times larger than it was in 1900, and the U.S. is, despite all the talk of China's emergence, by far the largest economy in the world. The U.S. can no longer be labeled "emerging" and has little chance of ever returning to that world-economic category. In fact, the only way the United States could ever return to that status is if it were first to collapse, and then rebuild from scratch. That's certainly not a scenario that bodes well for buy-and-hold.

I present a number of stock trading strategies in the Action section at www.JackassInvesting.com/actions that are based on rational, exploitable return drivers.

---

[16]   Louis Johnston and Samuel H. Williamson, "What Was the U.S. GDP Then?" *Measuring Worth* (2010). Retrieved February 14, 2011.

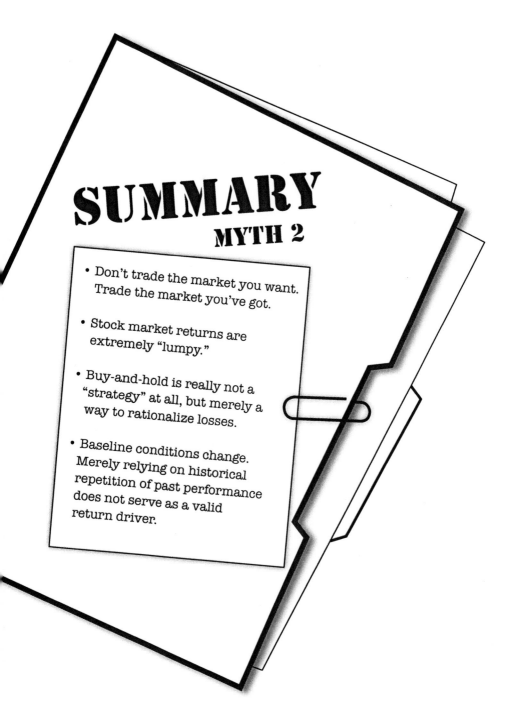

SUMMARY
MYTH 2

- Don't trade the market you want. Trade the market you've got.

- Stock market returns are extremely "lumpy."

- Buy-and-hold is really not a "strategy" at all, but merely a way to rationalize losses.

- Baseline conditions change. Merely relying on historical repetition of past performance does not serve as a valid return driver.

MYTH 3

You Can't Time
the Market

Ome of my favorite Seinfeld episodes is titled "The Opposite." In it, the
inimitable George Costanza, while standing on the beach reflecting on his
life, comes to the angst-filled conclusion that "every decision I've ever made,
in my entire life, has been wrong. My life is the opposite of everything I want it to be.
Every instinct I have, in every aspect of life, be it something to wear, something to eat ...
It's all been wrong."[17]

Going whole-hog with that premise as the basis for a radical and not overly coherent
behavior make-over, he immediately begins to do the opposite of everything he thinks
is right. The scene takes place at Jerry, George, Elaine, and Kramer's regular coffee shop
hang-out. A drop-dead, beautiful woman looks in George's direction and instead of
following his normal instinct to do nothing, he walks right up and introduces himself
with the line, "My name is George. I'm unemployed and I live with my parents."

Of course, it worked like a charm. George gets the super-hot girl, moves out of his parents'
house, and lands his dream job, working with Steinbrenner and his beloved Yankees.

---

[17] "The Opposite" is the eighty-sixth episode of the NBC sitcom *Seinfeld*. It first aired on
May 19, 1994.

We are all George Costanzas – but before the "opposite" revelation.

How often have you done what you thought – perhaps were even convinced – was "right" in managing your money, just to find out you were dead wrong? Buying a "sure thing" that almost immediately sold off. Selling out of a profitable position because it felt good to take a profit, only to see it rise significantly from that point of sale. I'm guessing quite a lot. Well, in actuality I don't need to guess. I know. Because the statistics show that in the aggregate, people lose. And lose big-time.

One of the best studies of the effect of human discretion on returns is that produced by DALBAR, Inc.[18] Their analysis is straightforward. They compare the returns of holding stocks, as measured by the return on the average stock fund, with the returns earned by an "average" person. The results (Figure 8) are quite revealing. Average fund participants, because of their tendency to panic and withdraw from their funds at low points, and add money to their funds at high points (based on a large dose of greed getting in the way of rational thought), underperform a static buy-and-hold scenario by 5.03% per year. That's right, 5.03% PER YEAR! From 1990 through 2009 the average stock mutual gained an average of 8.20% per year, while the average person in those funds earned just 3.17% per year.[19]

Growth in $10,000 Over 20 Years: 1990 - 2009

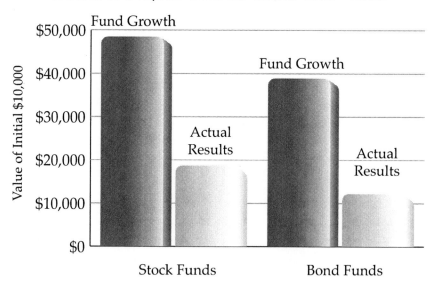

Figure 8. *Source: DALBAR, Inc.*

18   DALBAR, Inc., Federal Reserve Plaza, 600 Atlantic Ave., FL 30, Boston, MA 02210.
19   "2010 Quantitative Analysis of Investor Behavior," DALBAR, Inc. (March 2010): 2-3.

And this losing behavior is not limited to stocks. Over the same period bond mutual funds gained an average of 7.01% annually. People with money in those funds averaged a 1.02% annual return. Their timing decisions resulted in them underperforming the funds by 5.99% per year![20]

The cause of this dramatic underperformance is simple. The vast majority of people do not manage their money pursuant to a plan. They trade, er, gamble emotionally. They jump in at the top and bail out at the bottom. They get a tip and they buy a stock. That stock starts to drop and they get anxious and sell. Or they hang on in the *hope* that the price will at least rise back to where they bought the stock so that they can sell it there. Unless it doesn't, in which case they finally panic and sell it substantially lower. Confused? So are they. Virtually none of their buy/sell decisions are executed pursuant to a plan. Their results reinforce the cliché that "failure to plan is to plan for failure."

Statistics such as those published by DALBAR are often used by self-anointed financial gurus to induce people to "buy-and-hold" rather than to trade the markets. It's an easy argument to make and many people fall for it. Why even attempt to trade if the statistics are so clear that traders lose money? The truth is far different however. The people who are underperforming the very funds into which they place their money aren't traders (and they certainly aren't investors). They're gamblers. They are not trading pursuant to a plan. They are trading on their emotional instincts and placing trades with negative expected outcomes. That's gambling.

Importantly, "you" do not need to be part of "them." You can profit by exploiting the proven tendency for investors to time the market badly. You can do, in the real world of investment, what worked so well for George Costanza in his small-screen life quest. In fact, precisely because "they" can't time the market, you can. I'll show you how in this myth's Action section at www.JackassInvesting.com. Furthermore, whether you are aware of it or not, you are already functioning as an aggressive market timer.

Freewill and the hidden truth of market timing

In the chorus of the *Rush* song "Freewill," lead singer Geddy Lee's vocal pierces the air with Neil Peart's lyric "If you choose not to decide, you still

---

[20]   DALBAR, "Quantitative Analysis of Investor Behavior."

have made a choice."[21] Clearly, Neil was writing about market timing when he wrote those lyrics (even if he was unaware of it!). How does a rock song apply to investment strategy?

Do you own Brazilian stocks? No? Have you even considered trading Brazilian stocks? If not then you "still have made a choice" to be flat (out of) Brazilian stocks and likely thousands of other markets. Being flat with no position in Brazilian stocks is no different than being flat in a market you pay attention to, such as U.S. stocks. You are timing each of those markets simply based on the fact that "you've chosen not to decide." I realize this is an unconventional and potentially uncomfortable way to view market timing. But it does point out that you are making timing decisions whether you are "in" a market or "out." When you are flat U.S. stocks, it is no different from you being flat Brazilian stocks. You have no position in either market and are free to decide whether to enter either market long or short. Despite your predilection to focus on U.S. stocks, there is no difference between either decision. Looking at it in this fashion, everyone is a market timer. So if you're already timing thousands of other markets in addition to the U.S. stock market, why not do it right?

"Fine," you say. "But can we focus on just one market at a time, such as U.S. stocks. Should I attempt to time the U.S. stock market?" The answer, once again, is that you already are. The only variable is what time frame you are choosing.

Are you long stocks? If so, you've made the decision, whether conscious or not, that stocks are going up. That's a timing decision. Are you out of stocks? You've made the decision that the potential for gain does not offset the risk of loss. Going flat was a timing decision. Perhaps you say you never time the market. You are a disciple of buy-and-hold. Buy-and-hold is a timing decision as well. It's just the extreme example of the belief that stocks are going up. You will make a sale of those stocks at some time. It may be in ten years hence to pay for college tuition or out of your estate after your death, but there will be a sale associated with that long position eventually. In the case of a sale following your death, that just happens to be a timing decision that you left up to a higher power.

So if you are going to time the U.S. stock market anyway, why not do it in a systematic fashion, based on sound underlying principles that increase the probability that you will outperform buy-and-hope? Throughout history, virtually all of the world's greatest investors have applied this approach.

---

[21] "Freewill" was released in 1980 on Rush's *Permanent Waves* album.

"Buy when there's Blood in the Street"

Perhaps one of the most famous anecdotes related to market timing can be attributed to Baron Rothschild. In July 1870, Napoleon III, the nephew of Napoleon Bonaparte, threw France into a war with Prussia. The result was disastrous for France. In September 1870 the Prussian army began the siege of Paris.[22] After a massive bombardment of the city, on January 28, 1871, Paris surrendered and a new provisional government was formed. During the siege however, hundreds of thousands of Parisians became armed members of a citizen's militia known as the "National Guard," which held 400 cannons on the Butte Montmartre. The new government viewed this as a threat and ordered its own troops to seize the cannons. But instead, the government troops rebelled against the order and effectively joined forces with the National Guard. Fearfully, the government members fled to Versailles, leaving the Central Committee of the National Guard as the only effective government in Paris. In keeping with its democratic ideals, the Central Committee arranged for elections for a "Commune," which took place on March 26th.

Soon thereafter however, government forces returned from Versailles and besieged the city. Their forces, enlarged by French POWs released by Prussia, pushed back the National Guard. The siege reached its climax during "La Semaine Sanglante," or "The Bloody Week," in May 1871, when as many as 30,000 people were reportedly executed or killed in fighting. It was at that time that a young man, who had just received a large inheritance, called on the great banking firm of Rothschild to ask their advice on how best to invest his fortune. Here's a recounting of the story as published in a 1917 edition of The Gas Record:

> In 1871 when the Commune in Paris was at its height and the streets were red with blood, a young man called on the great banking firm of Rothschild to ask advice about a large fortune to which he had become heir. The head of the house told him to buy French Government Securities. "What: buy securities when the streets of Paris are running with blood!" was the young man's surprised exclamation. Baron Rothschild is reported to

---

[22] Prosper Olivier Lissagaray, *History of the Paris Commune of 1871*, (originally published Paris 1876, republished by New Park Publications 1976).

have said: "My young friend, that is the very reason that today you can buy securities for 50% of their face value."[23]

This led to the oft-quoted adage "Buy when there's blood in the street." Investment opportunities are presented to you at exactly the time you are least emotionally prepared to accept them. That is precisely why they exist.

Figure 9. *"Le siège de Paris" by Jean-Louis-Ernest Meissonier (1815 - 1891). Oil on canvas.*

Fortunately, investment opportunities do not *require* actual blood to be spilled. Far less dramatic opportunities are presented every day. And the world's greatest investors, in fact "The World's Greatest Investor," regularly employs market timing.

---

[23] "Opinions and Comments – Buy Securities Now," *The Gas Record* (July 11, 1917): 402.

"The World's Greatest Investor" (also known as The Oracle of Omaha)

"The World's Greatest Investor" (the phrase often used when referring to Warren Buffet), is a market timer. Buffet's company, Berkshire Hathaway, held $47 billion dollars, a full 28% of its market capitalization, in cash at the U.S. stock market peak in the fall of 2007.[24] This was the most cash ever held by Berkshire Hathaway and turned out to have been a great time to have been in cash, as stock prices fell by more than 50% over the ensuing 18 months. Rather than increasing his stock positions at unattractive prices he engaged in market timing by making the decision to hold a large cash position.

Conversely, as stocks began to collapse during the financial crisis of 2008, Buffet began to buy. First he picked up a distressed position in both Goldman Sachs[25] and General Electric.[26] In late 2009 he capped off his buying spree with a purchase of the remaining shares in Burlington Northern Santa Fe railroad that he didn't already own. At a price of $44 billion, this was, by far, the largest purchase Buffet's company had ever made.[27]

Buffet knows and uses what you learned in *Myth #1 – Stocks Provide an Intrinsic Return* - short-term stock prices are driven primarily by people following their emotional weather vane. When they are depressed about corporate prospects, as they were during the 2008 financial crisis, they drive the prices of stocks straight down.

> *Warren Buffet is a "value investor" only because people, through their knee-jerk buying and selling patterns, consistently provide him with the perfect opportunity to be one.*

Perversely, the recognition of this short-term behavior leads to Buffet's reputation as a long-term investor. Once he's made his opportunistic

---

[24] Berkshire Hathaway Inc. Form 10-Q for the quarterly period ended September 30, 2007. pg. 2.

[25] "Berkshire Hathaway to Invest $5 Billion in Goldman Sachs," *Goldman Sachs* press release (September 23, 2008).

[26] "GE Announces Common Stock Offering; Warren Buffet Announces Investment in GE," *General Electric* press release (October 1, 2008).

[27] "Berkshire Hathaway Inc. to Acquire Burlington Northern Santa Fe Corporation (BNSF) for $100 per Share in Cash and Stock," *Berkshire Hathaway* press release (November 3, 2009).

purchase, Buffet holds many of his stock positions for long periods of time. He is capturing the benefit of corporate growth, which dominates stock prices over long periods of time. He is hand-picking individual stocks. Not the market. He is interested in reaping the benefits of selecting strong, well-managed companies and being rewarded in higher stock prices for their individual corporate performance.

Stocks aren't the only financial instrument Warren Buffet market times. As Mr. Buffet succinctly describes in his 2007 letter to shareholders of Berkshire,

> The U.S. dollar weakened further in 2007 against major currencies, and it's no mystery why: Americans are a lot more excited about buying products made elsewhere than the rest of the world is about buying products made in the U.S. Inevitably, that causes America to ship about $2 billion of IOUs and assets daily to the rest of the world. And over time, that puts pressure on the dollar.[28]

And a few paragraphs later he describes a long position he entered into in the Brazilian currency, the "real," as a way to time the direction of the U.S. dollar:

> At Berkshire we held only one direct currency position during 2007. That was in – hold your breath – the Brazilian real. Not long ago, swapping dollars for reals would have been unthinkable. After all, during the past century five versions of Brazilian currency have, in effect, turned into confetti. As has been true in many countries whose currencies have periodically withered and died, wealthy Brazilians sometimes stashed large sums in the U.S. to preserve their wealth. But any Brazilian who followed this apparently prudent course would have lost half his net worth over the past five years. Here's the year-by-year record (indexed) of the real versus the dollar from the end of 2002 to year-end 2007: 100; 122; 133; 152; 166; 199. Every year the real went up and the dollar fell. Moreover, during much of this period the Brazilian government was actually holding down the value of the real and supporting our currency by buying dollars in the market.

---

[28]   Berkshire Hathaway Annual Letter to Shareholders for the year 2007 (December 31, 2007): 16-17.

Not only does Mr. Buffet reveal that he is a market timer, but that he is timing a currency which as a market has proven to be the antithesis of buy-and-hold. As he acknowledges, "during the past century *five* versions of Brazilian currency have, in effect, turned into confetti." As discussed in *Myth #1 – Stocks Provide an Intrinsic Return*, and clearly understood by Mr. Buffet, the past performance of a market is virtually irrelevant when considering whether to buy or sell it today. All that matters is whether the return drivers for that market *today* warrant a buy or sell decision.

"Sure," you say. "It's easy for The World's Greatest Investor to successfully time the market. That's why he's The World's Greatest Investor. But what about me?" The answer is: you can – precisely because most people can't.

It appears that people are hard-wired for investment failure. Because of that it is easier for financial professionals to instruct their clients to buy-and-hold rather than attempt to time the market, simply because most people *will* time the market incorrectly. But you don't have to be one of those people. You can exploit their behavior.

An opposite truth – most investors are gamblers, professional "gamblers" are rational traders

Johnny Chan is a world-class poker player. He's won the World Series of Poker ten times and was inducted into the Poker Hall of Fame in 2002. He was portrayed in the 1998 film *Rounders* and appeared as himself in the 2009 movie *Poker King*. He is a straight-A student of the game. Not only does Johnny understand all the statistical permutations when he sits down at a table, but he knows the other players as well. He uses this knowledge to create a plan prior to every game. Here's his story of how he won a $185,000 pot in a side game at the World Series of Poker, as he recounted it in an issue of *Trader Monthly* magazine.

> You need only to visit the World Series of Poker once to realize there's as much action, maybe even more, in various side games as in the Main Event itself. On one particular occasion, I was playing in a No-Limit Hold-'em side game with blinds of $300 and $600. It was a full ring game, with nine players dealt in on most hands. The stacks ranged

from a low of about $20,000 to a high of about $100,000 ~ which I had sitting in front of me, as did a couple other players.

Because a few players were inclined to pay off too easily, and I wanted to flop a hand with which to bust them, I was hoping to see a lot of flops relatively cheaply with mediocre hands. With a bit of luck, I'd make some hands that would reward me disproportionately.

That was a problem, though, because one of the players with a large stack was to my immediate left, and he had a habit of raising the pot when one or two players would limp in ahead of him. When he did that, he would usually over-bet the pot. He was seriously cramping my style, because he made it hard for me to limp in with mediocre hands. I would call for $600, and he would make it $5,000 to play. Because I had hands like ace-deuce suited, eight-five suited and jack-queen, I had to fold.

But I watched him for a while and noticed that if someone called his over-bet before the flop, he would over-bet the pot after the flop as well. Opportunity had presented itself as I figured out both how to take him out in a major way and clear a path for me to play my longer-term strategy for that game.

I decided to encourage him to continue stealing pots from me by temporarily becoming even more liberal in my pre-flop hand selections. I limped in with hands like eight-three off-suit, jack-seven off-suit and queen-deuce suited, willingly spending $600 a pop to allow him to raise me out.

True to form, he did exactly that. I folded to his raise almost every time to make sure I was training him well. Once or twice I strategically made a more serious investment, calling a flop for $5,000, then folding to his $25,000 over-bet when I didn't connect solidly with my hand.

Finally, though, I picked up a pair of aces and limped in. Sure enough, he raised the pot to $5,000, and I flat called. The flop produced a king of spades, a 10 of clubs, a four of hearts. I checked to him, and he went ahead and bet $25,000. Perfect. I waited a bit for effect, acted somewhat concerned and, with a shrug of my shoulders, raised all in. It didn't take him long to call.

The turn brought the eight of diamonds, the river - the four of spades, and I won a nice $185,000 pot against his king-jack. He left the game shortly thereafter, so I was able to start seeing a lot of flops with mediocre hands, making still more money later in the game on, among other hands, a straight I made with a nine-seven suited, trip fours I made with king-four suited and two pair I made with jack-nine.

The lesson here is first, know your facts (statistics) and second, know your opponent. Since at the top levels of poker play everyone knows the statistics, the difference - Johnny Chan's return driver - was his exploitation of the other hapless player's predictable consistency of behavior.

Although there is no doubt in anyone's mind that Johnny Chan is a professional poker player, his M.O. in that particular game made it, by definition, illogical to label him a gambler. A gambler is someone who takes unnecessary risks or trades with a negative return expectation. Johnny did neither. Although he almost certainly started with an edge over his opponents, by studying them closely he vastly improved his advantage. You can do the same.

Opposite attracts...money

Despite the fact that most pundits and advisors misuse the statistics that show how badly people underperform the stock market as an opportunity to preach their "stay the course" mantra, the DALBAR studies clearly spotlight the consistently poor results realized by the average person in efforts made to time the market. Johnny's opponent at the poker table was no different. In this case the study reveals a return driver that can be exploited by you. It doesn't matter that the exploit being revealed results in consistent losses – just that it's consistent. When a trading approach results in consistent losses it simultaneously reveals an opposite approach that is more-than-likely to result in consistent profits.

Changing your investment strategy habits can be at least as difficult as quitting smoking after a lifetime of smoke inhalation. Because of peoples' inability to change, they tend to keep on losing money in the market (justifying and rationalizing all the while) and are very prone to continue down that blind alley. They will not change. But you don't have to be one of "Them."

Follow a systematic approach

Throughout this book I advocate the need for you to take a systematic approach to building and maintaining your portfolio. For if you manage your money pursuant to a rational systematic process and not just ignore, but exploit the "myths" and other established doctrine being spewed by financial pundits and publications, you will have a repeatable investment edge. That said, I cannot over-emphasize the need for rational discretion in the initial research stage of that portfolio construction. This means that for every system you explore for inclusion in your portfolio, you must understand and accept the return drivers underlying that strategy's returns, and understand their potential of recurring in the future.

There is perhaps no clearer return driver for market timing than that revealed by the DALBAR studies. Based on the consistently horrendous market timing (in)abilities displayed by the average person, a systematic approach that is able to unemotionally evaluate what the "average" person is doing and then do the opposite could generate enormous returns. Think about that. You can exploit the emotional trading of others for your own profit. In the Action section for this myth at www.JackassInvesting.com I present a trading strategy based on the return driver that enables you to systematically exploit the poor market timing of others.

SUMMARY
MYTH 3

- Everyone is a market timer.

- On average, stock and bond market participants lose more than 5% per year by emotionally trading in and out of stock and bond funds.

- Since you're already timing the market, you might as well do it right. Follow a systematic process to exploit the emotional (gambling) behavior of others. Capture the 5% per year they are leaving on the table.

- Warren Buffet and other successful investors are market timers. They are considered "value investors" only because people, through their knee-jerk buying and selling patterns, consistently provide them with multiple opportunities to be one by buying stocks at depressed prices.

"Passive" Investing
Beats "Active" Investing

Before jumping into this myth, I need to make one key point:

passive *index investing is* **active** *investing.*

The only difference between the two is the percentage of stocks in the portfolio that are bought and sold each year (the "turnover"). But the reason that this is a myth and not a truth is the fact that the managers of the "passive" indexes, including the Dow Industrials, S&P 500 and NASDAQ 100, do not structure their indexes to provide people with maximum returns, but as I describe below, only to be "representative."

This means that the index managers don't follow a strategy intended to maximize returns, based on a sound return driver, for the inclusion of a stock in any of the major indexes. In fact, they don't follow a systematic strategy at all. John Prestbo, editor of Dow Jones Indexes, made the following statement in September 2008, "There are no predetermined criteria for a stock to be added or deleted, though we intend that all components be established U.S. companies that are leaders in their industries."[29]

He made that statement in a press release announcing the deletion of a stock from the Dow Jones Industrial Average; a stock that had been added to the Index just four years earlier. What company would you guess Dow Jones held in its index for just four years? The answer is: AIG. In just the four years that AIG was held by the Dow Jones Industrial Average its stock price fell by more than 97%.

Not an isolated example

The underperformance of AIG after its inclusion in the Dow Industrials is not an isolated example. In fact, in a research study conducted by William Hester, CFA, of the Hussman Funds, he showed that from 1998 through early 2005 it was actually better to put money in the stocks that got *deleted* from the S&P 500 Index rather than the stocks that were *added* to the index (Figure 10). Specifically, over that period the annualized returns of stocks added to the S&P 500 Index was 0.47%. In stark contrast, the average annualized return of the stocks deleted from the S&P 500 Index was +11.43%. The annualized performance of the deletions exceeded that of the additions by an enormous difference of almost 11%![30] Take a look:

"Passive" mutual funds or ETFs are those that follow a low-turnover approach, meaning they infrequently change the stocks in their portfolios. They often track market indexes such as the S&P 500. "Active" funds are those that trade more frequently.

29 "Dow Jones to Change the Composition of the Dow Jones Industrial Average," *Dow Jones Indexes* press release (September 18, 2008).
30 William Hester, "Deletions from the S&P 500 regularly outperform new additions," *Investment Research & Insight*, Hussman Funds (March 2005).

S&P 500
Effective Date through 3/15/2005
Annualized Returns in Percent

	Median Returns		Average Returns		Number Replaced
	Additions	Deletions	Additions	Deletions	
Full Period	2.93	15.36	0.47	11.43	63
2004	1.2	6.6	9.07	3.65	7
2003	22.8	79.5	24.37	77.19	4
2002	15.06	24.64	19.72	29.68	12
2001	0.01	14.61	-8.2	1.35	9
2000	-11.18	8.78	-11.97	2.6	22
1999	0.5	12.8	-1.59	-10.15	5
1998	6.78	7.58	3.56	5.11	4

Figure 10

So not only are the indexes *not* based on a strategy designed to maximize returns, but their performance indicates that they may actually be based on a process that results in *reducing* returns. The overt lack of a clear profit-motivated strategy may result in the index managers selecting stocks that dramatically underperform those stocks they delete from the indexes. Now let's look at the differences (or lack thereof) between "passive" index funds and "active" funds.

Comparison of "passive" index funds and "active" funds

The basis for stocks to be selected for inclusion in a "passive" index is no different from the one used in "active" stock selecting. The recipe used by both "active" and "passive" portfolio managers to select stocks for inclusion is based on a system, human discretion or a combination of the two.

A market index is a human creation. Someone had to develop it. Furthermore, no market index is static, someone has to manage it. In other words, the stocks that comprise the Index and the allocation they each have towards the index value calculation were developed using some underlying base methodology or system. Once developed, they are then actively managed (traded). Success in that management is based on two factors; the first: the system underlying the Index and the second: how actively it's managed (what is the portfolio turnover)?

It's only natural for a person to want and expect maximum return on their money. The stumbling block inherent here is that the major indexes themselves, such as the S&P 500, were never developed to provide maximum returns. In fact, as shown in the previous study, the "anti-index" approach, buying the stocks discarded from the indexes, can dramatically beat the indexes themselves. So why does this myth exist?

Why this myth exists

This myth that "passive" investing beats "active" investing exists for one key reason. By definition, not every fund manager can be above average. On average they're, well, "average." Now, add to that the fact that the fees charged to "active" U.S. stock mutual funds, as a group, are normally around 1% more per year than those charged to "passive" index funds. If index funds are truly representative of the average of stocks available to trade, and active fund managers historically stay in the "average" rating, then we would reasonably expect passive index funds to outperform active funds by 1% per year. But they don't. In a study made by David Blanchett and Craig Israelsen and published in the *Journal of Indexes*; during the period 1997 through 2006, index funds outperformed the average stock fund by just 55 basis points (a basis point is 1/100 of 1%).[31] This means that before fees, index funds underperformed active fund managers by a paltry ½ of 1% annually.

This tends to confirm the Hussman Funds study. The methodologies employed by the people managing the indexes result in those indexes underperforming the "market." Even active fund managers, before factoring in their higher fees, outperform the indexes. No surprise here. Just as all athletes are not of equal skill; equity traders, whether professionals or individuals, can't possibly be equally skilled. Some are talented, some just get lucky. Fortunately, you are not constrained to investing in either the traditional low-turnover, passive index funds or high-turnover active funds. In 2003, Cliff Asness and Robert Arnott published an article that showed that companies that distributed larger dividends subsequently showed higher earnings growth."[32] As we saw in Myth #1, earnings growth is one of the primary drivers of stock returns over the longer-term. So a portfolio consisting of stocks with high dividends, rebalanced

---

[31] David Blanchett and Craig Israelsen, "Active Vs. Passive," *Journal of Indexes* (January/February 2009).

[32] Robert D. Arnott and Clifford S. Asness, "Surprise! Higher Dividends = Higher Earnings Growth" *Financial Analysts Journal*, Vol 59, No. 1. (January/February 2003).

infrequently, is in essence an index fund based on a sound return driver. This realization set off a flurry of research that led to the development of a number of innovative indexes based on the desire to perform, rather than simply be representative; and a number of index funds have been launched based on these indexes. I will present some of these in the Action section for this myth at www.JackassInvesting.com.

But first, let's take a look at the three big boys of today's most-referred-to indexes: the Dow Jones Industrial Average, the S&P 500, and the NASDAQ 100. You will see that each index has not only been redefined multiple times, and the constituents have been reconstituted frequently (they are hardly "passive"), but that the indexes themselves were never developed to provide maximum returns, only to be representative of a specific subset of "the market" as selected by their creators.

....

The great grandfather of U.S. equity indexes – Dow Jones Industrial Average

It was November 1882 when Charles Dow and Edward Davis Jones first set up shop in the basement of a candy store, described by John Gerrity, one of Dow's $5-a-week messengers, as "a little ramshackle building," at 15 Wall Street in New York City.[33] They began producing a hand-written, two-page financial newsletter, titled *Customer's Afternoon Letter*. It was quickly nicknamed by its first readership, "the flimsies," based on the ultra-thin paper stock chosen.

Dow Jones would send a fleet of reporters and messengers around to brokers and company offices looking for relevant business news. The messengers ran the stories back to the office where they were then dictated to a group of writers. In long-hand, the information was then transcribed on thin sheets of tissue paper that had multi-layers of carbon paper (the copy machine of the era) placed between each of 24 sheets. The individual sheets were then hand delivered to subscribers several times a day. The business thrived, as Dow Jones gained a reputation for delivering news that was both fast and accurate. This was in direct opposition to the competition's overtly biased

---

[33] Bruce J. Evensen, "Dow, Charles Henry," *American National Biography Online* (October 2008 Update), Retrieved February 14, 2011.

articles written to promote individual companies. The *Customer's Afternoon Letter* became the burgeoning industry's standard for accurate, ethical, and credible information. Dow and Jones were able to parlay their new-found reputation into an expanded four-page format. It officially became *The Wall Street Journal* on July 8, 1889.

On July 3, 1884, Dow Jones founded Dow Jones Indexes and released the first Dow Jones Average, which consisted of 11 companies, primarily railroads, in the *Customer's Afternoon Letter*.[34] But it took until May 26, 1896 before the first Dow Jones Industrial Average was officially published.[35] It consisted of just 12 stocks. It wasn't until 1928, long after Charles Dow's death, that the Dow Jones Industrial Average was expanded to include 30 stocks.[36]

The Dow Industrials has been one of the least frequently modified of the major indexes. Between its inception in 1928 and year-end 2009 the Index was changed only 48 times.[37] The Index composition is rather bizarre however, and certainly not developed to produce optimal returns for a portfolio designed to track its performance.

How the Dow Jones Industrial Average is calculated

First, *The Wall Street Journal* editors determine which stocks are to be in the average. This is admittedly subjective, with stocks being added only if, in the words of Dow Jones Indexes, "the company has an excellent reputation, demonstrates sustained growth, is of interest to a large number of people and accurately represents the market sectors covered by the averages."[38]

Second, the weightings assigned to each of the 30 components of the Index are determined, not by their relative market capitalization, or even in a fashion designed to approximate the overall impact they have on the economy, but by share price. Essentially, the stocks with the largest share price carry the

---

[34] "Charles Dow," *NNDB* (Soylent Communications, 2011), Retrieved February 14, 2011.
[35] "What happened to the original 12 companies in the DJIA?," Dow Jones Indexes. Retrieved February 14, 2011.
[36] "Dow Jones Industrial Average History," Dow Jones Indexes, Retrieved February 14, 2011.
[37] "Dow Jones Industrial Average History."
[38] "Dow Jones Industrial Average Methodology," Dow Jones Indexes, Retrieved February 14, 2011.

largest weight in the Index. For this reason alone they could never include Berkshire Hathaway, with a share price of more than $100,000, in the Index. That single stock would account for more than 90% of the price movement of the Index, while the other 29 stocks would account for the rest.[39]

In addition, while the general criteria that The Wall Street Journal editors use to select stocks for inclusion in the Index are also representative of criteria that would most likely exclude the worst performing stocks, the editors in no way represent that they are selecting stocks that they feel have the greatest appreciation potential. That's bad enough, but of greater concern to we investors is the allocation methodology. It is clearly not logical to assume that merely because a stock has a higher price that it should receive a higher allocation in the index.

> A "stock split" may be effected by a company when its share price rises to a price that is well above that of similar companies. The company makes the decision to "split" the stock to make it appear more "affordable." A 2-for-1 stock split means that the company issues every shareholder an additional share of stock for each share they already own. This does not create any additional value, as the market price will immediately adjust for this by dropping to half its previous price.

Are the Berkshire Hathaway "A" shares, simply because the stock was never split and therefore maintains a higher share price, a better value than another stock that has split? Obviously not. Yet, because their share prices are higher than they would be had they split, the Dow Jones Industrial Average allocates more to the stocks of companies with shares that have not been split.

Similar to the S&P 500 and the NASDAQ 100, which I will discuss next, the manager of the Dow Jones Industrial Average makes no attempt to select stocks

---

[39] As of February 2011 the average price of a stock in the Dow Jones Industrial Average ("DJIA") was $53. If Berkshire Hathaway was added to the Index, with an "A" share price of $125,000, it would dominate the index performance, with more than 98% of the weighting in the index. Here's the calculation: $125,000 / (($53 x 29) + (125,000)) = 98.79%]. That means that a 1% move in Berkshire Hathaway would move the DJIA .98%, while a 1% move in all of the other 29 stocks in the DJIA would move the DJIA just 0.02%. Berkshire Hathaway did create "B" shares coincident with its acquisition of Burlington Northern Santa Fe in 2009, that were priced at 1/30 the value of the "A" share, but even those would have dominated the performance of the DJIA. In January 2011, however, Berkshire Hathaway further split the "B" shares (50 to 1) resulting in a share price of $70. These could now be successfully added to the DJIA. Same company. But before the split it was off-limits to inclusion in the DJIA because of its share price. A simple stock split makes it acceptable. That in itself points out the absurdity of the process used to calculate the DJIA.

with characteristics to indicate they will appreciate at a faster rate than any other stocks. The Index is merely designed to "represent the market sectors covered by the averages." This begs one simple question for people who invest in mutual funds and Exchange Traded Funds (ETFs) designed to match the performance of the Dow Jones Industrial Average:

> "Why would a person subrogate their investment process to the arcane and off-the-cuff process followed by *The Wall Street Journal* editors rather than manage their portfolio themselves pursuant to a clearly defined, objective, profit motivated, systematic, and repeatable set of rules?"

The S&P 500

The S&P 500 has become the principal index against which stock portfolios are measured. It has also long been the most actively traded of U.S. stock index futures contracts. According to Elliott Shurgin, a veteran member of S&P's index committee, about $1 trillion worldwide is invested in funds that directly track the results of the S&P 500 Index. Think about that. $1 trillion is invested pursuant to methods that S&P itself states, in virtually every press release related to additions or deletions to its index, that those "Additions to and deletions from an S&P equity index do not in any way reflect an opinion on the investment merits of the companies concerned."[40] *That's no basis for intelligent investing. And that's why you can do better.*

"ETF" is the acronym for "Exchange Traded Fund." These are similar to mutual funds, in that they track baskets of stocks, bonds, commodities or other assets, but trade like a stock on an exchange throughout the day.

But first a little history. As you'll see, clearly, the S&P 500 Index is not "passive", neither in structure nor in the composition of its components.

---

[40] "Standard & Poor's Announces Changes to U.S. Indices," *Standard & Poor's* press release (June 12, 2008).

History of the S&P 500 [41] [42] [43]

Standard & Poor's introduced the S&P 500 Index in 1957. At the time it was introduced, Standard & Poor's already had a track record of creating market indexes, having introduced the 233 Composite Index in 1923. That index contained 233 stocks divided into 26 industry groups. Both the 233 Composite and each of the industry group indexes were calculated for publication once each week.

In 1928 Standard & Poor's recognized the need to publish an index on a more frequent basis. In that era before computers, calculating the 233 Composite was deemed too tedious to do on what first became a daily, then an hourly, basis. Because of this Standard & Poor's created a more manageable index composed of a subset of stocks. This index, the S&P 90 Stock Composite Index, was comprised of 50 industrial, 20 railroad and 20 utility stocks.

Following the introduction of the S&P 90 Stock Composite in 1928, Standard & Poor's continued to calculate its original 233 Composite and industry sub-sets on a weekly basis. However, they also continued to modify the Index through the addition of new companies and industry groups. By 1941 the "233" Composite contained 416 companies in 72 industry groups. By 1957 it had expanded to become the S&P 500 Index.

By the time the S&P 500 was introduced in 1957 there was the need to create a history for the Index so that people could accurately evaluate its past performance. The new S&P 500 Index was combined with the 90 Stock Composite Index to create a daily record going back to 1928.

Composition and management of the S&P 500

The S&P 500 Index originally consisted of 425 industrials, 60 utilities, and 15 railroads. As a requirement, all 500 stocks were listed on the New York

---

[41] "A History of Standard & Poor's – S&P 500 Index," Standard & Poor's, Retrieved February 14, 2011.

[42] "History of the Standard & Poor's," Cool Fire Technology LLC (2004), Retrieved February 14, 2011.

[43] "Investing Classroom – Stocks 200 – The S&P 500," Morningstar.com, Retrieved February, 14 2011.

Stock Exchange. At the time these stocks represented 90% of the value of all common stocks listed on the NYSE. The base level of the S&P 500 Index was set at 10, retroactive to a base period during the years 1941-1943. This worked out to an index value of 46.67 at year-end 1956, roughly in line with the average price per common share of $49.12 on December 31, 1956.

The continued growth and evolution of the U.S. economy once again required Standard & Poor's to modify the Index in order for it to stay relevant. In 1976, the S&P 500 was changed to be comprised of 400 industrials, 40 utilities, 40 financials and 20 transportation stocks. The financial component was added to better reflect those companies' relative and growing importance to the U.S. economy. For the same reason, the railroad component was modified to include airlines, air freight and trucking companies. For the first time, American Stock Exchange and Over-The-Counter (OTC) stocks were also included in the Index.

The next major change to the Index took place in 1988 when Standard & Poor's began to vary the weighting of each industry sub-group to more accurately reflect each industry's weighting within the overall market. Perhaps most importantly, the Index is calculated on a "capitalization-weighted" basis. This means that the largest companies have the largest impact on the index value. So the biggest allocation goes to the biggest companies, not the companies that have the greatest potential for stock price appreciation.

Recent changes in the S&P 500 Index

In addition to major structural changes made to the S&P 500 Index over its history, each year certain stocks are removed and others added to the Index. The characteristics of these stocks have changed over time to reflect the changes in the overall stock market. As of February 2011, a company wanting to be considered for inclusion in the S&P 500 must:[44]

- Be a U.S. company that is an operating company and not a closed-end fund, holding company, partnership investment vehicle, or royalty trust.

  And have:

- Adequate liquidity and a "reasonable" price. S&P wants to see the ratio of annual dollar value traded to float adjusted market capitalization of

---

[44] "S&P U.S. Indices – Index Methodology," Standard & Poor's, Retrieved February 14, 2011.

1.00 or greater and a minimum of 250,000 shares traded in each of the six months prior to evaluation for inclusion.

- Market capitalization exceeding $4 billion.

- Financial viability, usually measured as four consecutive quarters of positive as-reported profits; as reported earnings are GAAP Net Income excluding discontinued operations and extraordinary items.

- A healthy public float, meaning that the percentage of shares outstanding, not held by corporate insiders, comprise at least 50% of the stock.

Once a stock is in the Index, it may violate one of the conditions and still not be deleted if Standard & Poor's deems the violation to be temporary. Standard & Poor's believes that excessive turnover in index membership should be avoided when possible. That said, even during periods when the Index rules did not change, the Index's composition did. During the ten years from 2000 through 2009, 306 stocks were deleted from the Index and 306 stocks were added in their place.[45] This was done in order to keep the index composition in line with the methodology most recently outlined by Standard & Poor's. This is an average portfolio turnover, as measured by the number of stocks bought and sold, of 6.1%. While this level of portfolio turnover is low by the standards of most mutual fund managers, it is also not "passive". Most importantly, the turnover is not based on criteria designed to maximize returns, but simply to maintain the "representative" character of the Index.

The composition of the Index is not passive. Instead, it's an actively managed subjective compilation of 500 stocks that employees of Standard & Poor's have selected to be included in the Index. Mutual funds that track the Index are following a system designed and managed by the staff at S&P. Logically, the same question I just asked regarding the Dow Jones Industrial Average comes up for those investing in mutual funds and ETFs designed to match the performance of the S&P 500 Index:

> *"Why would a person subrogate their investment process to Standard & Poor's rather than manage their portfolio themselves pursuant to some clearly defined, objective, profit-motivated, systematic, and repeatable set of rules?"*

---

[45] "S&P 500 Stocks – Index Changes, Component Stock List, Historical Earnings Reports and Stock Splits, Stock Quotes and Charts," Standard & Poor's, Retrieved February 14, 2011.

The answer that seems to be undeniable is that people who place money in mutual funds that track the Index feel that they are incapable of "beating" the Index. They don't want to risk losing to it when they can simply invest in it. However, Standard & Poor's freely acknowledges that their index was not developed with any attempt to select stocks that had characteristics that would help them outperform other stocks. It was merely created to mimic the "average" performance of the stocks of the most important companies in the U.S.

But it *is* possible to beat the Index. It's an extremely rational expectation since the managers of these indexes have not structured them to maximize performance. In recent years many researchers have developed systematic processes that result in indexes composed of stocks based on characteristics that *are* statistically likely to result in market outperformance. I present some of these indexes in the Action section for this myth at www.JackassInvesting.com/actions.

The NASDAQ 100

The NASDAQ 100 was launched in January of 1985. This trading index, based on market capitalization, represents the largest non-financial issues listed on the NASDAQ Stock Market. The most popular method for investing in this index is through the NASDAQ-100 Index Tracking Stock ETF, listed under the ticker symbol "QQQ."

The way it works is that each year, in early December, NASDAQ announces its list of annual additions and deletions to the Index via a traditional press release. Replacements are made effective after the close of trading on the third Friday in December. And, if at any time during the year a security listed in the Index is no longer traded on the NASDAQ Stock Market, or is otherwise determined by NASDAQ to become ineligible for continued inclusion in the Index, the security will be replaced with the largest market capitalization security not currently in the Index and that meets the Index' eligibility criteria. Over the ten years ending in 2010, 128 stocks were removed from the Index and 128 were added in exchange.[46] This is an annual turnover rate of almost 13%.

In addition to the annual and intervening additions and deletions of securities in the Index, NASDAQ also reviews and adjusts the weightings

---

[46] "Historical Data – NASDAQ 100 Index," NASDAQ, Retrieved February 14, 2011.

assigned to each security on a quarterly basis. These adjustments are generated by a proprietary algorithm that is triggered if certain pre-established weight distribution requirements are not met. The notable term here is "proprietary". NASDAQ does not reveal the method they use to construct the index. But we do know that, similar to the Dow Industrials and the S&P 500, there is no attempt by NASDAQ to select stocks that have characteristics pointing to their ability to appreciate at a rate any faster than the rest of the pack. They clearly state that the Index is merely designed to "represent the largest non-financial domestic and international securities listed on the NASDAQ Stock Market based on market capitalization."[47] We also know that the Index is in no way balanced across those 100 securities. As of December 31, 2010 Apple made up more than 20% of the Index and the top four holdings received more than 33%. The top 13 stocks accounted for half of the Index's weighting.[48] The NASDAQ 100 is clearly not a balanced, diversified index. And as I will show in the Action section for this myth, studies have shown that even a simple, equal-weighted index will outperform the more "sophisticated" weighting methods used by the index creators such as Dow Jones indexes, Standard & Poor's and NASDAQ.

Once again; the same question should shine in 30 ft. neon to those who place money in mutual funds and ETFs designed to match the performance of the NASDAQ 100 Index:

"Why would a person subrogate their investment process to NASDAQ rather than manage their portfolio themselves pursuant to some clearly defined, objective, profit motivated, systematic and repeatable set of rules?"

A rational person would not.

---

[47] "NASDAQ-100 Index," NASDAQ, Retrieved February 14 2011.
[48] Although NASDAQ doesn't freely disclose the weightings for each of the holdings in the NASDAQ 100 Index (they sell this information for $10,000), the PowerShares QQQ ETF, which attempts to track the NASDAQ 100 index, is required to report its positions to the public. The data for composition of QQQ as of December 31, 2011 was obtained from the Invesco Power Shares web site, Retrieved February 14, 2011.

SUMMARY
MYTH 4

- Passive index investing is active investing. The only difference between the two is the percentage of stocks in the portfolio that are bought and sold each year (the "turnover").

- The major market indexes were not created with the intent of maximizing performance, only with the intent of being "representative."

- A rational person would not subrogate their investment process to the index managers; rather they would manage their portfolio themselves pursuant to some clearly defined, objective, profit-motivated, systematic, and repeatable set of rules.

Stay Invested So You Don't Miss the Best Days

March 10, 2009 was setting up to be another bad day for Wall Street. Stock markets had already suffered their worst yearly start on record. In just 4 weeks the S&P 500 had shed more than 22% of its value. Panic reigned and people were petrified that they would suffer additional unrecoverable losses. They had started selling aggressively, and the weekly survey of investor sentiment by the American Association of Individual Investors showed that more than 70% were bearish. This was the highest level in the history of the survey, dating back to the mid-1980s.[49] The latest *Rasmussen Reports* survey found that 53% of Americans thought that the United States was at least somewhat likely to enter a 1930s-like depression.[50]

---

[49] AAII sentiment survey data available at: http://www.aaii.com/files/surveys/sentiment. xls. Retrieved February 14, 2011.

[50] "53% Say It's Likely the U.S. Will Enter a Depression Similar to 1930's," *Rasmussen Reports* (March 10, 2009).

The next day's morning news contained non-stop reports of financial disasters from every quarter of business and industry. A *USA Today* study showed that 24 million Americans had gone from 'thriving' to 'struggling' since just the beginning of 2008.[51] U.S. Federal Reserve chief, Ben Bernanke, told the Senate Budget Committee that he saw little reason to believe that the trend of economic weakening had reached bottom.[52] The Asian Development Bank reported that financial assets around the world may have lost "well over $50 trillion" of value in the prior year and called the decline "astounding."[53]

But, the next day, March tenth, the stock market did not immediately collapse. In fact it rallied sharply. By the 4pm close in New York, the S&P 500 had gained a full 6.3%! In effect, the market produced a full year's expected return (without dividends) in just one day! People were panicked and fearful that they would miss out on additional gains. With the blind faith and reckless abandon of drunken sailors rowing ever-faster, ignoring a giant hole in the bottom of their boat, they bought aggressively.

Fear of missing out

Clearly, the prospects for stocks didn't change significantly during the day on March 10, 2009. What did change were people's emotions and their emotional reactions. A significant number of market participants shifted from a *fear of losing* their money to a *fear of missing out* on making money.

There has been some great research conducted over the past few decades detailing the decisions people make when faced with or regarding risk. Some of the earliest and best research is a result of the collaboration between Daniel Kahneman and Amos Tversky. Their groundbreaking 1979 paper *Prospect Theory: An Analysis of Decision Under Risk*[54], laid the groundwork for what later became the field of Behavioral Economics. Mr. Kahneman won the Nobel Prize in Economics in 2002 for his

---

[51] Susan Page, "24 million go from 'thriving' to 'struggling'," *USA Today* (March 10, 2009).

[52] Ben S. Bernanke, "Current economic and financial conditions and the federal budget" (testimony presented before the Committee on the Budget, U.S. Senate, Washington, D.C., March 3, 2009).

[53] Claudio M. Loser, "Global Financial Turmoil and Emerging Market Economies: Major contagion and a shocking loss of wealth?," *Asian Development Bank* (March 9, 2009): 7.

[54] Daniel Kahneman and Amos Tversky, "Prospect Theory: An Analysis of Decision under Risk," *Econometrica*, Vol 47, No. 2. (March 1979): 263-292.

work.[55] It is generally agreed that Mr. Tversky would have also received the Noble as well, had he not died in 1996.

Others, including Richard Thaler, at the University of Chicago Booth School of Business, established how human behavior leads to market anomalies, such as mispricing of stocks and the creation of buying and selling trends.[56] Their work, and the field of Behavioral Finance, supports my long-held belief that, in general, people don't make rational investment decisions. Emotions completely dominate their decision-making process. I won't attempt to reproduce Thaler's findings here, but I can share an anecdote that will put it all in perspective.

I have a friend who decided to buy AOL Time Warner stock (now just Time Warner, TWX) in the early 2000s. This was shortly after Time Warner merged with AOL, in one of the most hyped and infamous mergers in recent history. It stands as an example of one of the greatest failed mergers on record. Shortly after the merger, the company's stock price exceeded $50 per share. As TWX started its swan dive into the upper teens, my friend held on. He was clearly upset by the losses he was incurring. But when I finally asked him about his plan for preserving the money he had put into TWX stock, his response proved that he wasn't as concerned with the losses he was suffering as he was with the prospect of missing out on any gains if he sold prematurely. He didn't want to sell the stock, he said, "because what if right after I sold it went up?!?" He was more comfortable taking the hit of a major loss than dealing with the "what if" factor. Wow! Talk about being married to a position. The punch line to this sad story is that TWX ended up falling below $10 per share by late 2008.

In contrast, I have another friend, Charlie, who made a small fortune trading in the gold market in the late 1970s. I traded with Charlie in the mid-1980s and got some insight into his trading approach. Charlie's vision was clear concerning the risk-return conundrum. "Picture the market you are trading as being a conveyor belt," he said, "with dollar bills flowing past. Most of them you will miss. Every now and then, just reach down and pick up the easy ones." In other words, you don't need to pick up profits on every trade. In fact, there are so many trades available every day that you'll miss the vast majority of them anyway. So logic dictates that you shouldn't get fixated on those very few that you happened to notice. It can drive you crazy thinking of every trade that "could've" been. Besides, it's detrimental to positive long-term performance.

---

[55] "The Sveriges Riksbank Prize in Economic Sciences in Memory of Alfred Nobel 2002 Daniel Kahneman, Vernon L. Smith," Nobel Prize (2002). NobelPrize.org. Retrieved February 14, 2011.

[56] "Richard H. Thaler," *University of Chicago Booth School of Business*, ChicagoBooth.edu. Retrieved February 14, 2011.

The conventional wisdom offered by financial pundits preaches the fear of missing out on profits. But it is not virtuous to maintain long positions simply out of fear of missing large up days in the market.

Only taking the best trades and avoiding the disasters? That's investing. Being afraid to cut losses for fear of missing out on profits? That's gambling.

When perception is reality

Remember the study that refuted the belief in Myth #1 that stocks always provide an intrinsic return? Over the longest periods the stock market's performance is driven by aggregate corporate earnings (and the growth of those earnings). In shorter time periods the market's performance is driven more by the multiple that people are willing to pay for those earnings. What the exaggerated stock market performance of March 10, 2009 illustrates is that

in the shortest time frames – hours to months – stock market performance is driven not by earnings, nor by the multiple people are willing to pay for those earnings; rather, they are driven by people's perception of what other people will be willing to pay for those earnings.

This naturally leads to another misperception, and this 5th myth...that it is important to stay invested in order not to miss the best days (strongest up surges) in the stock market.

How many times have you been told or read that if you trade in and out of the stock market you risk missing the "ten" (or some other number) best profit-making days? I've read the studies and heard the talking heads that preached this fear-based myth for years. And the investment experts and soothsayers who preach this "fear of missing out" philosophy are usually prepared to support their position with studies that show the unfavorable impact that missing those best days would have on the overall return. So let's check their facts.

At first blush, the results do seem to support the "fear of missing out" advocates. For example, if you had invested $1 in the S&P 500 on January 1, 1990, by the end of 2010 it would have been worth $3.56, assuming all dividends were reinvested. But if you happened to be out of the market and missed the ten best days during that 21 year period, the investment would be worth only $1.78, exactly half that amount. Whoa, better not do that!

But a trade based on fear – the fear of missing out on the best days in the market – is a losing trade. It's emotional. As I point out in the prior myth, emotions lose money. *The fact is you're losing out on big moves all the time.* Did you catch the 500% run-up in the uranium market during 2005-2007? How about the doubling in the price of the Baltic dry freight (shipping rates) index during the first two months of 2009? There are thousands of such trading opportunities every year. Guess what? Most people missed them all! Most people are so fixated on stocks and a few other markets that they don't even know these other opportunities exist.

There's a lot of activity taking place in a lot of markets virtually every day. Here's just a small sampling of the profit opportunities you likely missed during the recent past. Every one of these markets is tradable. Every one of these price moves occurred in just one day. You can open an account to trade these markets as easily as you can open an account to trade stocks.

- On December 31, 2008 crude oil prices jumped almost 10% from $53.50 to $58.73 per barrel
- On September 10, 2009 natural gas prices climbed almost 7% from $4.64 to $4.95 per mmBtu
- On October 9, 2009 orange juice prices rocketed almost 10% from less than $0.99 to more than $1.08 per pound of concentrate
- On December 3, 2010, cotton prices rose more than 5% from $1.17 to over $1.23 per pound

I realize that for some of you, these opportunities will only translate to an increased anxiety level. You may be thinking, "OMG! I'm missing out on all these profit opportunities!" Of course instilling panic is not my purpose here (I missed each of these trading opportunities as well). My purpose is to illustrate the following:

Missing a big day in the U.S. stock market is no different than missing a big move in the uranium market. Give it no more thought. Profit opportunities abound. It's irrational to be fixated on one – being long stocks – at the virtual exclusion of all others.

Watch your back!

The fact of the matter is that if you insist on using fear as your strategy, then it's the *worst* trading days of the year that you should be concerned with, not the best. *Missing the worst down days improves returns by more than the amount gained by capturing the best up days.* Using the $1 invested example previously discussed, while missing the ten best days lowers your return by $1.78, missing the ten worst days more than doubles your return, increasing it by $4.03. That's right, your $1.00 turned into $7.59. It gets even better. As Figure 11 shows, missing out on the twenty or thirty worst days can dramatically boost your returns.

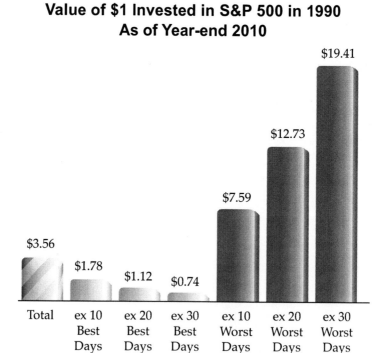

**Value of $1 Invested in S&P 500 in 1990
As of Year-end 2010**

Figure 11

Although the benefit of missing the worst days is obvious, a fair question to ask would be, "what would happen if you missed *both* the ten best and the ten worst days?" In this case, the investment would be worth $3.79, even better than the $3.56 figure for staying in the market. Similarly, if you miss the twenty best and the twenty worst days, the investment would be worth even more, $3.99; and missing the thirty best and worst improves performance still more, to $4.06 (Figure 12).

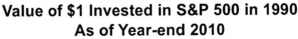

Value of $1 Invested in S&P 500 in 1990
As of Year-end 2010

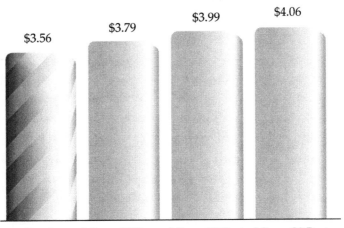

| Total | Minus 10 Best
& Worst Days | Minus 20 Best
& Worst Days | Minus 30 Best
& Worst Days |

Figure 12

This simple study clearly illustrates the tremendous benefit of managing risk and being out of the market during the losing periods. Even if you also give up the same number of the best market days, you are better off financially. That is because the positive impact on a portfolio of avoiding the worst days is far greater than the value of capturing the best days. Most successful investors understand this. A friend of mine, Jack Schwager, wrote a book titled *Market Wizards*.[57] I highly recommend the book if you haven't read it, and I'd recommend it highly as a re-read if you have. It contains interviews with some of the top traders of that time, many of whom remain top traders today. One theme resonates throughout the book: preserve your profits and cut your losses short. Trader after trader makes it clear that their success had more to do with minimizing losses than with maximizing gains. Staying invested in order to avoid missing the best days is exactly counter to this successful mentality.

---

[57] Jack D. Schwager, Market Wizards (New York: HarperCollins, 1989).

Armed with the information presented above, it is clear that avoiding loss can have a dramatically positive impact on portfolio performance. It can have an even bigger positive impact on your psyche.

The data needed to avoid the worst investing days and make the right buying choices is readily available to every person. So why aren't they able to avoid the fallacy perpetuated by the myth? Why are they instilled with the erroneous fear that they will miss out on profits rather than the fear they will be exposed to tremendous losses?

My answer is three-fold. First, as I also point out in *Myth #2, "Buy and Hold Works Well for Long Term Investors*, buy-and-hold only serves as another way to rationalize losses. Financial advisors are famous for preaching that it is necessary to regularly accept big losses to ensure you are still invested when those "big up" days come around.

A second reason is a result of across-the-board conflicts of interest, leading directly to a loss of objectivity on the part of financial pundits and press. It's just a fact that many financial professionals have a vested interest in people maintaining their long stock positions, as they often have no valid alternative to offer them.

Finally, the third possible reason is that it's highly probable that the investment pros are taking the easy road and only telling their clients what they have historically wanted or expected to hear. If an advisor attempts to avoid large losing days but instead misses out on big profits, he risks being fired by his company or his client. Doing what other financial advisors are doing, even if it's wrong, is the safer "career" move. But, at the end of the day, why should you care about their rationalizations, conflicts of interest, or career risks. Your only concern and focus should be your own profit and peace of mind.

Angry Environments

"Angry Environments" exist. These are periods when market conditions are least suitable to any given market or company. To be in such an environment and not adapt is not smart. Would you walk around in the cold all winter without a coat? No. So don't do the same with your positions in the stock market. Cover up.

If we are able to detect when we're in an angry environment, or better yet, when we are about to enter into an angry environment, we can take the necessary steps to avoid losses. In the case of the U.S. stock market, these steps could include reducing position sizes or going flat stocks. Another option is to enter into long positions in stocks that are likely to perform best in that environment and short positions in stocks that are likely to underperform. And, as shown in our study, even if in our attempt to miss the largest losing days we also miss the largest profitable days, we'd be better off. So rather than simply spouting the overused fear-based mantra about staying invested to avoid missing the best up days, let's react rationally to the market conditions with which we are presented.

In the Action section at www.JackassInvesting.com/actions, I present specific strategies you can employ to do this. In Action #3 I present a strategy that uses investor sentiment to time the overall market. In Action #7 I present a momentum-based timing strategy that takes both long and short positions in global markets. In Actions #8 and #16 I present two strategies that vary allocations among market sectors and countries that are most likely to outperform other sectors or countries. In Action #10 I present two mutual funds that use individual stock fundamentals and technical indicators to create more balanced portfolio of both long and short stocks. And in Action #12 I present ways to access global trading strategies that provide tremendous diversification of both global markets and return drivers. Each of these Actions will assist you in sidestepping, minimizing and even profiting from the losses suffered by the buy-and-holders during angry environments.

SUMMARY
MYTH 5

- Investing is the process of taking the best trades and avoiding the disasters. Gambling is being afraid to cut losses for fear of missing out on profits.

- You are missing big moves in numerous markets virtually every day. Missing a big day in the U.S. stock market is no different than missing a big move in any other. Give it no more thought. Profit opportunities abound. It's irrational to be fixated on one – being long stocks – at the virtual exclusion of all others.

- "Angry Environments" exist for every market. Rather than simply spouting the overused fear-based mantra about staying invested to avoid missing the best up days, a rational investor will follow a systematic process that will allow them to react rationally to the market conditions with which they are presented, thereby sidestepping or profiting from Angry Environments.

Buy Low, Sell High

It was the heyday of the great equity bull market of the 1990s and I was chatting with a friend in the wealth management business. He zealously employed a buy low, sell high strategy for his clients who were all extremely pleased with the results. When I asked him the specifics he let me in on his secret.

"We start by targeting a buy price on a stock that is below the current price. If a stock is at $50 we may place limit orders at $48. Then if we get filled we place a sell order at $52. After we get filled on the sale we do it all over again."

"But what happens if you buy at $48 and the stock doesn't make it up to $52, but instead keeps falling?" I asked.

"We may buy more. But we're patient and only buy good stocks so the price will eventually come back."

Well, what my friend was seemingly blind to is that the "be patient" M.O. he was prescribing for his clients is, by no means, bankable. Since history has proven that good stocks have an annoying habit of turning into bad stocks, his clients were being exposed to open-ended risk. Trading with that strategy in the hope of capturing a limited profit, but remaining exposed to open-ended losses, will eventually lead to the equivalent of trading death - a poor-folio. It's gambling.

My friend was not the only one who employed this strategy. In fact, I heard it from friends at the gym, a tech consultant my business hired (he only did it with Intel stock, because he *knew* that company better than others), and many others. The fact is, in a bull market, virtually *any* strategy that involves buying first and selling later produces profits. If a stock sells off and you buy it you will soon be rewarded with higher prices. And as I will point out in the next myth, this "winning" behavior is reinforced, even if it's wrong. This behavior is what drove the doubling of the P/E ratio of the S&P 500 Index from 20 in January 1995 to more than 40 in April 2000.[58]
In fact, this change in investor sentiment (to "irrational exuberance") is the major factor that *caused* the great bull market of the 1990s.

That said, how can anyone argue with that or say that an approach of buying low and selling high is bad. After all, profit is defined by the approach. The answer is that doing it is a far cry from simply defining it.

"Testing – testing" buy low, sell high

A "drawdown" is what occurs when the value of any investment falls from a peak price to a lower price and is usually expressed in percentage terms. A drop from $10 to $8 for example is a drawdown of 20%. The "maximum drawdown" is the largest percentage loss that occurred in a drawdown before the previous peak price is once again exceeded.

As a test of buy low, sell high, I looked at the performance of the S&P 500 from the start of the most recent secular bull market on August 11, 1982 through August 10, 2010. Over this 29-year period the S&P 500 produced an average annual return of 9.09%. As we know however, this return did not appear without causing widespread angst. Significant drawdowns occurred throughout that period, causing considerable emotional stress for buy-and-holders. So I am not preaching the buy-and-hold mantra. As you will continue to see throughout this book, there are lower risk ways to manage your money. What I am saying is that as bad as buy-and-hold is;

---

[58] The P/E ratio is calculated using the Cycle-Adjusted Price-to-Earnings ("CAPE") that divides the current stock price by the average annual earnings over the prior 10 years. The P/E ratio using price to just the prior year's reported earnings shows a similar doubling in the P/E over the period, from 15 in 1995 to 30 at year-end 1999, as reported on the Standard & Poor's Index Services website. Retrieved February 14, 2011.

buy low, sell high is worse. You may expect a strategy of buying low and selling high to limit the maximum drawdown experienced, since you will not be entering the market with a buy until after the market has already at least partially sold off. But here is where investment reality deviates substantially from standard expectations.

Figure 13 and Figure 14 compare the performance of buying-and-holding the S&P 500 with buying after a 10% drop and then selling out following a 20% rally from that purchase price.

S&P 500 Performance: Buy-and-Hold Compared with Buy Low – Sell High

	Buy & Hold	Buy Low, Sell High
Years	29	29
Average Annual Return	9.09%	4.69%
Annualized Volatility	18.14%	15.94%
Maximum Drawdown	-54.07%	-52.71%
% Profitable Days	53.29%	53.28%

Figure 13

Performance of S&P 500 Buy-and-Hold Compared with Buy Low – Sell High

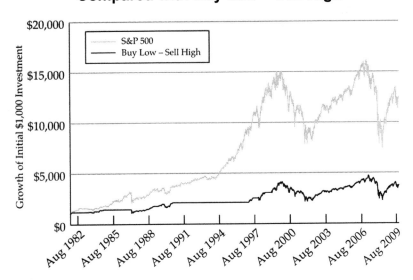

Figure 14

Two statistics immediately jump out. First, the annualized return drops dramatically, from 9.09% to just 4.69%. Second, the maximum drawdown barely changes. That is because although the strategy may have bought after a dip in prices, the market still rallied after being bought, but not the 20% required to sell out of the position. Then it proceeded to drop. Since this strategy doesn't limit losses, only profits (by selling out at a pre-arranged profit), a person using this strategy would have been in for the brunt of the declines.

Buying after a 10% decline and selling after a 20% gain is only one of many parameters that a person could have chosen to trade this strategy. To ensure that this was not just an inconvenient selection of a poor parameter set, I tested this same strategy looking at every 5% buy point during selloffs of between 5% and 30%, and then exited those trades following gains of the same amounts. This resulted in a total of 36 separate parameter sets being tested. None of the sets produced a return that exceeded those of buy-and-hold. In fact, the average annual return across the 36 parameter sets was just 3.21%. Even worse, despite this substantially reduced return the average maximum drawdown remained quite high at 44.44%. The end result was that the ratio of return to drawdown was less than half that of the buy-and-hold approach. *Buy low, sell high is clearly an inferior method of trading.*

The "feel good" method of trading

The buy low, sell high way of thinking remains extremely popular despite its obvious inadequacies. The myth extols the consistent, beneficial results, supposedly "baked in" to the system – making it a "feel good" style of trading. When you buy something, such as a stock, and then sell it after it subsequently rises in price, it always feels good. That's basic. But what should you do if the stock continues to rise after you sell it? In the 'feel good' method of trading, you wait for it to once again fall in price, preferably to below the level where you sold it, and then buy it again. In a bull market the followers of buy low, sell high get rewarded, as do all long-biased traders (those who maintain long positions in the hope of ever-rising prices). But in a bull market the price often doesn't fall back to below where you sold it, leaving you to either 'chase' the stock and buy it at a higher price (missing the intervening gains) or give up on buying it altogether. As a result, as a group, buy low, sell high traders do worse than if they simply held on to their positions throughout the bull market.

Conversely (and perversely), in a bear market you will almost certainly get the opportunity to buy the stock back at a lower price, only to be rewarded with ever lower prices as the bear mauls the stock. The end effect is the same. Over time you will underperform even a simple buy-and-hold approach.

However, that doesn't stop people from habitually employing this method. Millions do. They do so for a variety of reasons, many of which they often don't know or understand themselves. While those employing this method will claim their motivation is purely profit; their real motivation is very often quite different. People have told me how trading makes them "feel alive" – that they like the "action" that trading provides. While they're making money they are provided with great day-to-day, temporary satisfaction. When buy low, sell high works, people often experience a misplaced feeling of being *in control*. Feeling any of these emotions should serve as a warning light. If it's the *trading* that makes you feel good and not the *profits* at the end of the trade, you're gambling. If profits are truly your goal, then once again it's time to pull a u-turn and put "The Opposite" approach to good use.

In the next chapter I'll show you exactly how to profit by buying strength and selling weakness and in the Action section for this myth at www.JackassInvesting.com I present a profitable time-tested trading strategy that exploits the losing behavior of the buy-low, sell-high crowd. It does this by including a requirement that the stocks you buy must be within 10% of their 12-month highs – exactly the opposite of a buy low, sell high strategy.

SUMMARY
MYTH 6

- Buy low, sell high is clearly an inferior method of trading in that it preserves losses, yet limits profits.

- Attempting to buy low and sell high, as it's practiced by the vast majority of people, will eventually lead to the equivalent of trading death – a poor-folio. It's gambling.

- Buy low – sell high creates a misplaced feeling of being in control. If it's the trading that makes you feel good and not the profits at the end of the trade, you're gambling. If profits are truly your goal, then once again it's time to pull a u-turn and put "The Opposite" approach to good use. I'll show how in the next myth.

It's Bad to
Chase Performance

In early 2001 I received a call from a woman asking if she could come by my office and take me out for lunch. She had read about me in the book *Bulls, Bears and Millionaires*[59] and thought I could help her.

The author had dedicated a chapter to how I had started trading with just $5,000 (in 1979) and worked my way through fits and starts and ended up building a thriving trading business. She had started with $10,000 a few years before our lunch and, chasing performance all the way, fully participated in the technology stock rally, growing her initial 10k into a fortune of a few million dollars.

Unfortunately, she had no exit strategy. Within months after the tech market peaked, she had lost it all, as the "dot bomb" exploded with full force. She had chased performance and lost.

---

[59] Robert Koppel, *Bulls, Bears and Millionaires: War Stories of the Trading Life* (Chicago: Dearborn Trade Publications, 1997), 16-32.

The problem however was not that she chased performance, nor her choice of what to chase; rather that she did so without any plan. It wasn't a question of "if," it was just a question of "when" the tech bull market was going to come to an end. She had made no plan for that eventuality. Worst yet, even after the tech bubble burst and stock prices fell, she never cried "uncle," never gave in, and remained eternally hopeful that prices would once again rise. As a result she rode her account down until the broker stepped in and made her decision for her by closing out her positions.

She was not alone. In fact, it was the aggregate behavior of her and thousands, perhaps millions, of other people like her that created the bubble in the first place. While trends can often be based on market fundamentals, this is not a mandatory requirement for a trend to take place. Instead, there is a common psychological return driver that underlies all trends. It is this fact:

Winning behavior is reinforced, even if it's wrong

When a market rises, those who believed it would, and got in early, become true believers. They tell their friends. Their friends tell their friends. More people buy and the market continues to go up. With every buy they are eventually rewarded. At some point, the price of that market loses touch with its true value. But that doesn't stop the price from climbing. Sure, underlying fundamentals can trigger or exacerbate the trend, but the trend continues primarily as more people profit from their past buys, convincing themselves and others that their act of buying was "right." Even when pricing gets way out of line with reality they become true believers and rationalize why "this time it's different." This crowd behavior creates trends - sometimes mega-trends. And those trends, in turn, create opportunity.

Statistical evidence of trends

If the distribution of returns in a market were randomly distributed (also called a "normal" or "Gaussian" distribution) and did not "trend," a graph of the monthly percentage moves would trace out a perfect bell shaped curve. But markets don't behave that way. Figure 15 displays the frequency distribution of the monthly percentage moves made in the S&P 500 over the past 60 years. What pops out as obvious is that the distribution of monthly returns is not bell shaped. It's both skewed towards lower returns and simultaneously displays "thicker tails" than a normal distribution.

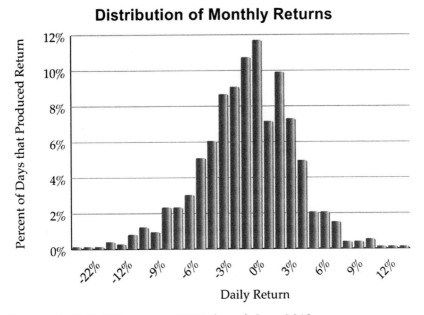

Figure 15. *S&P 500 January 1950 through June 2010*

This is significant and in fact unsurprising. Significant because it provides trading opportunities, which I will present here. Unsurprising, because the evidence of the returns of the market being skewed towards being more negative than positive was already laid out in *Myth #5 – Stay Invested So You Don't Miss the Best Days.* In exposing that myth we saw that by avoiding the "worst" market days your portfolio performs much better than had you avoided the same number of "best" days. That's telling us that the worst days are worse than the best days are best. This tendency for returns to be skewed towards larger negative performance is cleverly defined by statisticians as negative skew. And in fact the *"skewness"* of the distribution of the S&P 500 monthly returns is -0.436.

The second observation, that the tails are thicker than what should be expected in a normal distribution is what statisticians call positive "kurtosis." Thick tails are *positive* kurtosis and thin tails are *negative* kurtosis. The kurtosis of the distribution of the S&P 500 monthly returns is +1.761. Whereas a bell curve is indicative of a random distribution of prices, this positive kurtosis is evidence of trending market behavior. When any particular market trends it is possible to exploit that trend by chasing performance and profit over time. In the Action for this chapter at www.JackassInvesting.com, we'll create a strategy that does just that. But first, let's take a look at Standard & Poor's approach to tracking the profit potential of this trending behavior.

The Standard & Poor's Diversified Trends Indicator

Standard & Poor's, which manages the S&P 500 Stock Index, also maintains and calculates the performance of the Standard & Poor's Diversified Trends Indicator (S&P DTI).[60] This is an index that uses a simple trend-following strategy to take positions in 24 futures markets. Specifically, towards the end of the month the strategy looks at the price of each of the markets and if that price is above the exponential moving average of the past seven months, a long position is taken. If the market price is below the price of the exponential moving average, a short position is taken. Don't let the term "exponential moving average" scare you. There's nothing complicated about it. A moving average is simply the average of a specified number of prices. A seven-month moving average therefore is simply the average of the closing prices at the end of the past seven months. An "exponential" moving average simply weights the value of the current months more than the oldest months. Before I display the performance of the S&P DTI let me first describe how it is structured and point out some risks that can creep into trading strategy development.

The temptation to tweak – the flaw in the S&P Diversified Trends Indicator

As is evident from the description, the S&P DTI is a "trend following" based trading strategy. If the trend is up the strategy will indicate a buy. If the trend is down a short position will be signaled in each of the markets. Well, almost. While this trading strategy actually allows long positions to be taken in all 24 markets, it doesn't allow short positions to be taken in the four energy markets that are in the indicator. S&P rationalizes this uneven application of the trading criteria, and not shorting the energy markets, as being due to the fact that energy is subject to continuous demand with supply and concentration risk – hence they don't want to be caught short. But I believe that their prohibition against short-selling the energy markets is almost certainly a result of the developers of the trading strategy "curve-fitting" their strategy to ensure that it performed well on the past data. This is a common flaw in trading strategy development. When a strategy underperforms in a back-test, developers often modify it to perform better and subsequently rationalize the change. I see the prohibition on short selling energy markets by S&P as just such a rationalization. Here's **why;**

---

[60] "S&P 500 Diversified Trends Indicator (DTI)," *Standard & Poor's*. Retrieved February 14, 2011.

"Backwardation" in Energy Futures

Futures markets give traders the opportunity to buy and sell a wide range of markets for "future" delivery. This means that a trader can sell crude oil futures for delivery a year from today, rather than sell the actual physical commodity today. This enables them to lock in a price today at which they will sell their commodity in the future. Often, the futures contract for a specific commodity trades at a premium to the current cash price. For example, as I am writing this, the cash price of corn is approximately $3.90 per bushel, while the futures price for corn to be delivered in one year is $4.40. This structure, when the futures price is above the cash price, is referred to as "contango." As time marches forward, eventually the date of the futures contract becomes today's date and the contract expires. At expiration, the futures price, by definition, is set to the cash price at that time. In the case of the corn example this means that the futures price will drop $0.50 over the next year unless the cash price changes. This produces a strong headwind to those who bought corn at $4.40 and a tailwind to those who sold. (Figure 16).

Theoretical Price Convergence of Corn Futures to Cash
(Cash at $3.90 & 12-month Futures Price of $4.40)

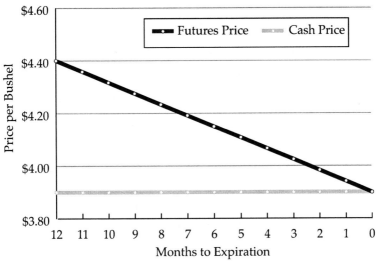

Figure 16

For much of the back-test period of the S&P DTI, however, the energy markets traded in "backwardation." Backwardation simply means that the futures prices are trading at prices *lower* than the current cash price. When a trading system enters into a short position in a futures contract at a price that is lower than the cash price, it is trading against the equivalent of a headwind. Ultimately, that futures price will converge with the cash price. In the process, even if the cash price stays even and doesn't rise, the futures price will rise to meet the cash price and there will be losses suffered on the short position entered in that futures contract.

It is because of these losses suffered in back-testing energy futures that I believe the developers of the S&P DTI prohibited short-selling in energy futures. They then rationalized a reason – that energy is subject to continuous demand with supply and concentration risk – for never taking short positions in the energy futures markets. The proper approach would have been to take all short trades in addition to all long trades. An alternative would be to add a filter that eliminates all trades where the risk doesn't warrant the trade. In that case, they could filter out short trades in markets trading in steep backwardation and long trades in markets trading in steep contango (upward sloping forward curve). But instead, they simply prohibited short positions in energy markets.

Applying trading systems inconsistently across different markets is a common temptation among trading system developers. They uncover a sound return driver but in back-testing discover that it incurred substantial losses, or at least underperformed, in certain markets. Rather than applying the system uniformly, or, better yet, fully understanding the reason for the system's failure in certain markets, they eliminate those markets from the portfolio. Unfortunately, this results in misleading back-tested results that are *not* predictive of future performance.

Performance is not its primary goal

But that's not the only flaw in the S&P DTI. Similar to the stock market indexes such as the Dow Industrials and S&P 500, the S&P DTI was not constructed with performance as its primary goal. In fact, Standard & Poor's explicitly states that the markets in the Indicator were not selected as "a means for achieving performance per se,"[61] but were chosen based on fundamental characteristics and liquidity. In fact, the financial markets in the Index were selected based on their "economic significance" and the agricultural markets

---

[61] "Standard & Poor's Diversified Trends Indicator - Methodology and Implementation," *Standard & Poor's* (January 2007): 4. Retrieved February 14, 2011.

and their allocations were selected based on their levels of production. Both these criteria were probably necessary for Standard & Poor's to achieve its goal of having the Indicator accepted by institutional investors (see *Myth #15 – The Largest Investors Hold All the Cards*), but neither economic significance nor production levels are of great consequence if the goal was performance.

But these foibles inherent in the construction of the S&P DTI don't negate the fact that trend following – chasing performance – works. The summary performance table (Figure 17) and chart (Figure 18) that follow show the performance of the S&P DTI compared with that of the S&P 500 TR Index from January 1988 through December 2010. The performance of the S&P DTI is calculated by Standard & Poor's using back-tested data prior to 2004 and by calculating the performance in real-time from January 2004 through December 2006. The performance from March 2007 through June 2010 is that of the Rydex|SGI Managed Futures Strategy H fund (RYMFX). This is an actual fund that you can put money into that trades pursuant to the S&P DTI.

Performance Comparison, S&P 500 TR vs. S&P DTI

	S&P 500 TR	S&P DTI
Years	23	23
Average Annual Return	9.73%	8.82%
Annualized Volatility	15.99%	6.70%
Maximum Drawdown	-50.96%	-16.62%
% Profitable Months	64%	69%

Figure 17

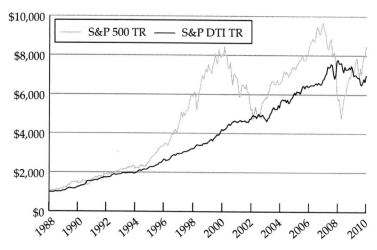

Growth of Hypothetical $1,000 in the S&P Diversified Trends Indicator & S&P 500 Total Return Index

Figure 18

The performance of the S&P DTI not only shows that trend following works, but also that true portfolio diversification can reduce risk. As shown in the table and chart, the S&P DTI delivered annualize returns that were just 1% lower than those of the S&P 500 TR Index, but with only 42% of the volatility. Perhaps more importantly, the S&P DTI suffered a maximum drawdown of just 16.6%, versus a drawdown of more than 50% for the S&P 500 TR Index. This last point is highly significant because the drawdown (maximum peak-to-trough loss) is a true measure of the "pain" felt by a person while holding a position.

"Volatility," also referred to more precisely as "Standard Deviation," is a measure of the variability of returns. It can be calculated either daily, monthly or annually. The figure represents the range of returns, around the mean return, that can be expected to occur in two out of every three periods. For example, if the annualized return is 10% and the annualized volatility is 8%, then in two out of every three years it can be expected that the annualized return will range from 2% to 18% (10% ± 8%).

The fact is that chasing performance, meaning systematically identifying the strongest trends and allocating money to them, is a valid and proven strategy that captures the return driver based on this self-reinforcing behavior. Many successful professional investors use this trend-following methodology, which is sometimes also referred to as *momentum trading*, to take both long and short positions in a wide variety of markets including equities, currencies, and commodities.[62]

The key is to ensure that you are the trend follower, not the trend creator. There's a big difference. One reacts to the markets in a disciplined, systematic fashion and makes money, while the other trades emotionally and loses. People who chase performance without a plan, in the aggregate, lose money while creating the trends, jumping out at the bottom and in at the top. Trend followers, on the other hand, systematically identify trends and ride them until their strategies indicate they have ended. In the Action section for this myth I'll present a trend following strategy that profits from chasing performance. This demonstrates the following:

> *A simple trend following strategy employed across a diversified portfolio of uncorrelated markets can produce returns relative to volatility and drawdowns that easily exceed that of a buy-and-hold strategy in stocks.*

Diversification – when less is more

The reason for the superior risk-adjusted performance of the S&P DTI relative to the S&P 500 TR Index is two-fold. First, despite the fact that the S&P DTI trades in just 24 markets – less than 5% of the 500 stocks held in the S&P 500 TR Index – the smaller S&P DTI portfolio is actually more diversified, as it incorporates many markets that trade independently of each other. As a result the S&P DTI is not subject to the same single "event" risk that underlies a position in the S&P 500 TR Index. Losses in its constituent positions are unlikely to all occur at the same time. Second, the trading strategy underlying the S&P DTI is adaptive while the buy-and-hold strategy employed by the S&P 500 TR Index is not. When people's sentiment changes and they start selling certain markets, driving their prices lower, the trading strategy powering the S&P DTI adapts, entering into short positions in those down-trending markets. In contrast, the S&P 500 TR Index naively maintains its long positions in every stock, incurring losses.

---

[62] One author and trader, Michael Covel, has written several books that chronicle the lives of trend following traders and the use of trend following strategies. See more at: http://www.trendfollowing.com/trend-following-book.html.

The performance of the S&P 500 TR demonstrates that simply increasing the number of markets in a portfolio does not, in and of itself, result in diversification. This is strategically significant and highlights one of the core tenets of this book. Simply buying hundreds of stocks, spread across all sectors, does *not* provide portfolio diversification. Yet this belief is repeated across numerous publications and by numerous investment advisors and industry professionals. (I will cover this concept in more detail in *Myth #12 - Futures Trading is Risky, Myth #18 – Diversification Failed in the '08 Financial Crisis,* and *Myth #20 – There is No Free Lunch.*)

This comparison points out a truth that, all by itself, dramatically questions, if not refutes, conventional "investment" wisdom.

> *If you were to make a single investment and had to choose between the S&P 500 and the S&P DTI, the clear, logical decision is to place the money in the S&P DTI.*

Yet the conventional wisdom has people doing the exact opposite, placing a substantial percentage of their portfolios in the less diversified and much riskier S&P 500.

SUMMARY
MYTH 7

- Trends exist and are perpetuated because winning behavior is reinforced, even if it's wrong.

- The distribution of stock market returns shows strong evidence of trending behavior.

- A simple trend following strategy employed across a diversified portfolio of just 24 uncorrelated markets can produce returns relative to volatility and drawdowns that easily exceed that of a buy-and-hold strategy in stocks.

- If you were to make a single investment and had to choose between the S&P 500 and the S&P DTI, the clear, logical decision is to place the money in the S&P DTI.

Trading is Gambling – Investing is Safer

My friend Mark is an experienced professional trader. He started his career in the early 1970s, on the floors of the New York Stock Exchange and New York Mercantile Exchange. He was then tapped by Merrill Lynch to form what became their Financial Futures and Options Group. In 1983 he co-founded a successful commodity trading advisor (CTA) firm and today runs an investment firm that manages billions of dollars in institutional investor's money.

Mark is also a very disciplined trader. Before he even thinks about incorporating a new market or trading strategy into his portfolio, he thoroughly researches its underlying return drivers and carefully tests its viability while risking limited capital. He's intent on making sure he has a competitive edge (fully understanding his return drivers) before committing any substantial capital.

Over dinner one night he told me about a new trading program he'd been researching and participating in over a couple of years' time. Sticking with his super-disciplined style, he started small, risking less than $1,000 per trade. As he gained more skill in his approach he increased his exposure. At the time we were sitting down to that dinner he had increased his risk to a few thousand dollars – and was regularly profiting on each trade.

Mark had a clear understanding of the statistics that drove this new program. But it was his understanding of the other market participants' behaviors that gave him the extra edge. This is similar to the edge I identified in *Myth #3 – You Can't Time the Market*. In the Action section for that myth I present a trading strategy that exploits human nature, the tendency for people to emotionally chase performance and end up buying near tops and selling near bottoms. Unfortunately, as good as Mark became at employing his new program, he would never be able to incorporate the strategy into client accounts. In fact, outside of specific locales, the strategy is illegal to pursue. For Mark, in addition to his day job as a professional money manager, had become a skilled practitioner of poker, in particular, Texas hold 'em.

Using his same set of analytical skills and healthy dollop of discipline, he was winning on a regular basis. We talked to each other about how poker, like trading, is a game of skill combined with an element of luck. Poor poker players consistently lose (with an occasional lucky win), while disciplined skilled players, over time, are able to walk away with the less skilled players' money.

Sounds a lot like what most people consider to be "investing," doesn't it? In fact, virtually every pursuit incorporates both skill and an element of luck.

> *It is not the pursuit itself – be it stock trading, poker playing or starting a business – that determines whether the participants are engaged in gambling. Instead, gambling is defined by each individual participant's behavior.*

Mark, although he plays poker, is not a "gambler" - by definition. He carefully analyzes each hand, each situation into which he is dealt, evaluates the likely behavior of his adversaries, and then makes his informed, rational decision. Most people, although they "invest" in stocks, are gamblers. They react emotionally to price changes, news reports and other daily distractions. They do not follow a systematic plan that gives them a statistical edge.

This is supported by the DALBAR figures that show that people massively underperform a passive approach to buying-and-holding mutual funds. Yet most governments consider poker to be gambling, while any transaction in stocks, bonds or other financial asset is considered "investing." All 50 states in the U.S. have laws controlling gambling, which they define as being games with three elements:

1. A prize of value

2. Consideration, meaning it costs something to play; and

3. An outcome determined predominately by chance, not skill.[63]

Here's why the states are wrong about what they define as gambling and why, even under their definition, professional poker isn't gambling (but what most people consider to be investing, is).

Investing, Trading and Gambling

Investing is often thought of as an act of entering into a position and leaving it on for an extended time. It's been historically touted as being the virtuous approach. Trading is the description used to explain the act of changing those positions more frequently. It is considered "speculative' and often referred to as gambling. The fact is that investing and trading are neither.

You may have noticed that I have frequently refrained so far in this book from referring to people as "investors." I realize that is the common term used to describe people who place money at risk in stocks and other financial instruments, but that's not my definition.

> *Investing is the process of identifying the best, most rational opportunities for profiting within your means, and then unemotionally following a process that combines those opportunities into a portfolio that has a high probability of achieving the greatest returns possible while limiting risk over a specific time period.*

Trading, and the development of trading strategies, is the method used to achieve that return and thus is a component of investing.

---

[63]　I. Nelson Rose, "Gambling and the Law: Is poker -- like chess -- a game of skill?" *Casino City Times* (October 10, 2008), Retrieved February 14, 2011.

In contrast, gambling is entering into or maintaining trades with a negative expected outcome or taking unnecessary risks. The process people have been taught to follow to earn a return on their money is not investing. It's gambling.

A person who is 60% long stocks and 40% long bonds is taking unnecessary risk. They are gambling.

It's not that there is a problem with being long stocks. It's that exposing 60% of a portfolio to *anything* is gambling. That includes government bonds, treasury bills, and other "riskless" investments. Because, as we discussed previously in this book, nothing is permanent. Not even the U.S. financial system or the "full faith and credit" of the U.S. government.

In addition, angry environments exist. This is articulated in *Myth #5 – Stay Invested In Order to Avoid Missing the Best Days* and further defined as being the periods when market conditions are least suitable to any given market. To be in such an environment and not adapt is not smart. My friend Mark varies his poker play based on the hand he is dealt and the expected behavior of his opponents. He adapts. He's not a "gambler." That's one of the reasons he wins at poker. The same applies to trading stocks. Put a process in place to ensure that when you're dealt a "bad hand", you adapt. If you don't, you're gambling.

Another way to determine if you are gambling, and not investing, is to objectively evaluate your psyche.

If you are acutely aware of every fluctuation in the U.S. stock market then you certainly have too much riding on the outcome. You are gambling.

If it keeps you up at night then it *is* a certainty you have too much exposure. If you weren't gambling on the U.S. stock market you wouldn't care any more about the movement in U.S. stocks than you would in the movement of orange juice, wheat, oil, or Australian dollars, which are components of the S&P Diversified Trends Indicator described in *Myth #7 – It's Bad to Chase Performance.* Or you may hold short positions in U.S. stocks, based on a trading strategy such as that outlined in the Action section for *Myth #10 – Short Selling is Destabilizing and Risky.*

The fact is that there are a myriad of strategies that can be incorporated into an investment portfolio. Picking just a couple, such as being long U.S. equities or long fixed income securities is intentionally limiting and exposes the portfolio to unnecessary and avoidable risks – gambling. To be clear, diversifying by buying developing market stocks, small cap stocks, large cap stocks, growth stocks, and value stocks is NOT truly diversifying. Under "normal" environments, over longer periods, the returns from each stock are dominated by the performance of each company. To some extent this provides portfolio diversification. But during angry environments that may last for years, there is one dominant return driver: people's sentiment towards stocks. This, more than any other force, dominates stock performance. Because of that, there are scenarios where all these strategies will perform similarly. That is the inherent risk involved. And if you create a portfolio of strategies that are all underpinned by the same return driver, you have taken on avoidable risk and have inadvertently become a gambler.

Sad-but-true...that is the state of the majority of today's "investment" advice. The financial press and investment pundits consider allocating capital among stocks of different industries to be diversifying. Let's examine their mistake in logic.

Correlation kills (performance)

Figure 19 shows the correlation of returns among stock sectors during the period October 2002 through October 2007.[64]

This was a favorable period for being long stocks, as virtually all sectors rose. The lighter shaded cells illustrate the lowest correlations and the darker shades highlight the higher correlations. What is apparent is that during this "favorable" market environment, when all sectors rose, the various sector relationships were only moderately correlated.

---

[64] A perfect correlation of 1.0 means that one sector moves up and down at exactly the same time and same amount as another sector. A correlation over 0.6 indicates a high correlation and a figure of less than 0.3 is generally indicative of two markets that are uncorrelated to each other.

Monthly Correlation among U.S. Stock Market Sectors
During the Bull Market Period Oct. 2002 – Oct. 2007

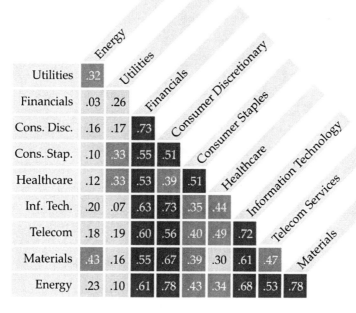

Figure 19. *Sectors show just moderate correlation to each other as individual stock and sector fundamentals affect returns.*

That all changed during the financial crisis of 2008 however. Virtually all sector returns became highly correlated with each other, providing no diversification benefit. All sectors fell (Figure 20).

Monthly Correlation among U.S. Stock Market Sectors During the Bear Market Period Nov. 2007 – Feb. 2009

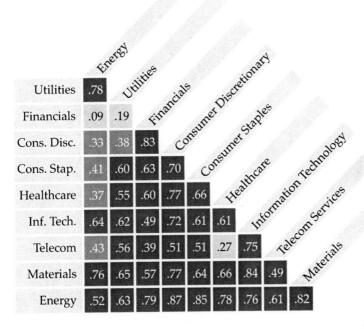

Figure 20. *Sectors show increased correlation to each other as fundamentals are swamped by overall investor sentiment.*

Figure 21 further illustrates this high correlation of performance among stock sectors. There was very little difference in both the timing and extent of the losses suffered by each sector.

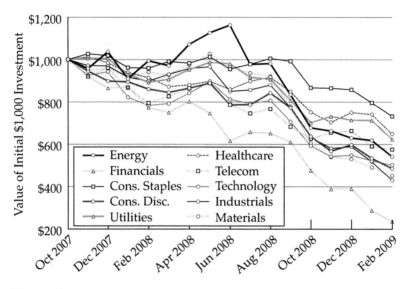

Performance of U.S. Stock Market Sectors During the Bear Market of 2007-2009

Figure 21

This is exactly the trait you *don't* want to see. When one sector is falling you want to see other sectors rising or at least falling much less. That would provide you with some diversification benefit. But instead, in bear markets, when the benefits of diversification are most needed, sector diversification does not provide the benefit. Yet investment gurus continue to promote stock diversification as a method of reducing portfolio risk. This simple study is yet more proof that their definition of diversification falls far short of functionality.

Understanding return drivers

During the favorable period covered in the first table displayed in this myth, the performance of at least some of the stock sectors were driven primarily by factors specific to each stock in that sector, lowering the correlation of the returns of that sector relative to others. But once the global economic crisis took hold, performance of virtually ALL sectors became dominated by the same return driver, the overwhelming disdain and mistrust across the country for stocks of any type. As a result all stocks fell in price. People who thought they were diversified found out they were not.

Anytime your money is committed to a single strategy, such as being long financial assets (stocks, bonds, real estate, cash), you should expect that there will come a time when a single return driver will overpower all others and dominate your performance, turning your portfolio into a poor-folio. And that usually occurs, as displayed above, during angry environments that are detrimental to your portfolio's value.

Spreading your money across multiple market sectors does not diversify your portfolio. It leaves you dangerously dependent on a single return driver and exposes you to unnecessary risk. As a result, *investing, as it's been taught, is gambling.*

Trading

So if what has long been preached as "investing" is really gambling, then what is the truth behind trading, which is often referred to as gambling?

The truth is that every decision is a trade. Any decision you make to buy a stock is based on the facts you have at your disposal at that time. You've evaluated those facts and decided to make an educated, informed decision. That's a trade. Maintaining that position is a continuation of that trade. If the facts change and the environment becomes unfriendly for your long position it certainly doesn't make sense to maintain the position just because, at sometime in the past, you made a decision to buy. You should sell. The alternative, holding on to the position in the face of an Angry Environment is called hope, and in some cases, delusion. It's not investing. It's gambling.

But it's also easy to understand why the myth - that trading is gambling - exists. Study after study shows that the more frequently people trade; the more they lose. The reason for this is actually quite simple and based on two facts:

- Every decision incurs a cost, with commissions and price spreads being among the largest. More decisions, more costs; and

- In the aggregate, people make the wrong decisions when trading their money. The more decisions they make, the more wrong decisions are likely to be made. The DALBAR study exhibited in *Myth #3 – You Can't Time the Market*, gives a clear long term example supporting this fact.

While the first bullet point can be minimized but not avoided, the second is *entirely* avoidable. In fact, that is a primary purpose of this book.

Trading is essential for successful investing, but not the irrational, emotionally-charged trading that most people engage in. For the majority of people, to trade successfully they need to employ multiple systematic trading strategies based on valid and logical return drivers.

There are many easily employable trading strategies that can be used to ensure your portfolio is truly diversified, many of which are presented in this book; and that diversification is the very essence of successful investing. I present one trading strategy, related to trading the stock sectors presented in this myth, in the Action section for this myth at www.JackassInvesting.com.

Gambling

Gambling is entering into or maintaining trades with a negative expected outcome or taking unnecessary risks.

In *Myth #3 – You Can't Time the Market*, you were introduced to Johnny Chan. Johnny is not a gambler. He may play poker for a living, but he does it in a studied, systematic fashion carefully calculated to give him an edge over his opponents. Each hand is a trade. By understanding the environment (his card, the other cards showing, the behavior or the "tells" of the other players), Johnny can craft his trading strategy to provide him with a positive return expectancy – the essence of trading.

My friend Mark, who I introduced you to at the start of this myth, is also not a gambler. He took years honing his poker skills, learning the strategies necessary for success under various conditions.

In contrast, most people, in their approach to investment, are nothing but "white-collar" gamblers working without a net, without any systematic plan. They commit money to trades without a systematic plan. They expose their money to a single dominant return driver, and they respond emotionally as the environment changes.

SUMMARY
MYTH 8

- Gambling isn't defined by a game, market or frequency of trading. It is defined by a person's behavior.

- Investing is the process of identifying the best, most rational opportunities for profiting within your means, and then unemotionally following a process that combines those opportunities into a portfolio that has a high probability of achieving the greatest returns possible while limiting risk over a specific time period.

- Gambling is entering into or maintaining trades with a negative expected outcome or taking unnecessary risks.

- A person who is 60% long stocks and 40% long bonds is taking unnecessary risk. They are gambling.

Risk Can Be Measured Statistically

In the early 1990s, after three years of research, I conducted a number of meetings with potential investors for my newly developed Brandywine Benchmark trading program. The program traded across more than 100 futures markets using three dozen separate trading strategies. During the meetings I presented the return drivers and back-tested performances of many of the individual strategies. While the overall performance of the Benchmark trading program showed consistent returns over more than a decade of back-testing (on a blind data set), many of the three dozen individual trading strategies exhibited inconsistent back-tested performance.

This was expected. Each of the individual trading strategies, by definition, lacked the diversification that was present in the complete Benchmark trading program. As a result, there were years during the back-test period when some of the individual return drivers were ineffective and certain trading strategies suffered losses. But because the overall Benchmark program was broadly diversified, those losing periods in one trading strategy were often offset by profits in another. As long as each trading strategy's return drivers were based on a sound logical premise, over time there was a high probability that each trading strategy would produce a profit.

It's a simple concept with which by now, this far into this book, you are completely familiar. That's exactly why I was caught by surprise with the reaction I encountered from the potential investors. It's a generic truth that people strongly prefer to invest in programs that exhibit strong returns while also demonstrating low volatility. The Benchmark trading program displayed this combination. But this group extended their belief in the need for low volatility to each of the individual trading strategies that comprised the overall trading program. They simply did not like the idea that many of the individual trading strategies within my Benchmark trading program displayed volatile returns. To me, that volatility was inconsequential. What was important was the significance of the return drivers responsible for those returns – and the high probability that those returns were likely to repeat in the future.

Critically, almost none of those people were concerned about the significance of the results with which they were presented. They assumed that if a track record was long enough then the future performance would approximate the past. None of them asked me about return drivers or the baseline conditions necessary for the trading program to continue to succeed.

Among this group of naysayers, one client stood out more resistant than the rest. I showed him the performance of one of my more innovative trading strategies. It was one that, based on its return drivers, had a high probability that its future performance would approximate the past. The bad news was that its past performance, despite being profitable, was highly volatile. In fact, the return earned by that strategy was less than 1/5 the magnitude of the maximum drawdown suffered by that strategy.

This volatility of returns was not a concern to me. First, because I was confident that the strategy would continue to perform in the future as it had in the past, meaning that over an extended period it would produce a profit. Second was the fact that none of the other strategies in the Benchmark trading program were based on return drivers that were similar to those driving the returns of the "volatile" strategy. So there was a good possibility that when the volatile strategy was losing money, many of the other strategies could be earning profits.

But the client I had singled out to convince categorically refused to consider any of this. He bluntly told me that he would never even think about investing in any trading strategy that didn't show a historical return at least ten times that of its greatest loss. The numbers he demanded were 50 times better than the return/drawdown ratio of the U.S. stock market! He ended our conversation by predicting that in one year (after failing with my approach) I'd see it his way.

I was floored. There is no such single investment that will, over time, sustain a 10:1 level of return to risk. Yet he was confident that such strategies existed. Not only that, he claimed to have had actually invested money in them. I was disappointed. Not because I didn't get the investment, but because after presenting my research and trading philosophy to him for more than an hour, he didn't see the logical point-by-point clarity of my approach. At the time I thought that I had utterly failed in my efforts to convince him that:

- sound, rational return drivers were the key to any successful trading strategy; and

- the volatility of past returns of any single trading strategy was irrelevant when considering the risk of a portfolio. I discuss this in *Myth #20 – There is No Free Lunch.*

I answered a phone call over a year later, and...it was him. He was calling asking me for a job! In our conversation, he told how he had come to understand my philosophy, only after suffering sizable losses, *gambling* on his safe "investments."

This encounter led me to think quite seriously about risk, and more specifically, how risk is perceived and measured by people. It seemed clear to me that if people are consciously avoiding trading strategies that are sound, their paranoia would necessarily open up a bank of trading opportunity windows for the rest of us. Profit would be there for the taking by employing those "unexploited" trading strategies. Before I tell you how risk should be measured and exploited for profit, let me relay an example to describe how the vast majority of people define and measure risk.

Is volatility an indicator of risk?

People have long associated volatility of investment returns with risk. Increasingly, over the past few years I have noticed a tendency for people to strongly favor trading strategies with lower volatility of returns. These "investments" are considered "safer" than others that exhibit higher volatility return streams. I disagree. While volatility may be a great indicator of risk in a *random* return stream, it is not a great indicator of risk for any given trading strategy. The risk inherent in a trading strategy is simply a function of the validity of its return drivers.

By focusing on the return drivers rather than statistical measures of volatility of returns, it becomes apparent that some strategies, although they may exhibit high short-term volatility, may actually present very little longer-term risk of loss. In contrast, other strategies may go for long periods exhibiting very little volatility, yet be subject to substantial, almost assured, longer-term risk of loss.

Moths to a flame

In the mid-1990s I accepted money into one of my funds from a European family office, historically ultra - conservative in their investment style. They were my clients for one month. In those thirty days we lost a few percent, and because of that they immediately withdrew their money; despite the fact that our published track record (and all discussions we had with this family) clearly showed that a loss of that amount was ordinary and was to be expected. Their immediate, knee-jerk reaction was to say, "Waiter...check please." As it turned out, this was their normal course of action. Over the next few years I heard the same story from other traders with whom they had "done business." What this family was searching for was consistent monthly gains, without any noticeable monthly losses. Unfortunately for them, they found it, or so they thought.

In early 2009 I heard their name come up in the news. They were on a list of "investors" that each lost hundreds of millions of dollars in the Madoff Ponzi scheme. (For more on the Madoff scam, see *Myth #14 – Government Regulations Protect Investors*). It turns out that Madoff reported just the type of steady month-after-month profits they desired – and we now know just how legitimate that data was. In addition to the Madoff allocation, their desire for consistent,

A "reversion-to-mean" trading strategy takes a position in a market when the price of that market diverges significantly from the normal, or "mean," price of that market, or its relationship to other markets, with the expectation that the price will "revert" back to the mean.

low-volatility returns led them to place their money in highly similar positions; because if a certain style of trading had been producing consistent returns with low volatility then most practitioners of that style of trading were also displaying similar performance. This led to a concentrated, rather than diversified portfolio. It also led to them focusing solely on performance, to the exclusion of the most important criteria, the return drivers responsible for that performance.

One type of trading that appealed to that European family office was the use of "mean reversion" strategies. Quite often these types of strategies produce consistent returns with low volatility over extended periods. As a result, the lure of the low volatility associated with reversion-to-mean strategies attracts people like moths to a flame, with a similar result. In the next two sections I'll show how this attraction can lead to disaster.

TED Spread

The "TED spread" is the difference in the interest rate between "risk-free" U.S. Treasury bills and the LIBOR (London Interbank Offered Rate) rate. The "TED" acronym is explained by the fact that the TED spread began as the difference between interest rates on three-month U.S. T-bills (the "T in "TED") and three-month Eurodollars (the "ED" in "TED").

The difference in the rates is due to the fact that people view the U.S. T-bill as "risk-free." Meaning that there is a 100% chance that the U.S. government will repay you the money you use to buy a T-bill. The LIBOR rate is the rate at which banks in London agree to lend money to each other. The difference in the two reflects the uncertainty that the banks will repay their loans.

Under "normal" conditions the TED spread is confined to a reasonably narrow range of between 10bp and 70bp ("bp" is an acronym for "basis point," which is 1/100 of 1%). This normal environment is displayed in Figure 22.

It's quite easy for a trader, especially a professional trader, to trade the TED spread by buying T-bills and short-selling LIBOR contracts when the spread is at the low end of the range and doing the opposite when the spread is at the high end of the range. This is a classic reversion-to-mean strategy. Over the three year period displayed in Figure 22, a trader employing this strategy would have exhibited reasonably consistent profits with occasional small losses. A statistical analysis of that trader's results would likely be quite impressive and attract a significant amount of money from other people. But the results would be nothing more than a statistical illusion.

TED Spread for the "Normal" 3 Year Period 2002 - 2004

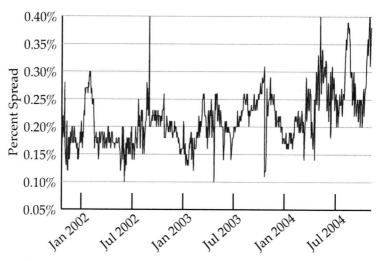

Figure 22

Figure 23 displays the TED spread for the period January 2006 through August 2008. Following years of consistently bouncing around in the range of 10bp to 70bp, in August 2007, during the subprime mortgage crisis, the TED spread rapidly blew out to more than 200bp.

Any trader who had shorted the TED spread at 40 or 50 or 60 expecting the usual reversion back towards 10 or 20 would have suffered enormous losses. Many did. But that was only the beginning. Figure 24 expands the range of the previous chart to include the effect on the TED spread of the 2008 financial crisis. The spread continued to expand in 2008, ultimately reaching more than 450bp. Translation: Any trader who utilized a reversion-to-mean strategy was wiped out.

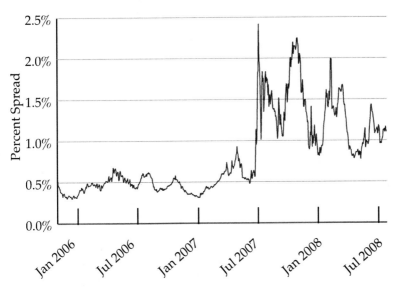

Figure 23

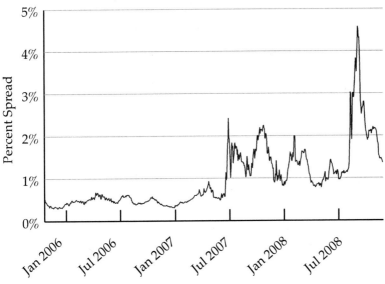

Figure 24

Clearly, the historical range of the TED spread was in no way indicative of its future range. The only method for determining the risk of the strategy was to fully understand the return drivers and baseline conditions underlying the strategy. Doing so would have likely pointed out the potential for the spread blowing out to 200, 300 or even more than 400bp, as did occur. A person could have employed the most sophisticated statistical analysis of the risk of trading the TED spread in early 2007 and never been able to anticipate the turmoil that followed almost immediately. In fact, that statistical analysis could have easily led the person to conclude that the trade entailed so little risk that it warranted, or even required, the use of leverage to compound the return potential.

There's a tendency to think that extremely wealthy people, with easy access to the most brilliant investment advice and statisticians, would not be lured by the statistical illusion of a low-risk investment. But that's not the case. My ex-client, the European family office, is a perfect example of a well-off investor completely beguiled and trapped by the lure of low-volatility returns. They not only invested in funds that employed similar "risk-free" strategies, but they also insisted on applying leverage in order to enhance their returns. It wasn't uncommon for them to invest up to four times their available cash. The result: a loss of 10% might actually destroy 40% of their cash invested.

But the illusion of safety results in additional damage. It is common for people to extrapolate past success into the future and, as a result, concentrate their portfolio on those strategies that produced the greatest profits in the past. Reversion-to-mean trading strategies are perfect traps for this behavior. Statistically, they are likely to produce a long series of profitable trades prior to the one trade that produces a large loss. If the person gains increased confidence in the trading strategy as a result of the string of gains, and increases their commitment to the strategy as a result, they will, by definition, have the greatest percentage of their assets committed to the strategy at the time when it suffers its greatest loss.

When genius failed

In 1995 I had a due-diligence visit from an institutional investor. During his visit he mentioned a new fund that had been set up in Greenwich, Connecticut by the head of bond trading at Salomon Brothers, one of the top investment firms during the 1980s. The founder had a few of the nation's top economists and mathematicians (including two future Nobel Prize winners) working with him at the firm. I was pretty much cloistered in my own world, which at that time was a century-old townhouse office jammed with people, computers and wiring that got so hot the electrician couldn't add additional circuits until we shut enough equipment down to lower the temperature of the electrical box. As a result of my semi-hermit business style at that time, I really had no idea who those designated geniuses were and I remember saying, without hesitation, "I'd never trust a fund whose trading decisions were based solely on mathematical models without any clear understanding of the risks inherent in the underlying return drivers." My belief then, and even more so now, was that statistics alone could never provide a full understanding of risk. Risk could only be determined through a full understanding of the return drivers underlying any given trading strategy.

For the next three years I ate those words. The fund that I criticized, Long Term Capital Management, produced large, consistent profits of 40% per year throughout the mid-1990s. They grew to manage more than $4 billion. It became "clear" to many people that they were right (and I was wrong). At least until they weren't.

I became aware of the collapse of Long Term Capital Management on a windy New York City day in September 1998 while walking past the World Trade Center. A discarded Wall Street Journal lay on the sidewalk. While I'm not generally in the habit of trash-picking used newspapers, the headline caught my eye. It said that a major fund, Long Term Capital Management, had lost billions on bad trades.[65]

How that happened is an interesting story. And if you're interested in learning more than what I will present here, I highly recommend the leading book on the subject: *When Genius Failed: The Rise and Fall of Long-Term Capital Management*, written by Roger Lowenstein and published in 2000.[66]

The geniuses behind Long Term Capital Management – and they were geniuses – developed trading strategies that capitalized on small mispricings in the credit, equity and derivatives markets. But because those mispricings would only produce a few basis points of profit each, the trading strategy also required substantial leverage to produce a reasonable profit. In other words, if they could leverage each trade 10 times, then a 10 basis point gain would equate to a 100 basis point (1%) profit for the fund. Because their models indicated such a low probability of loss on each individual trade, they were confident that they could support this substantial leverage without exceptional risk. The methods behind many of their trading strategies were actually quite straightforward. Here's one example.

---

[65]   Anita Raghavan and Mitchell Pacelle, "A Hedge Fund Falters, So the Fed Persuades Big Banks to Ante Up," *The Wall Street Journal* (September 23, 1998).
[66]   Roger Lowenstein, *When Genius Failed: The Rise and Fall of Long-Term Capital Management* (New York: Random House, 2000).

From bonds to bondage

U.S. government bonds are considered as safe an investment as a person can make. They are backed by the full faith and credit of the U.S. government and promise to pay back a fixed amount of interest prior to the full repayment of the bond. In the 1990s the U.S. government was regularly issuing bonds to people and institutions. The differences in the bonds' present value were minimal, and if there were differences it was assumed by economic theory that those differences would be eliminated by arbitrage. However, due to the "liquidity" of different bond issuances, small price discrepancies regularly arose between the newest bond and the bond that had been issued a few months before.

Long Term Capital Management's Ph.D.s developed trading methods that allowed them to buy the cheaper bond (the less-liquid and so-called "off-the-run" bond that was issued a few months previously) and sell the more expensive "on-the-run" bond. Their methods profited when new bonds were issued and the values of the existing bonds came into alignment.

Throughout the mid-1990s this strategy, and numerous others like it, produced out-sized profits for Long Term Capital Management and those people and institutions who had entrusted it with their money. Better yet, those out-sized returns were produced with low volatility. People interpreted this low monthly volatility as being low risk. But the reality was far different. This became evident in the last half of 1998 as baseline conditions changed.

On August 17, 1998, the Russian government and the Central Bank of Russia issued a Joint Statement announcing that they were declaring a moratorium on payment to foreign creditors and defaulting on their domestic debt. Overnight, the baseline conditions upon which Long Term Capital Management had built its trading models had changed. There was a rush to own the safest and most liquid financial instruments available. In the minds of most people the place to be was in the on-the-run U.S. Treasury bond, the same bonds that Long Term Capital Management's trading models had shorted. A rise in the price of these bonds, relative to older bonds, resulted in losses for their position.

These losses were compounded by the leverage that Long Term Capital Management had employed as part of their strategy. To earn a reasonable return they needed to hold large positions relative to their cash position. This was reflected in the fact that at the beginning of 1998 Long Term Capital Management had capital of $4.7 billion and held positions whose face value exceeded $124 billion – for a debt to equity ratio of more than 25 to 1.

Most people know that this leverage likely represents a lot of risk. If you buy $2,500 worth of a stock but only put down $100 to do so, a small 4% drop in the stock's price will result in a total loss of your $100. Of course, the Ph.D.'s at Long Term Capital Management were well aware of this. But they had enormous confidence in their models and as a result were comfortable with taking on 25 to 1 leverage.

They shouldn't have been. Their confidence was misplaced. While the geniuses at Long Term Capital Management thoroughly understood the math behind their models, they failed to acknowledge the importance of the baseline conditions that were required to make that math work. Their trading strategies took advantage of minor disruptions in prices among bonds, stocks and derivative contracts, entering into positions in anticipation that prices would eventually revert to their "normal" relationships. When they developed their trading strategies they calculated, based on historical price movements, that price anomalies such as those caused by the Russian default weren't expected to occur more than once every 20,000 years. But they did occur. What they failed to account for was the potential change in baseline conditions. When those changed, so did the odds. Once every 20,000 years was transformed into a certainty. The math couldn't have predicted it. But a better understanding of the required baseline conditions could have. My friend Mark (the poker player) likely would have changed his approach to adjust to the new odds. But long Term Capital management did not. The Long Term Capital Management debacle clearly points out that *statistics are a bad predictor of risk*. As a result of their reliance on statistics, Long Term Capital Management collapsed in a spectacular fashion, requiring a $3.6 billion bailout organized by the Federal Reserve Bank of New York.

Risk is what risk does

You may recognize the sub-title to this section as being a paraphrase of the "stupid is as stupid does" saying from the movie *Forest Gump* or perhaps the "pretty is as pretty does" proverb from Chaucer's *The Wife of Bath's Tale*. The message here is that you shouldn't interpret the *surface* appearance of a trading strategy as being at all indicative of its riskiness any more than you should interpret a person's appearance as being indicative of their qualities.

Instead, base that decision on a deeper understanding of the return drivers and baseline conditions underlying each trading strategy's returns. The volatile trading strategy that I had unsuccessfully presented to my potential investor – turned job-seeker – continued to display high volatility. But it also continued to produce profits. What was important was that the back-tested performance was and continues to be *accurate*. The trading strategies that he had put his money and faith behind, while appearing to be much safer statistically, eventually (rather quickly for him) encountered losses that exceeded anything predicted by the "bullet-proof" statistics. Similarly, both the European family office and Long Term Capital Management fell victim to the illusion of safety, produced by previously low volatility and steady returns. Many prefer the illusion to the reality. However, risk is what risk does.

The previous examples showed how the illusion of low volatility led to financial disaster. In the remainder of this myth I'll show you how it can also present you with profitable trading opportunities.

The illusion of volatility as a measure of risk

The mean-reverting strategy trading the TED spread and the bond(age) strategy traded by Long Term Capital Management were both examples of trading strategies that appeared low-risk because their returns initially exhibited low levels of volatility, but ultimately proved to be highly risky. Is it possible for the opposite to be true – for a low-risk strategy to exhibit high volatility? Let's take a look.

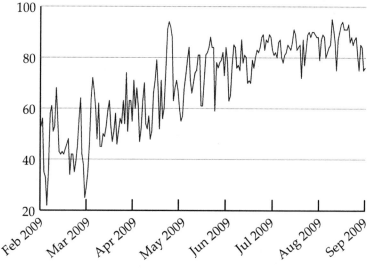

Mystery Market Performance February 2009 through August 2009

Figure 25

Figure 25 illustrates the performance of a market for the period February 1, 2001 through September 1, 2009. This 2009 price pattern is highly representative of the historical pattern for this market.

A basic understanding of the underlying fundamentals of this market points toward the high probability that profits will be earned by utilizing a seasonal strategy that systematically buys on February 1 and sells on September 1 each year. Using moderate leverage assumptions, in 2009 this simple strategy would have produced the following performance characteristics:

Strategy Performance Characteristics

Total Return:	5.5%
Annualized Return:	9.4%
Annualized Volatility:	32.4%

Despite the positive return, many people would consider this to be a strategy too risky to consider. The annualized return is less than one-third that of its annualized volatility. At a 32% annualized rate, volatility is approximately twice as high as that of the S&P 500 Index. The truth, however, is that the volatility measure is totally misleading and completely unrepresentative of the risk inherent in this strategy. While no trading strategy can ever be considered a sure-thing, this strategy comes close, despite its high volatility.

Why am I so confident of the continued long-term success of this strategy? Because it's based on a sound, logical return driver that has a high probability of producing similar results year after year. The return driver is the predictable cyclicality of seasons.

The chart shows the daily high temperatures for 2009 in degrees Fahrenheit for Philadelphia, Pennsylvania. Once you understand the underlying return driver for this "strategy," it becomes clear that the intervening short-term volatility exhibited by the daily high temperatures between February and September in no way represents "risk." For example, no one can seriously argue that risk increased (and the probability of temperatures rising decreased) when the daily high temperature dropped from 68 degrees on February 11th to 25 degrees on March 2nd. In fact, the opposite was true. There was even a higher probability that temperatures would increase. Yet a naïve statistical analysis of the risk (volatility) and return of this strategy would confidently conclude that it is highly risky, thus reducing the probability of achieving the tested results.

Betting on temperatures rising in Philadelphia from February through August is as close to a sure thing as you can get. When the temperature dropped on March 2nd, "buying" in anticipation of a reversion to the mean temperature of 60 degrees would have been the "safe trade". Risk didn't increase when the temperature dropped sharply. It decreased.

Unfortunately, not all return drivers can be captured in a trade. In analyzing Philadelphia's monthly temperatures, it's highly unlikely that you could find anyone willing to take the other side of the bet. That's because most people are well aware of the high probability that temperatures in Philadelphia would rise between February and September. Who would bet otherwise?

Many traders are on the look-out for similar "sure-thing" trades. They religiously run gigabytes of data through their computers, desperately looking for relationships among markets that can be profitably exploited. These "quants" (short for "quantitative analysts") then trade the most successful of these back-tested relationships. While they often achieve periods of success, their approach is a ticking time-bomb.

Don't get me wrong. I believe strongly that trading strategies must be quantitatively developed and systematically applied. But their initial conception must be based on solid fundamental concepts that are clearly understood. That also means that their failure can also only be determined by evaluating changes in the baseline conditions that affect the return drivers... and never solely through statistical measures.

The Oracle of Omaha's take on volatility

To be fair, not all people are enamored with low volatility returns. In particular, Warren Buffet once said "Charlie Munger and I always have preferred a lumpy 15% return to a smooth 12%." In other words, it's not the road that matters most, but the destination. A great example of this philosophy is Warren Buffet's purchase of a significant stake in the parent company of *The Washington Post* decades ago.

Warren Buffet, who learned directly from value investing pioneers David Dodd and Ben Graham, marveled in his 2001 shareholder report on his ability to have been able to purchase his sizable investment in

Washington Post Company in 1973 at a price equivalent to just one-fourth of the then per-share business value of the enterprise. Despite this being a great investment over decades for Mr. Buffet, it was seemingly not that obvious to other people, who had been responsible for pushing the price down to such low levels. In fact, the stock continued to fall after his purchase and by year-end 1974 his Washington Post Company holdings showed a loss of 25%.

As I demonstrate in *Myth #1 – Stocks Provide an Intrinsic Return*, the problem is that, in the short term, a stock's price is not based on a company's value or earnings potential, but instead almost entirely on people's enthusiasm towards owning stocks. With the perfect vision of hindsight, The Washington Post long remained as one of Buffet's premier investments, as the stock rose several-fold from his purchase price.

The belief that volatility is equated with risk prevents people from employing many trading strategies containing sound return drivers. There are other value approaches that exploit this same aversion to volatility. While these trading strategies may exhibit high volatility on their own, as part of a diversified portfolio they can dramatically reduce risk by being based on unique return drivers that earn returns when other strategies incur losses. Here's one I have personally employed.

"Juicing" your returns

In 2004 the Atkins diet craze was in full force. First introduced by Dr. Robert Atkins in a book he published in 1972, the diet required participants to virtually shun carbohydrates in favor of a diet rich in meats, fish and eggs. At the height of its popularity in 2004, 9% of North American adults were on the diet.

The effect was widespread. Sales of many carbohydrate-rich foods, such as pasta, rice and orange juice declined. This led to lower prices of these commodities, as production easily outran demand. But it also exposed a return driver and opportunity to develop a successful trading strategy.

The production cost for physical commodities can reach a low point at which producers begin to lose money. When that occurs, producers of that commodity will stop investing in producing that commodity and instead shift to producing other commodities or stop producing all-together. Immediately thereafter the supply of that commodity will fall, bringing it more into line with demand. When supply and demand come into alignment, prices stabilize. This process creates a natural support level for prices and can serve as the return driver for a "marginal cost of production" (MCP) trading strategy.

To develop the MCP trading strategy we first established a list of commodity markets that were tradable and contained reasonably accurate cost-of-production data with relatively stable production cost structures. We then systematized a process for entering into long positions when those commodities had current prices that were trading at, near or below their marginal cost of production. The result was a trading strategy based on a sound, logical return driver – the profit motive of producers – that underscored virtually all rational business decisions. (You may also notice the similarity to value investing in stocks.)

In 2004 I applied this strategy to the orange juice market. In early 2004 the OJ supply was abundant and both Florida and Brazilian production was on the rise. Most importantly, because of the Atkins diet craze, orange juice, being high in carbohydrates, was shunned. Demand fell. As a result, in May 2004 prices hit a 27-year low of 55 cents per pound of frozen concentrate. My fund began buying orange juice when the price first dropped below $0.70 per pound of frozen concentrate. We continued to buy and incurred losses as prices dropped an additional 20%.

It was "obvious" to most market participants that prices would continue to fall as carbohydrate consumption shrank and production of orange juice continued to rise. But instead, orange juice prices bottomed in late May and by October the price had risen to 90 cents, as displayed in Figure 26.

While this price rise wasn't directly attributable to orange growers cutting back production, a long process since orange trees have many years of production once they reach maturity; production *was* reduced. During August and September of 2004 hurricanes Charley, Frances, Ivan and Jeanne battered Florida orange groves, reducing Florida's production by 40%. Market sentiment shifted overnight from concerns of over-supply to panic over the need to ration limited supplies. While my fund didn't plan for the hurricanes to hit, it was well-positioned in a low risk trade when they did. Prices ultimately reached more than $1.50 per pound. These types of trades do not occur often, but when they do occur they can become highly profitable and with limited risk. While orange juice had the potential to rally in price by $1.00, its price was highly unlikely to fall in price to below zero.

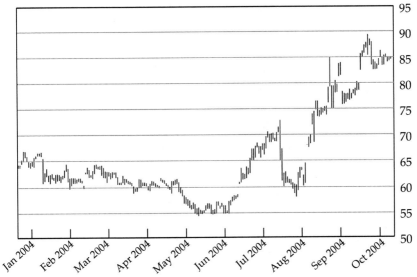

Orange Juice
Front Month Futures Prices
(Cents per Pound)

Figure 26

While this trading strategy is based on a sound return driver capable of producing positive returns when consistently applied, it was widely viewed by people I showed it to as being too risky. Their inability to see the viability of my strategy was based on misreading two observations.

First, they correctly perceived my strategy's returns as being volatile. My fund incurred losses as orange juice prices dropped from $0.70 to $0.55. Most futures brokers required less than 10% of the contract's face value as collateral for the trade. Even using less than half of that leverage would have resulted in a complete loss of the money committed to the trade.

Second, they saw the returns from the strategy as being inconsistent. In fact, when markets are trading at a high price, levels well above the marginal cost of production, there are no trading opportunities for this strategy at all. As a result, any capital committed to this strategy would be used inefficiently while it awaited a trading opportunity.

But while others were dismissing the strategy based on its standalone qualities (high volatility and inconsistency of returns), I was looking at it based solely on its sound return driver and high probability of producing profits over time, *within the context of a diversified portfolio.* You too can take advantage the tendency for other people to misinterpret risk by employing trading strategies in your portfolio that are underexploited by others but have sound return drivers capable of producing profits over time. I present the use of such trading strategies in *Myth #20 – There is No Free Lunch,"*and in the Action section at www.JackassInvesting.com.

SUMMARY
MYTH 9

- Sound, rational return drivers are the key to any successful trading strategy.

- Risk can only be determined by an understanding and evaluation of the return drivers underlying any given trading strategy. Risk is not determined by the volatility of the returns of a trading strategy.

- The volatility of past returns of any single trading strategy is irrelevant when considering the risk of a portfolio. Highly volatile trading strategies, if based on a sound, logical return driver, can be a "safe" contributor to a portfolio.

- The Long Term Capital Management debacle, marginal cost of production strategy and Philadelphia temperature chart presented in this myth are just a few examples that point out that statistics are a bad predictor of risk.

Short Selling is
Destabilizing and Risky

By September of 2008 the nation's recognized "Titans of Finance" such as Morgan Stanley CEO, John Mack, and Lehman Brothers CEO, Richard Fuld, were literally short-circuiting in panic mode. Mack wrote a warning memo to Morgan Stanley employees stating, "Short-sellers are driving our stock down. The management committee and I are taking every step possible to stop this irresponsible action."[67] The previous April, Lehman Brothers' Fuld had gone on record with his shareholders threatening that he wanted revenge on those he felt were responsible for the drop in his company's stock price, "I will hurt the shorts – and that is my goal."[68]

Unfortunately for Mack and Fuld, the shorts were right on point. Morgan

---

[67] Memo from Morgan Stanley CEO John Mack to Morgan Stanley employees sent September 17, 2008. As referenced in an article published by Emily Thornton, "Morgan Stanley's John Mack Swings Into Action," *Bloomberg Businessweek* (September 17, 2008). Retrieved February 14, 2011.

[68] Andrew Ross Sorkin, "Lehman Brothers takes on rumors from 'the shorts'," *The New York Times* (July 8, 2008).

Stanley's stock price fell from $40.83 at the end of August 2009 to $23.00 at the end of September and $17.47 at the end of October, before bottoming under $10/share in December. Lehman Brothers fared even worse and it had nothing to do with the "irresponsible action" of the shorts. It was Fuld who had been irresponsible. Under Fuld's leadership, on September 15, 2008, Lehman Brothers collapsed into the largest bankruptcy in the history of the United States. Their stock didn't become worthless because of the shorts. It became worthless as a result of the back-to-back quarterly losses of $2.8 billion and $3.9 billion the company suffered as a result of irresponsible trading of sub-prime mortgage securities and other financial instruments.

However, that didn't stop in-fighting politics from proceeding as usual. Pressure to impede short-sellers quickly spread to the institution responsible for regulating such action, the U.S. Securities and Exchange Commission (SEC). On September 19, 2008, the SEC issued a ruling that temporarily eliminated the ability of people to sell short 799 stocks of companies in the financial industry (ultimately increased to more than 950 stocks).[69] This "emergency order temporarily banning short-selling of financial stocks will restore equilibrium to markets," promised SEC chairman, Christopher Cox.[70]

His promise was empty.

··········

What short-selling is

Virtually everyone understands the concept of buying a stock with the expectation of profiting when it rises in price. This is called "going long." Not as many people are familiar with the concept of "selling short" and profiting when a stock drops in price. The procedure is relatively simple.

A person expecting a drop in a stock's price can borrow that stock from their broker, who may own the stock itself or have a client who owns the stock. If that's not possible, the broker can borrow from another broker who has a client who fits the bill. Once the stock is borrowed the person can then sell it. This is called "selling short," and is no different than if they had owned the stock themselves – except that at some point the person must "close" out the short position by buying

---

[69] "Statement of Securities and Exchange Commission Concerning Short Selling and Issuer Stock Repurchases," *U.S. Securities and Exchange Commission* press release (October 1, 2008).

[70] "SEC Halts Short Selling of Financial Stocks to Protect investors and Markets," *U.S. Securities and Exchange Commission* press release (September 19, 2008).

the stock back and returning it to their broker. If the stock price is at a lower price when they buy it back, they earn a profit. If higher, they take a hit and lose money.

Short interest, the percentage of a company's stock that is sold short, typically makes up less than 5% of outstanding shares. The depressing effect on stock prices is minimal. We don't need to theorize about this. The SEC ban in September of 2008 provides a perfect example of how "successful" any imposed restriction to short selling was to the stabilization efforts. The results show that the SEC was going down the wrong strategic road.

Theory (conventional "wisdom") meets reality

Over the two and a half weeks beginning on September 19th, 2008, the length of time that the short-selling ban was in place, the Dow Jones Industrial Average plummeted more than 2,000 points, or 18.7% and the S&P 500 dropped 21.5%. Even worse, financial stocks in the U.S. - the very stocks that were "protected" by the short-selling ban - fell a much greater 31.7%, as exemplified by the Financial Select Sector SPDR (XLF).

Performance of Financial Stocks vs. Broader Market

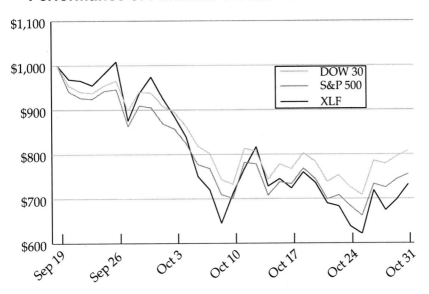

Figure 27

Figure 27 clearly displays the negative performance of the financial stocks, both relative to the overall market and in absolute terms, following the ban on the short-selling of financial stocks on September 19, 2008.

Clearly, the ban on short-selling did little to prevent an accelerating collapse in financial stocks. In fact, financial stocks fell even faster when the short-selling restriction was put in place and bottomed out following the end of the restriction. While this actual market experience doesn't prove that short-selling is good, or even that it doesn't destabilize markets, it certainly does show that markets are more than capable of being unstable even in the absence of short-selling.

The U.S. government's ban on short-selling was far from being the first time that short-sellers were accused of being the cause of falling stock prices. The belief that short-selling destabilizes markets is a myth that traces its roots back to the very first recorded short sale.

History of short-selling

In 1602 the Dutch government granted the Dutch East India Company a 21-year monopoly to trade with Asia. As a result the company (actually called Verenigde Oostindische Compagnie or "VOC") became the world's first multi-national corporation. The grant of monopoly attracted investors, one of whom was a 44 year-old merchant named Isaac Le Maire. In 1602 he invested 85,000 guilders in VOC.[71]

VOC was not a safe bet, however, and Le Maire knew it. Trading conflicts between the British and VOC led to the constant threat of attacks on their ships running the Baltic routes. Furthermore, VOC had issued no dividends or even financial statements. As a result, in 1609, Le Maire decided to sell off his shares. But he didn't stop there. In addition to the shares he owned, Le Maire shrewdly contracted to sell additional shares, which he had not yet purchased, for future delivery. This was the first recorded "short" sale.[72]

Although the strategy proved profitable for Le Maire, Dutch dignitaries quickly banned the practice with the issue of the first stock exchange

---

[71] "Dutch invented short selling in 1609," *nrc handelsblad* (September 22, 2008).
[72] Daniel Trotta, "Short sellers have been the villain for 400 years," *Reuters* (September 26, 2008).

regulation in 1610.[73] This was also the first recorded ban against short-selling. The ban was reiterated in 1621, 1630 and 1636.[74] So, the very moment short-selling appeared on the investment horizon, as a viable tactic, a ban was put in place to stop it. This didn't prevent the most famous financial bubble of all time though – Tulipmania.

Bubble trouble

In his classic book, published in 1841, *Extraordinary Popular Delusions and the Madness of Crowds,*[75] Charles Mackay details the events surrounding major speculative bubbles such as the Mississippi bubble, the South Sea bubble and Tulipmania. In each of these speculative manias, now commonly referred to as financial "bubbles," people came to accept new rationalizations that supported ever higher prices for businesses, entire industries, or even, during Tulipmania in Holland, tulip bulbs.

Tulipmania has become a metaphor for speculative manias. Introduced to the Netherlands in the late 16th century, tulips grew in popularity due to their brilliant colors and profusion of varieties. During the first part of the 17th century the flower became a luxury item and status symbol. By the 1630s speculators began entering the market. Their motivation for buying the bulbs far surpassed any actual interest in owning tulips. They were purchasing tulip bulbs with the expectation that rising demand would allow them to quickly sell at greatly escalated prices. And prices did escalate rapidly.

Because it takes seven years for a tulip seed to produce a bulb, demand quickly outpaced the supply of new bulbs. In 1636 a farmhouse was sold in exchange for three rare bulbs. But prices continued to rise, reaching a peak that winter, when single bulbs were exchanged for more than ten times the average annual salary of a skilled laborer. At a charity auction of 70 fine tulips left to benefit seven orphans by their father, one rare "Violetten Admirael van Enkhuizen" bulb sold for 5,200 guilders, more than 30 times an annual salary.[76]

[73] Seraina Gruenewald, Alexander F. Wagner and Rolf H. Weber, "Short Selling Regulation after the Financial Crisis – First Principals Revisited," *University of Zurich, Switzerland* (October 25, 2009): 2.

[74] Peter M. Garber, "Famous First Bubbles," *The Journal of Economic Perspective*, Vol. 4, No. 2 (Spring, 1990): 35-54.

[75] Charles Mackay, *Memoirs of Extraordinary Popular Delusions and the Madness of Crowds* (London: Office of the National Illustrated Library, 1848).

[76] Mike Dash, *Tulipomania – The Story of the World's Most Coveted Flower* (New York: Three Rivers Press, 1999).

But suddenly, following Newton's classic truism, "What goes up must come down," prices started a rapid swan dive. The first indication came at a routine bulb auction in Haarlem, the epicenter of the industry's trading activity, where prices failed to rise. Panic spread like wildfire throughout the country as speculators observed a sudden lack of interest in the "precious" bulbs that had been, just days earlier, such a hot commodity. Within months the average price had fallen more than 99% (Figure 28). What is interesting to note and remember is that all this speculation and the resulting collapse in prices took place without the benefit of short selling. The Dutch government had reiterated its ban on short-selling in 1636.

Tulip prices didn't collapse because short sellers targeted the tulip market. Tulip prices collapsed because they had reached levels which were clearly unsupportable. An entire estate was sold in exchange for three tulip bulbs. When rationality returned, prices collapsed. Nevertheless, throughout the centuries, when stock prices sold off sharply, short-selling was often blamed. Dick Fuld and U.S. regulators did not invent the practice.

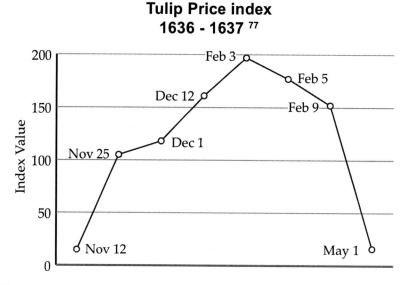

**Tulip Price index
1636 - 1637** [77]

Figure 28

Even if short selling isn't destabilizing, it certainly is risky, right? Here again, the truth proves itself to be a far cry from the accepted myth.

[77]   Earl A. Thompson and Jonathan Treussard, *"The Tulipmania: Fact or Artifact?"* David K. Levine (April 2003): 6.

A Front Row Seat to Insanity – Anecdotes from the Internet Bubble

As spectacular as Tulipmania was, it was eclipsed in both magnitude and breadth of participation by the Internet bubble of the late 1990s. What happened there was amazing and truly crazy. I know. I was a part of it.

In 1996 I founded a company called spree.com. Spree evolved into becoming one of the first ecommerce communities. We provided people with the ability to create their own online stores, using technology we created and name-brand products we sourced for them. Some of those partners were household names. For example, spree.com was the exclusive ecommerce partner and fulfillment service for PGA Tour merchandise. Spree grew rapidly and by late 1998 we were ranked among the top-10 ecommerce sites by traffic. When I left the company following venture capital (VC) funding at the end of 1999 we had more than 250,000 affiliates who had created web stores in the spree.com community. But spree.com wasn't profitable. And a big reason for that was that competition wouldn't allow it.

Within two years of starting Spree, hundreds of other companies jumped in as competitors. Many of these were well-financed by venture capitalists and followed the mantra of growth at any cost. They meant it. Most of these competitors sold their products at a loss, supporting those losses with their VC funding.

But those VCs expected a return on their money and they would expedite that return in one of two ways: sell the companies they funded to other, larger companies; or sell them to the public. In the late 1990s, selling to the public became the preferred method for one simple reason: the public would overpay.

A company is sold to the public through an Initial Public Offering (IPO). In the U.S. this requires a formal registration with the SEC. Once that registration is approved the company is free to enter into a "road show" where the "underwriters" (the investment bankers representing the company) and the company's executives travel the country telling their story and getting people fired up to buy the stock. Once the underwriters are convinced that enough people are interested; they conduct the IPO, taking money from people and in exchange, issuing them stock in the company.

As I point out in *Myth #1 – Stocks Provide an Intrinsic Return*, a stock's price is based on a combination of its earnings and the price that people are willing to pay for those earnings. With Internet stocks in the late 1990s, people were not only willing to pay huge multiples for earnings, but were also willing to pay huge multiples solely for potential earnings, as most of the companies were unprofitable. Here's an example of that.

TheGlobe.com

TheGlobe.com was started by two Cornell undergrads and launched in 1995. The company enabled clients to create their own websites that were hosted by TheGlobe.com. Within a couple of years they had millions of people using their service. Their business model relied on advertisers paying to place advertisements on those websites, as the users were not charged for the service. Despite losses of more than $10 million in the first nine months of 1998 and nine-month revenues of just $2.7 million, the company filed for an IPO, which took place on November 13, 1998.[78]

What happened that day was unprecedented. TheGlobe.com shares, priced initially at $9 per share, immediately soared and closed their first day of trading at $63.50. This was a record first day move of more than 600%! The two founders were then each worth close to $100 million and the entire company was valued at more than $800 million.[79] Despite the lack of a sound business model the founders, supported by their newly minted fortunes, exhibited extreme hubris. On a CNN profile, filmed in 1999, a camera panned in on one of the partners as he danced, wearing a pair of tight, shiny leather pants on a table-top at a trendy Manhattan night club. Another camera slowly zoomed to the right, revealing his model-girlfriend shimmying by his side. The riveting visual accompanied the founder taunting, "Got the girl. Got the money. Now I'm ready to live a disgusting, frivolous life!"[80] That picture of over-the top, decadent life-style was being funded by the emotional investors who paid him real money by buying his stock from those who flipped it to them following the IPO.

With the Internet imprimatur bestowing millions in riches on seemingly unworthy subjects and their followers, even "old school" ultra-conservative companies were lining up to get in on the game.

---

[78] Dawn Kawamoto, "TheGlobe.com's IPO one for the books," cnet News, (November 13, 1998).
[79] Kawamoto, "TheGlobe.com' IPO one for the books."
[80] Stephan Paternot, A Very Public Offering: A Rebel's Story of Business Excess, Success and Reckoning (New York: John Wiley & Sons, 2001).

Hooked on speculation

K-Tel was about as non-tech as they come. The company started in business in the 1960s as a mail order seller of cookware and knives.[81] The "Veg-O-Matic" was one of their popular products. It was developed by Seymour Popeil, the founder of Ronco, but sold by K-Tel. Although it was not part of its original business plan, shortly after its founding the company began selling music in the form of compilation albums. These combined multiple artists onto one album centered on a single theme. You are probably familiar with the "Hooked on... series," including such titles as "Hooked on Classics." They flew off the shelves.

In the midst of the Internet bubble in April 1998 K-Tel announced they were expanding their business to the Internet. Nothing significant would be changing in the operation of the company. After all, it started as a direct marketing company and the Internet would simply be another distribution channel for its products.

Nevertheless, on the day of the announcement K-Tel stock more than doubled in price. Over the next few weeks the stock continued to rise, climbing from $3 per share to, ultimately, $33.93 per share.[82] This price was an increase of more than ten times from its price prior to the "Internet" announcement. The main explanation for the jump in the stock's price was that it had been officially declared an Internet company and, as a result, its stock should be priced as such.

Yes, that's exactly as dumb as it sounds...the same company, with the same earnings. In fact, based on my experience with spree.com, K-Tel's earnings prospects were potentially less, as they would now be competing with all those Internet music companies that were selling *their* products at a loss.

But none of this over-powered the fact that people had been repeatedly told by analysts, and through experience came to believe, that Internet companies should command a higher multiple for their earnings than other companies. As a result they eagerly paid more for the same earnings. In the short term they were rewarded for this behavior. Others were equally willing to overpay, thereby pushing prices even higher. Of course, in the longer-term, this behavior would prove to be irrational.

---

[81] About K-tel International" *K-tel*. Retrieved February 14, 2011.
[82] "K-Tel Fails to Meet NASDAQ Listing Criteria," *The New York Times*, (November 18, 1998).

In The End...

Anyone who shorted either of these stocks, at any point during their existence, made money. That's because the stocks of both companies became worthless. The stock of TheGlobe.com fell from a high of $97 to less than 10 cents per share by 2001. Today it is worthless. K-Tel suffered a similar fate. The stock fell rapidly after the launch of its Internet store in mid-1998 and ultimately was taken private in a 1 to 5,000 reverse stock split on July 18, 2007.[83] People who put their money into these stocks were essentially wiped out. Clearly, the risk in those stocks was borne by those who held long positions. Short sellers profited handsomely.

The Risk of Selling Short

In early 2002 a friend introduced me to a friend of his who was making tons of money trading stocks. His friend asked to come by my office and meet. "Sure," I said. I'm always interested in talking with other traders, especially successful ones.

The meeting heated up, from my perspective, when this trader began to outline his particular method. It started with a leveraged account at a day trading firm. Using their structure he was able to obtain leverage of up to ten times his capital. Then, if the stocks he was watching rallied, he sold them short because, as he said "it's obvious the market is going down. I don't know why everyone doesn't know that." Well, I've met a lot of long-term successful traders and the one common trait is that they are humble, objective people. They lack hubris. Not so of this trader. What was obvious to him was simply an observation, based on historical patterns that happened to fit with his bias. He thought stocks were going lower and they did. He leveraged that single belief as much as ten to one. When that trade worked he did it again. His winning behavior was reinforced, even though it was a terribly flawed strategy. I cautioned him politely and as he left the office, I just knew his time in the trading world would end badly.

It did. When the bear market of 2000 – 2002 came to an end this short-seller continued to sell on every rally. He did this until he ran out of money. He lost everything. But it wasn't short selling that put him at risk. It was his biased behavior and lack of a sound trading strategy.

---

[83] SEC filing, Amendment No. 4 to Schedule 13E-3 made by K-Tel International, Inc. on July 18, 2007.

You probably noticed the similarities between this story and my story of the woman I met for lunch who bought tech stocks on margin all the way up, only to lose everything once the bull market peaked and turned into a bear. Only this story is in reverse. Just as it wasn't the bear market itself that produced the woman's losses, but rather her lack of a strategy to adjust to the bear market, he didn't employ a strategy that could adjust to the shift from bear back to bull. In both cases they thought they were making money because they had a special insight on the market's direction. They didn't realize the truth, which is that the market activity simply happened to match their bias. The truth only hit them (probably like a ton of bricks) only after they had both lost everything. Neither one of them had employed any trading strategy based on a sound logical return driver; that and that alone, was the cause of their trading nightmare. The mistake doesn't lie in making the choice between short selling and buying long. Because of the fact that a long position can only fall to zero and the risk on a short position is that the stock runs to infinity, the conventional wisdom has always been that selling short is riskier than buying long. However, entering into any position, long or short, without a coherent exit strategy is what creates the risk, not whether that position is a long or a short. And, in fact, an analysis of stock price movements indicates that short selling is actually *less* risky than buying long. Here's why.

Long risk exceeds short risk

I'll start with the obvious. When you buy something, the inherent risk involved is that it can go down in price. When you sell something the risk is that it goes up in price. So to understand the relative risk of long and short positions, we need to know the relative magnitude of up and down price moves.

In *Myth #5 – Stay Invested So You Don't Miss the Best Days* we saw that by missing both the 30 best performing days and the 30 worst performing days in the stock market we could improve our overall performance over the past 20 years. This indicated that the worst days produced more damage to performance than the best days contributed. And then in *Myth #7 – It's Bad to Chase Performance* we saw the statistical evidence that the distribution of returns of the U.S. stock "market" are negatively skewed, indicating a tendency for stocks to have larger down moves than up moves. This indicates that *the short-term risk to a long position (it selling off) is greater than the upside risk to a short position.*

There are risks "baked-in" to the short-selling process. But whether a stock is underpriced or overpriced, there is an underlying return driver we can exploit.

In this case the return driver is based on the excessive multiple people are occasionally willing to pay for potential earnings. In the Action section for this myth I'll present you with investments you can make that enable you to benefit from short selling. Before that however, let me show you how the overall market and financial system benefits from short selling.

The virtues of short selling

Short-sellers habitually seek out bad companies and short their stocks. This provides numerous benefits to the stock market in general and holders of long stock positions in particular.

First of all, as I describe in *Myth #1 – Stocks Provide an Intrinsic Return*, the stocks of well-run companies, those with growing earnings, will rise over time.

> *If short sellers incorrectly target the stock of a well-run company and aggressively push down its price; this provides those who understand the company's true value an additional opportunity to buy the stock at an attractive value.*

You'll hardly ever hear the management team of a well-run company complain about short-sellers. One reason is that their stock is seldom the target of short-sellers. Investors who prefer the short-sell strategy are busy seeking out poor-performing businesses. But additionally, a well-run company's management is well aware that as their companies perform, the short-sellers will eventually be forced to repurchase the shares they sold short, thereby boosting the company's stock price. Secondly,

> *short-sellers keep the market honest – they have a financial incentive to uncover companies engaged in fraud and other misdeeds.*

They have done their homework about the companies they short. They tend to pour over financial statements, including the oft-ignored footnotes, and closely compare the utterances of management with the actual deeds of the business. There is a long list of companies whose misdeeds have first been uncovered by short-sellers, long before regulators became aware of problems. These include some of the biggest scams in history, including Enron and WorldCom, plus over-hyped stocks such as Krispy Kreme. Third,

short-sellers provide the stock market with liquidity.

When General Motors filed for bankruptcy on June 1, 2009, the stock rose from $0.75 on the day prior to the filing to as much as $1.60 over the subsequent week. This was the result of short-sellers, who had previously shorted the stock in anticipation of just such a bankruptcy filing, taking their profits and buying back their shorts once the bankruptcy became official. This short-covering bounce gave people who held long positions the opportunity to sell off their stock. Without the short-sellers, this liquidity would not have existed.

Ultimately though, in any case where a company is not fraudulent or about to go bankrupt, anyone planning on short-selling will need to repurchase that stock in order to return the shares they borrowed. If the company is well-run, with growing profits; their stock price will eventually rise. If short sellers truly are capable of pushing a stock down to well below its real value, true investors

> A "short squeeze" occurs when the price of a stock rises and investors who sold the stock short rush to buy it to cover their short positions. As the price of the stock increases, more short sellers feel driven to cover their positions, thereby pushing the stock price up even further.

should welcome their actions. It gives them the ability to buy that stock at a highly favorable price.

In addition, the buying pressure created by those short sellers who repurchase their shares will add to the overall, upward pressure. This creates what is known as a "short squeeze." The results can be spectacular and highly profitable to people who hold long positions.

In the crash of 2008, many companies saw their stocks become the target of short-sellers. These included Barnes & Noble, MGM Mirage, Citigroup and Goodrich Petroleum. In these companies, the percentage of their outstanding shares that had been sold short ranged between 24% and 34%. When the stock market rebounded out of the March 2009 lows, these stocks, in turn, exploded in price (Figure 29). A big contributor to their rallies was the short squeeze brought on by the large percentage of shorts that were covering (buying back) their short positions.

Heavily Shorted Stocks' Performances
Following the Market Low of March 9, 2009[84]

Stock	% of Shares Sold Short	Return from 3-9-2009 to 4-15-2009
Barnes & Noble - BKS	34%	68%
MGM Mirage - MGM	31%	305%
Goodrich Petroleum - GDP	25%	76%
Citigroup - C	24%	205%
Hovnanian - HOV	24%	400%
Green Mountain Coffee Roasters - GMCR	44%	97%
Bankrate - RATE	36%	47%

Figure 29

Why do some of the world's most sophisticated investors, such as Goldman Sachs and the Harvard and Yale universities' endowments, actively engage in short-selling or place their money with hedge-fund managers who are active short-sellers? Because it is irrational *not* to short-sell.

In fact, Richard Fuld, the failed executive I introduced at the start of this chapter, and John Mack, both headed up firms that engaged sizable trading operations that employed short-sellers. You're correct in sensing a bit of hypocrisy here. At the same time their companies were aggressively shorting the stocks of other companies, they were calling on the federal government to provide them protection against those who were short-sellers of *their* stock. The reality was, they knew the truth: Short-sellers profit by shorting the shares of poorly-run companies. At that particular time both Morgan Stanley and Lehman Brothers were poorly-run companies. The short-sellers were right on target and profited from their strategy.

---

[84] Dan Caplinger, "Now It's time for Short-Sellers to Panic," The Motley Fool (May 5, 2009). Retrieved February 14, 2011.

SUMMARY
MYTH 10

- The short-term risk of a long stock position selling off is greater than the upside risk to a short position.

- If short-sellers incorrectly sell short stocks of strong companies, long-term investors will benefit by being able to buy those good stocks at lower prices than would otherwise have been available to them (had the short-sellers not pressured the stock lower with their sales).

- Short-sellers keep the market honest by uncovering companies engaged in fraud and other misdeeds. Those short-sellers profit by identifying and shorting the stocks of those companies and profiting as those stocks fall in price when others learn of the misdeeds.

- Short-sellers provide the stock market with liquidity when they step in to sell short stocks that become overhyped and bid up by emotional buyers.

Commodity Trading
is Risky

I read an article a number of years ago where people were surveyed regarding new sources of energy. An audience was asked whether they thought any of the sources described looked promising and practical enough to be considered as viable for their personal use.

One of the sources presented seemed especially compelling for a number of reasons. It was clean, its use allowed the U.S. to dramatically lower its dependence on "unfriendly" or unstable energy providers, and it could make use of existing infrastructure with only minimal retrofitting. But it had one serious drawback. It was dangerous and highly explosive. In fact, research had shown that it was likely to result in dozens of deaths per year. It was that death toll which caused the vast majority of those surveyed to reject it as a potential option. Many respondents even went so far as to say that they would never consider any energy source that would result in even one death per year.

The energy source? Natural gas. Obviously, millions of Americans already use natural gas to heat their homes and businesses, and to cook their food. It has been widely accepted for years. Although it can be explosive, when properly used, its benefits far outweigh its risks. The same is true of commodity trading.

I have been a commodity trader all of my adult life. I placed my first trade, buying gold options, in 1979. Most people consider commodity trading to be exotic. They consider commodity trading to be risky, especially as compared to trading stocks. The reality is that commodities have been traded since the advent of human civilization. Stock trading is a much more modern pursuit. And which action is more exotic: dealing in a tangible physical commodity that you can eat or use to create shelter, or a piece of paper or electronic entry that promises partial ownership in a legal entity. Still, the myth that commodity trading is risky persists. Let's look at three causes for why this myth came into being and how you can profit from that belief.

Comparing commodities to stocks

Despite my objection to using volatility as a proxy for risk, for reasons I provide in Myth #9, most people associate higher volatility with higher risk. So if commodities are more volatile than stocks that could be the basis for the myth that commodities are risky (certainly compared to stocks). Let's take a look by comparing the volatility of individual stocks with that of individual commodities.

Figure 30 shows the daily standard deviation for the ten year period 2000 - 2009 for a cross-section of common and well-known stocks and commodities. Within each category the markets are ranked from the most volatile to the least volatile. As is clear from the table, most commodities are not only considerably less volatile than technology stocks, but are also less volatile than more stable, large capitalization stocks such as Exxon Mobil, Berkshire Hathaway and GE.

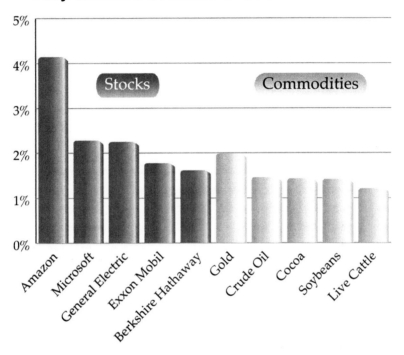

Daily Standard Deviation of Selected Markets

Figure 30

So if volatility does not lead to the perception that commodities are risky, what does? There is one strong candidate for this answer – the misuse of leverage.

Gambling with leverage

The reason commodities are viewed as risky has nothing to do with the markets themselves, but rather with the structure available to trade them. People who put money into U.S. stocks are limited in the amount of leverage they can use to trade any individual stock. SEC regulation T limits the amount that can be purchased on margin to 50%. That means that to buy $10,000 worth of stocks a person must deposit at least $5,000 with their broker. In fact, most stock traders do not use margin at all, preferring to put up the full amount of the stock price.

When most people speak about commodity trading, what they're usually referring to is "futures" trading (I'll discuss other myths associated with futures trading in the next chapter). Most commodity futures markets allow for leverage of ten times or more. This means that a trader need only deposit $1,000 to secure a position worth $10,000. And many commodity traders make full use of this leverage, holding positions in their accounts that are five or ten times larger than their account equity. This means that a 10% move in a commodity against a person's position would result in a 50% or 100% loss of the money deposited. It is this leverage that makes commodities look risky. Obviously, the use of leverage increases the effective volatility of each market substantially.

I know first-hand the structural risks of using leverage in commodity trading. I've suffered multi-million dollar losses more than once. The root cause of those losses was not leverage or that fact that the markets were commodities, but simply that I lacked discipline and failed to follow a set strategy. In fact, losses were often incurred in non-commodity futures, such as stock indexes. It wasn't commodities that were risky. Nor leverage. It was my behavior.

As an example, on Thursday October 15, 1987 I was highly bearish on U.S. stocks. I had written articles outlining my views on how the U.S. stock market was in an unsustainable bull run and due for a dramatic collapse. Sounds good so far right? (Just four days later, Monday, October 19, 1987 witnessed a U.S. stock market decline of 22%, the largest one-day decline in history). The market on October 15, 1987 was weak all day and I started out with a large short position in S&P futures contracts. But at the very end of the day the futures market rallied after the cash market closed (the S&P futures contract at that time traded until 4:15pm ET, while the actual stock market closed at 4:00pm ET). I covered my short positions and bought into that rally. By the close of futures trading I was long S&P 500 futures contracts worth many times the value of the cash in my account. The market fell throughout the following day, ending with a sizable loss of more than 4%.During that time I liquidated my position at a loss.

Watching the historic and gargantuan collapse of the stock market on Monday October 19, 1987, a collapse which I had predicted, only succeeded in rubbing salt into my already gaping wounds. It all went down without my participation. I had taken myself off the playing field the previous Friday, simply by abusing the leverage available to me as a futures trader. It was my abuse of leverage that created the risk, not the "commodity markets" in which I was trading. In fact, I wasn't trading a "commodity" at all, but a stock index.

Despite the fact that commodities themselves are no more risky than stocks, this myth persists. But the financial services industry, always creative, discovered a way to get people to put money into commodities. Their angle?... create commodity funds that have the look and the feel of stock index funds that are already well-accepted and have attracted more than a trillion dollars in savings.

Commodity index funds

During the 1990s and 2000s a number of "investible" commodity indexes were created. Similar to the S&P 500 and other long-only stock indexes, each is based on holding long positions (they are never short) in a single commodity or portfolio of commodities. While some of these buy the actual commodity (such as the SPDR Gold Trust (GLD), which holds gold bars), many others use their money to buy a portfolio of commodity futures contracts. The people who put money into these funds have the unrealistic expectation that they will profit from rising prices of the commodities held by those funds. Much like the average "blind date," the result does not always live up to the expectations.

One such index was developed by Goldman Sachs to track the prices of 25 (since revised to 24) commodity markets. The rights to the index were purchased by Standard & Poor's in 2007 and it's now known as the S&P GSCI.[85] The Chicago Mercantile Exchange (now the CME Group) began trading futures and options on this index in 1992 and in 2006 the iShares S&P GSCI Commodity Indexed Trust (GSG) was first offered as an opportunity for people to participate in the performance of the index.

"ETN" is the acronym for "Exchange Traded Note." This is similar to an ETF, which was defined in Myth #4, in that it tracks baskets of stocks, bonds, commodities or other assets. It differs in that the note is issued by a financial firm and therefore faces the risk that if the issuer goes bankrupt, the ETN may not repay the promised return.

Jim Rogers developed another such index and spent the most part of a decade popularizing its use. His book "Hot Commodities: How Anyone Can Invest Profitably in the World's Best Market"[86] became a hot commodity itself. Published in 2004, it introduced many people to the concept of holding a diversified

---

[85] "S&P GSCI," *Standard & Poor's*. Retrieved February 14, 2011.
[86] Jim Rogers, *Hot Commodities* (New York: Random House, 2004).

portfolio of long positions in commodities. This accelerated the interest in long-only commodity index funds and ETN's (Exchange Traded Notes).

Unfortunately, while commodity index funds have received a lot of attention as a way for people to "safely" invest in commodities, they are actually every bit as risky as stock index funds and expose people to unnecessary risk. This has nothing to do with the commodities they track, but is instead due to a flaw in the trading strategy underlying many of the funds (I first discussed this flaw in Myth #7). Because commodity futures contracts have limited life-spans, these funds are required to roll their long positions from one contract month to the next active contract month prior to the expiration of the first contract. There is a cost incurred in doing so. This cost is made up of the obvious components, such as brokerage commissions, but also some which are less transparent. Because there's a cost in storing a commodity, the price of that commodity for future delivery is often greater than that commodity's current cash price. This price differential is referred to as the "cost of carry." When the cost of carry is positive, more distant futures contracts will trade at a higher price than the current contracts. In this scenario the market is said to be in "contango." Figure 31 shows an example of a market in contango.

What the chart shows is that on February 22, 2010, the March 2010 price of coffee was approximately $1.30 per pound. The price of coffee for delivery in December 2010, however, was almost 9 cents per pound higher, at just under $1.39. More distant contract months were trading at even higher prices. This contango term structure has negative implications for a long-only commodity fund.

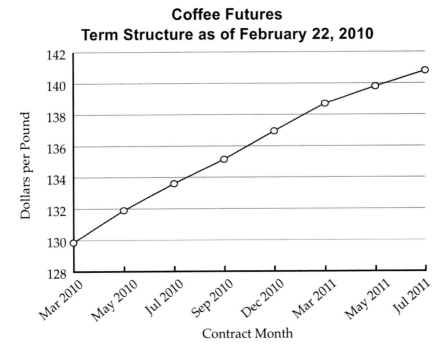

Figure 31

Every time a long-only commodity fund rolls from one coffee futures contract into a more distant contract month it pays more for that future contract than it is receiving on the sale of its current contract. In this example, over the course of one year this amounts to almost 9 cents, which is more than 6% of the current price of a pound of coffee. What this means is that coffee prices need to rise 6% annually just for the long-only commodity fund to break-even on its long coffee position.

Backwardation

Not all futures markets always trade with a contango term structure. At various times they may trade in "backwardation." Backwardation refers to the condition whereby current contracts trade at prices higher than those of more distant contracts. Figure 32 shows an example of the crude oil market when it was in backwardation in August 2007.

Crude Oil Futures Term Structure
as of August 31, 2007

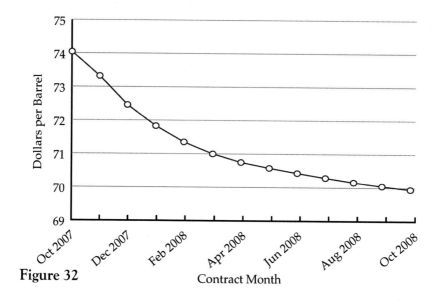

Figure 32   Contract Month

For much of the 1990s and 2000s, this was representative of the term structure of the crude oil futures market. It traded in backwardation, producing "roll premium" to long-only commodity funds with crude oil exposure. Roll premium refers to the profit produced when a futures contract is bought a few months distant, at a discount to the actual cash price. This profit source exists even if prices remain flat (or, up to a point, even if they decline!). Long-only commodity funds were structured to take advantage of this term structure. In fact, some of those funds, such as ones based on the S&P GSCI Index, derived the majority of their profits from this roll premium. While many people thought that putting money into those funds would provide them with a hedge against rising commodity prices, their actual returns were primarily produced by the roll premium, not rising commodity prices.

Of course, the situation can reverse as well. As discussed previously, a contango term structure, where the more distant futures contracts are trading at a premium to the near-term futures contracts, results in losses every time a position is rolled from one futures contract to the next. The negative effect of this term structure was blatantly obvious during early 2009 in the performance of the iShares S&P GSCI Commodity Indexed Trust (GSG), the largest fund structured to track the S&P GSCI Index (see Figure 33).

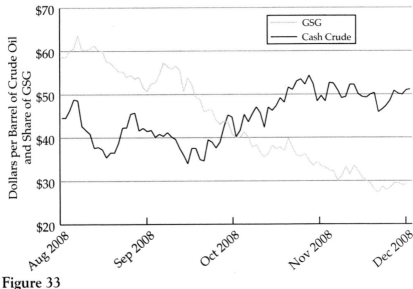

GSG Compared with Cash Crude Oil Prices
January through April 2009

Figure 33

Although crude oil prices rose 14.6% over the period displayed in the chart, and although crude oil makes up 46% of the S&P GSCI Index, GSG actually lost more than 50% of its value over the period! This loss was primarily the result of the roll cost incurred in the trading of the fund each month.

GSG was not the only fund to suffer losses due to the cost of rolling from one futures contract into the next. The PIMCO Commodity Real Return Strategy Fund (PCRAX), PowerShares DB Commodity Index Tracking fund (DBC), and United States Natural Gas (UNG) are all long-only commodity funds that lost money over the past few years, despite the strong performance of the markets in which they were trading. Perhaps it's the public's recent exposure to funds like these that has helped perpetuate the myth that commodities are risky. But once again, it wasn't commodities that were risky, but the way people traded them that turned these funds into losers. This is not uncommon. In playing to people's belief in the myths, financial firms often focus on creating products they know people will buy rather than products most likely to make those people money. But you don't need to lose along with the others who placed their money in these funds. In fact, in the Action section for this myth I will show you a method you can use to profit from this same term structure that produced losses for these and other long-only commodity funds.

SUMMARY
MYTH 11

- Commodity prices are no more volatile than stock prices, and many commodities are much less volatile than many stocks.

- Large losses that result from the abuse of leverage is a primary reason that commodities appear riskier than stocks.

- Long commodity index funds, such as GSG, earn the majority of their profits not from rising commodity prices, but more so from the backwardation inherent in many of the commodity futures markets that make up the major long-only commodity indexes.

Futures Trading
is Risky

This myth is so widely "known" it has become conventional wisdom. You constantly hear the stories about how most people who open a futures trading account end up closing it at a loss. Going by that statistic, trading in futures has to be riskier than skydiving with an unchecked parachute. But this losing behavior in futures trading simply confirms what we already learned in Myth #3. On average, people who trade in and out of mutual funds greatly underperform the return they would receive by leaving their money in the funds. And the more they trade, the more they lose. Compounding this losing behavior even further, the more leverage they employ, the greater their loss. And...most individual futures traders trade a lot and use a lot of leverage. The result: they lose a lot of money.

But what's important to know is that the fault lies not with the products but with the players. The majority of futures traders are not traders or investors, they're gamblers. As described in Myth #8, this distinction is not defined by the markets or instruments they trade, but by their behavior. They trade emotionally and without a systematic plan based on sound return drivers. Mirroring the conclusion of the DALBAR study presented in Myth #3, the fact that the vast majority of people lose money trading futures is not to be viewed as a depressing statistic. It is an exciting opportunity.

The money lost by the majority of futures traders is captured by the rational disciplined traders, just as the 5% left on the table each year by the mutual fund gamblers accrues to the more disciplined stock market participants.

Don't take my word for it. Various organizations have been tracking the performance of professional futures traders for decades. They've compiled these performances into indexes, similar to how Dow Jones and Standard & Poor's have created and tracked stock indexes. These provide us with an objective look at the performance of professional futures traders. Let's take a look at two indexes. These have similar returns but dramatically different risk levels, as measured by the losses (drawdowns) suffered during the history of each index.

A comparison of futures performance

I'll start by summarizing the returns of the first index, which is diversified across fewer trading strategies than the second index. As a result, it incurs substantial risk in relation to its returns.

During the period between January of 1987 and December 2010, this index produced 9.5% average annual returns. Not bad. But it did so while exposing its followers to high risk. In fact, as shown in Figure 34, the index suffered multiple losing periods in excess of 20%, with one loss actually destroying more than half of the index value.

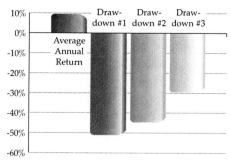

Figure 34

Now let's look at the performance of a second index (Figure 35). This one is clearly comprised of traders who employ a more conservative approach. The result is that the index suffered no losing periods of greater than 20%.

In addition, despite the substantially lower risk, the second index produced a greater annualized return than did the first index: +9.6% to +9.5%. This favorable combination of greater gains and lesser losses is the ideal goal sought after by most rational investors. However, because of the belief in the myth that futures trading is risky, most people did not benefit from the performance of the second index. For this index tracks the performance of professional futures traders. Specifically, it represents the returns earned by the BTOP 50 managed futures index.

The BTOP 50 is a composite index created and managed by Barclay Hedge that tracks the performance of commodity trading advisors (CTAs) that represent 50% of the assets being managed in the industry.[87] It can be considered the "S&P 500" index for managed futures. Despite the word "commodity" in their designation, CTAs are not restricted to trading just commodities. In fact, CTAs trade a broad diversity of futures contracts, including currencies, interest rates, and global stock indexes, as well as commodities such as crude oil, gold, and soybeans. In addition to trading in a diversity of markets, the CTAs that are represented in the BTOP 50 Index also incorporate a wide variety of trading strategies designed to adapt to changing market conditions. In early 2008 for

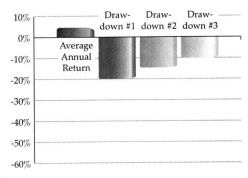

**Index #2
Solid Return, Lower Risk**

Figure 35

example, many of these CTAs profited by being long crude oil and many other commodities, as well as short global stock indexes. When the financial crisis hit hard and those commodities fell in price, many of those same CTAs reversed into short commodity positions, garnering healthy profits from both those positions and their short positions in global equities.[88] In stark contrast, the risky first index did not adapt, and as a result suffered extensive losses. Perhaps it is this behavior pattern that has led to the erroneous myth that futures trading is risky. But this argument crashes to earth like a skydiver

---

[87] More information about Barclay Hedge and the BTOP 50 Index can be found at www.barclayhedge.com.

[88] The monthly returns of the BTOP 50 Index available at: http://www.barclayhedge.com/research/indices/btop/index.html. Retrieved February 14, 2011.

without a parachute when it is disclosed that the first index isn't a futures trading index at all. It is the S&P 500 Total Return Index.

A long stock position has historically and persistently been promoted by financial advisors and the mainstream financial media to serve as the core holding for every portfolio created. And this same conventional wisdom has consistently espoused the view that futures trading is risky, certainly too risky to be included in a "conservative" portfolio. But the exact opposite conclusion should be reached. Managed futures, with their superior risk-adjusted returns, should receive a solid allocation in every portfolio.

*If it was true that "risky" investments have no place in
a conservative portfolio, then no one would own stocks.
They're too risky!*

Why stocks are riskier than futures

The fact that the BTOP 50 managed futures index displays more consistent returns than the S&P 500 TR Index should come as no surprise. Buying-and-holding stocks is a single trading strategy that, in the short-term, is dependent on a single return driver, investor sentiment. When an event occurs that turns this sentiment negative, such as the 2008 financial crisis, the strategy will suffer extensive losses. This is known as "Event Risk." Event Risk reveals the commonality of return drivers across positions in a portfolio and manifests itself in across-the-board losses when baseline conditions become unsuitable for the common return driver.

In stark contrast, the performance of the BTOP 50 is derived from a diversity of sources. This is because the trading strategies employed by the CTAs represented in the Index are driven by a wide variety of return drivers. In fact, just one of these alone, a simple trend following strategy similar to that used in the S&P DTI described in Myth #7, applied across just five global stock indexes, dramatically reduces risk while maintaining similar returns. This is illustrated in Figure 36. The trading strategy employed is described in the Action for Myth #7.

Performance Comparison – S&P 500 TR vs. Trend Following in Five Stock Index Futures for the 20-year Period 1991 – 2010

	S&P 500 TR	Trend Following
Years	20	20
Average Annual Return	9.11%	9.11%
Annualized Volatility	15.06%	9.79%
Maximum Drawdown	-51%	-27%
% Profitable months	65%	63%
% Profitable Rolling 12-Months	72%	84%
% Profitable years	73%	85%

Figure 36. *The specific composition of the Five Stock Index Futures portfolio is detailed in the Table of Figures section.*

But it's not just the flexibility of the trading strategies employed by the CTAs in the BTOP 50 index that make the BTOP 50 less risky than buying and holding stocks. It's also the fact that the individual markets that comprise the managed futures programs' portfolios are far more diverse and substantially less correlated with each other than the stocks that make up the S&P 500. This means that while one market may be moving higher, another may be moving lower. They are affected by different return drivers. As a result, an event that may cause one market to fall may cause a different market to rise. The financial market collapse in the fall of 2008 illustrates this point perfectly: Commodities such as soybeans and heating oil took a dive in price while others, such as gold, actually rose. This lack of market correlation provides diversification benefits which can markedly decrease the negative potential of event risk in a futures portfolio.

The BTOP 50 contains the performance of CTAs trading in more than three dozen global equities markets; dozens of currencies and cross-rates; more than 100 interest rate contracts and yield curve permutations; precious metals (such as gold, silver and platinum); base metals (such as copper, zinc and aluminum); energy markets (including crude oil, gasoline and natural gas); and dozens of other commodity markets (including soybeans, corn and other grain markets; livestock and other foods). And the trading systems incorporate a variety of return drivers, including those based on trends, fundamental supply-demand factors, the sentiment of market participants, arbitrage opportunities, intermarket relationships, and the effect of seasons and geopolitical events. As a result, the BTOP 50 index exposes people to substantially less event risk than does a position held in the S&P 500.

The benefits of managed futures

I can't claim credit for revealing the truth behind this myth. The secret has actually been out for more than 25 years. Harvard professor Dr. John Lintner presented a seminal paper at the 1983 annual conference of the Financial Analysts Federation in Toronto, in which he stated that "The combined portfolios of stocks (or stocks and bonds) after including judicious investments in appropriately selected sub-portfolios of investments in managed futures accounts (or funds) show substantially less risk at every possible level of expected return than portfolios of stocks (or stocks and bonds) alone."[89]

More recently, researchers from the CME Group and AlphaMetrix Alternative Investment Advisors updated the Lintner study. Their results not only continue to support the conclusion reached by Dr. Lintner in 1983, but state that "the results are so compelling that the board of any institution, along with the portfolio manager, should be forced to articulate in writing their justification in not having a substantial allocation to... managed futures."[90]

Figure 37 and Figure 38 show just why Dr. Lintner and other knowledgeable investors have been such strong proponents of managed futures. They compare the performance of the BTOP 50 with the S&P 500 TR since the start of the BTOP 50 in 1987. While the overall returns from both are virtually identical, the performance of the BTOP 50 was much more consistent and less risky than that of the S&P 500 TR.

---

[89] John Lintner, "The Potential Role of Managed Commodity-Financial Futures Account (and/or Funds) in Portfolios of Stocks and Bonds" (presented at the Annual Conference of the Financial Analysts Federation, Royal York Hotel, Toronto, Canada, May 16, 1983.

[90] Ryan Abrams, Ranjan Bhaduri and Elizabeth Flores, "Lintner Revisited: "The Benefits of Managed Futures 25 Years Later," CME Group (2010): 7.

Performance Comparison Graph
BTOP 50 Managed Futures Index &
S&P 500 Total Return Index
(Since the start of trading in the BTOP 50 Index)

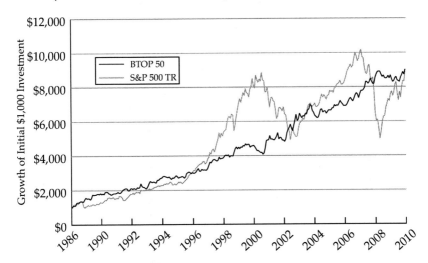

Figure 37

Performance Comparison Table
BTOP 50 Managed Futures Index &
S&P 500 Total Return Index
(Since the start of trading in the BTOP 50 Index)

	S&P 500 TR	BTOP 50
Years	24	24
Average Annual Return	9.59%	9.60%
Annualized Volatility	15.79%	10.59%
Maximum Drawdown	-51%	-13%
% Profitable months	64%	58%
% Profitable Rolling 12-Months	77%	86%
% Profitable years	79%	92%

Figure 38

In addition to providing higher returns with substantially lower risk, Figure 39 shows how the BTOP 50 profited during all but one of the worst-performing quarters for the S&P 500 TR over the past two-plus decades.

Performance of the BTOP 50 Managed Futures Index During the 10 Worst Quarters for the S&P 500 Index
(Since the start of the BTOP 50 Index in January 1987)

Period	Event	S&P 500	BTOP 50	Difference
Q4 1987	Black Monday Crash	-23.2%	16.9%	40.1%
Q4 2008	Bear Market in Equities	-22.6%	8.7%	31.3%
Q3 2002	WorldCom Scandal	-17.6%	9.4%	27.1%
Q3 2001	Terrorist Attacks - 9/11	-15.0%	4.1%	19.1%
Q3 1990	Iraq Invades Kuwait	-14.5%	11.2%	25.7%
Q2 2002	Continued Bear Market	-13.7%	8.5%	22.3%
Q1 2001	Continued Bear Market	-12.1%	6.0%	18.1%
Q2 2010	European Debt Crisis	-11.4%	-1.9%	9.5%
Q3 1998	Russia Defaults on Debt	-10.3%	10.5%	20.8%
Q1 2008	Credit Crisis	-9.9%	5.9%	15.8%

Figure 39

The numbers don't lie. Futures are not risky and, moreover, when properly traded by professional managers, they provide solid returns with lower risk. In addition, they hold the potential for profits when stocks slip into a nosedive. When viewed in this light, it becomes glaringly obvious it's those who cling to the "buy & hold" strategy in their stock trading that are the ones taking on excessive risk – certainly in relation to the prospective return. Conversely, those engaged in futures trading are involved in the more rational process of maximizing returns while minimizing risk.

An "Accredited Investor" is roughly defined as a person with a $1 million net worth or an annual income of $200,000. Many CTAs also require an investor to be a "Qualified Eligible Person (QEP)," which is a higher standard and requires the person to own investments with a market value of more than $2 million. The complete definitions are quite complex and the summary descriptions provided here are highly simplified.

If there is nothing else you take away from this book it's that what others revere as financial truths are quite often proven wrong when that notion is exposed to the clear light of factual analysis. Throw away your preconceived biases. Let the rest of the field jump to their conclusions without proof while you, the rational investor, gain the true, bottom-line advantage.

Unfortunately, although some managed futures funds are available to the "Regular Joe" demographic, the majority of managed futures programs are only available to the wealthy. This uneven playing field is created by regulatory impediments dictating that the majority of managed futures funds be privately offered and available only to "accredited investors." Many CTAs are also restricted to accepting investments from people who are considered to be Qualified Eligible Persons (QEPs), which is a higher standard and requires a person to own investments with a market value of more than $2 million. The complete definitions are quite complex and the summary descriptions provided here (and in the "Glossary") are highly simplified. In addition, the companies that offer these programs can't engage in pro-active advertising and marketing campaigns like a mutual fund can. As a result, because of the general public's inaccessibility to the product, most people remain unaware of its existence. In *Myth #14 – Government Regulations Protect Investors*, I discuss how regulations often interfere with people's ability to make the necessary allocations to create a truly balanced and diversified portfolio.

In the Action section for this myth I present some of the funds that are readily available to the general public and a few keys to gain entry to some of the more restricted investment tools in managed futures.

SUMMARY
MYTH 12

- The "average" futures trader loses money; similar to the "average" person who places money in stock and bond funds, as indicated by the DALBAR studies. The money lost by the average futures trader is captured by the rational disciplined traders, just as the 5% left on the table each year by the mutual fund gamblers accrues to the more disciplined stock market participants.

- The diversification of trading strategies incorporated in managed futures portfolios provides the ability for investors to earn greater returns with less risk than if they put their money into an S&P 500 index fund.

It's Best to Follow
Expert Advice

A selling frenzy shook the stock market on the morning of Wednesday, January 7, 1981. Immediately following the familiar sound of the opening bell that officially starts the hectic business day on Wall Street, trading volume soared to record highs as stocks plummeted to alarming lows. By the end of the day a record 92 million shares had been traded on the New York Stock Exchange and the Dow Jones Industrial Average fell more than 2%. Stocks fell an additional 1.5% the following day.

Such sell-offs are usually the result of global upheaval or international tragedy of some measure – the outbreak of war or the death of a president. On that day in 1981 it was the result of a phone call. To be specific...three thousand phone calls.

The calls were made to wealthy clients all over the world, on vacation in the Caribbean, in their penthouses overlooking Manhattan, or skiing in the Alps. These people all had one common bond. They had each paid $750 to subscribe to Joseph Granville's "Early Warning Service."[91] Their subscription entitled them to receive a telephone call or telex alerting them to the seer's latest prognostication. Late on the night of January 6 and into the early morning hours of January 7, Granville's staff of 34 called to wake their clients with the simple message, "Sell everything. Market top has been reached. Go short on stocks having sharpest advances since April." By 2:45 that morning, Eastern Time, the calls were completed.

The market's reaction was a testament to the clout of Joe Granville. His influence had been building over the prior six years as his *Granville Market Letter* grew its subscriber count to more than 13,000. But his reach extended well beyond that number, as each market call he made was met with ever-greater news media coverage.

The news media and Granville's subscribers weren't the only ones enamored by his market calls. So was Granville himself. A 1981 *People* magazine article quoted him as saying "I will never make a serious mistake in the stock market again."[92] Having mastered the market, Granville expanded into truly Nostradamus-level predictions. At a seminar in Vancouver, British Columbia in early 1981, Granville announced that he had adapted his stock market forecasting system to predict earthquakes. He specifically predicted that an earthquake would "shred" California 23 miles east of Los Angeles. He knew this, he said, because he developed and followed 33 earthquake indicators.[93] Alas, his skill fell far short of his self-confidence and massive ego. There was no earthquake. That blunder, along with errant predictions the prior year that both San Francisco and Santa Barbara would be hit with temblors,[94] began to shake the public's confidence in Granville's prognostication abilities.

Those "not-even-close" misses also marked the peak in Granville's fame. Over the following decades, his popularity collapsed along with the accuracy of his predictions. In 2005, Mark Hulbert, who, in his *Hulbert Financial Digest* tracks the performance of market gurus such as Granville by recording each of their buy and sell recommendations, stated that the *Granville Market Letter* "is at the bottom of the *Hulbert Financial Digest's* rankings for performance

[91] Edward E. Scharf and John Thompkins, "Granville Stuns the Market," *Time Magazine* (January 19, 1981).
[92] Kristin McMurran, "When Joe Granville Speaks, Small Wonder That the Market Yo-Yos and Tickers Fibrillate," *People Magazine*, Vol. 15, No. 13 (April 6, 1981).
[93] McMurran. "When Joe Granville Speaks, Small Wonder That the Market Yo-Yos and Tickers Fibrillate."
[94] Craig Unger, "Good-bye to L.A. Says Market Wiz," *New York Magazine* (May 12, 1980): 16.

over the past 25 years – having produced average losses of more than 20% per year on an annualized basis."[95] His subscribers paid far more than $750 per year to follow his advice.

....

Experts aren't

The December 20, 2007 issue of *BusinessWeek* (since purchased by Bloomberg L.P. and renamed *Bloomberg Businessweek*) contained an article titled "Where to Put Your Cash in 2008."[96] In the article, *Businessweek* polled seven well-known stock market analysts about their views on the direction of the stock market during 2008. As we all know now, 2008 proved to be one of the most calamitous years on record for the world's stock markets: $30 trillion in value was wiped out from the world's equity markets during the year. The S&P 500 fell 38%, which actually ranked it among the better performing markets. The MSCI Emerging Markets Index fell 54% and the MSCI World Index fell 42%.

Yet in the *BusinessWeek* article, every analyst predicted higher stock market prices for 2008. On average they predicted a 12.76% rise in the Dow Jones Industrials and a 12.61% rise in the S&P 500. Perhaps of even more interest was the fact that their predictions varied by very little among themselves. Their forecasts for the Dow Jones Industrials ranged from a gain of +8.56% to +15.35%. They were in consensus on their forecasts. At least they could take comfort in being wrong together.

Why is it that experts, people who make it their job to understand and forecast markets or events, can get it so wrong? Are they trying to do too much by predicting the movement of an entire market? Perhaps they'd do better with more limited predictions, such as the earnings of individual companies. Unfortunately, wrong again.

In the April 2010 issue of *McKinsey Quarterly*, the authors reported the results of a quarter-century-long study of stock analysts' earnings forecasts. Stock analysts are paid big money to understand in detail the operations of specific companies and, based on that in-depth knowledge, make forecasts of how much each of those companies will earn in future years. The

---

[95] Mark Hulbert, "Gambling on Granville," *Market Watch* (March 16, 2005). Retrieved February 14, 2011.

[96] William Greiner, "Where to Put Your Cash in 2008," *Bloomberg Businessweek* (December 20, 2007).

results of the study reinforced those of a prior study conducted a decade before. Analysts, they found, "were typically overoptimistic, slow to revise their forecasts to reflect new economic conditions, and prone to making increasingly inaccurate forecasts when economic growth declined."[97]

Specifically, over the time frame studied, analysts' forecasts were almost 100% off the mark. They estimated average annual earnings growth ranging from 10% to 12% per year. Actual earnings growth came in at just 6%. Figure 40 tells the story.

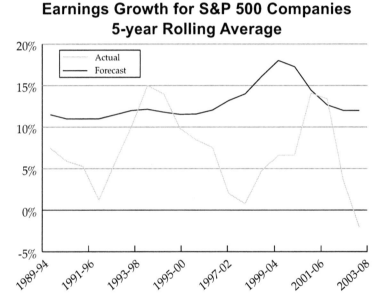

Figure 40

So perhaps we are still expecting too much from the experts. Perhaps forecasts of corporate details, such as cash reserves or earnings, are too difficult to predict. Perhaps the experts would do better with still more limited predictions, such as the simple future viability of a company. Then again, perhaps not.

On March 11, 2008, SEC Chairman Christopher Cox, when asked about the financial stability of firms such as Bear Stearns and Lehman Brothers, said "We have a good deal of comfort about the capital cushions at these

---

[97] Marc Goedhart, Rishi Raj and Abhishek Saxens, "Equity analysts: Still too bullish," *McKinsey Quarterly* (April 2010).

firms at the moment."[98] Just three days later, drained of most of its cash, Bear Stearns was forced into a hastily arranged marriage with JP Morgan Chase.

In June 2008, only three months before the demise of the now infamous Lehman Brothers (which I discussed in *Myth #10 – Short Selling is Destabilizing and Risky*), an analyst at the Boston-based financial consulting firm Celent assured the media, "Lehman's survival as an independent entity should not be at stake."[99] September of 2008 proved his analysis to be as inaccurate as a prediction can possibly be. Lehman Brothers went into collapse mode, and was forced to declare the largest bankruptcy in history.[100]

But these woefully inaccurate experts are not alone. An entire industry of "experts" exists for the purpose of rating the credit-worthiness of corporations and governments. Specifically they are highly paid to inform people as to the likelihood of companies and governments being able to repay their debts. It's the credit rating industry.

Ratings agencies – the "experts" on credit risk

When a company wants to raise money but not dilute its shareholders through the issuance of stock, one way for it to do so is to issue notes or bonds. These are simply loans that the company makes to people who provide money in return for a promise from the company to pay interest (usually in the form of a semi-annual payment, called a coupon), and, eventually, a return of the original cash lent to the company, called the principal. The loan is often called a "note" if its term (the time between the lending and repayment of the principal) is less than 10 years and a "bond" if the term is 10 years or longer.

For centuries, the buyers of corporate notes and bonds (I'll simply refer to these as "bonds") relied on their individual skill (or luck) to evaluate the ability of the issuing company to make the obligated interest and principal payments. Eventually however, the quantity and complexity of new bond offerings created the opportunity for specialized firms to fill the analysis role. These firms, which today include the big three of Standard & Poor's, Moody's, and Fitch, began

---

[98] Stephen Labaton, "Agency's '04 Rule Let Banks Pile Up New Debt," *The New York Times* (October 2, 2008).

[99] "Lehman Brothers posts $2.8 billion 2Q loss," *Associated Press* (June 16, 2008).

[100] Sam Mamudi, "Lehman folds with record $613 billion debt," *MarketWatch* (September 15, 2008).

providing ratings on railroad bonds in the early 20th century.[101] The most credit-worthy bond issues – those most likely to be repaid by their issuing companies or governments – would receive a rating of AAA (triple A). In keeping with this variation on a high school grading system, lower-rated bonds would receive lower letter grades, with any issue rated below B generally considered "junk."[102]

Initially, the customers of these bond ratings were financial institutions looking to buy bonds. They paid the ratings agencies for their analysis. That began to change when, in the 1930s, federal regulators began using the ratings to evaluate the soundness of the bonds held by banks. Because of this, any company that wished to have their bonds purchased by banks was essentially required to get each of their bonds rated. As a result, the business model of the rating agencies shifted. Instead of getting paid by the purchasers of the bonds, they began to require payment from the issuers of the bonds in order for those issuers to receive the required rating on each of their bonds.

This "issuer-pays" model, despite the obvious conflicts it created, became formalized in 1975 when the U.S. Securities and Exchange Commission deemed certain ratings firms to be "nationally recognized statistical rating organizations" (NRSROs).[103] It became increasingly necessary to receive an NRSRO rating before various government agencies or commercial banks could purchase a bond. It also became standard practice for buyers to rely on the ratings assigned to each bond by these NRSROs, rather than conduct their own individual due diligence. In other words, they subrogated their own research responsibilities to the research conducted by the "experts" – the rating agencies. As long as a bond was sufficiently rated by an NRSRO, the individual responsible for buying that bond at a bank or government agency was unlikely to lose their job if the bond defaulted. They were simply following the rules as established over the years through government regulations and industry convention. This subrogation of not only due diligence but also common sense, led to the near-collapse of the world's financial system. In the next two sections I'll articulate this chain of events, which at its most fundamental level was supported by the ratings provided by the NRSRO "experts."

---

[101] Lawrence J. White, "A Brief History of Credit Rating Agencies: How Financial Regu-lation Entrenched this Industry's Role in the Subprime Mortgage Debacle of 2007 – 2008," *Mercatus on Policy, Mercatus Center – George Mason University*, No 59 (October 2009): 1.

[102] "Moody's Rating Symbols & Definitions," *Moody's Investors Service* (June 2009): 8.

[103] White, "A Brief History of Credit Rating Agencies: How Financial Regulation En-trenched the Industry's Role in the Subprime Mortgage Debacle of 2007 – 2008:" 2.

The subprime crisis

Between 2002 and 2007, banks lent an estimated $3.2 trillion to homeowners with bad credit and undocumented incomes.[104] Despite the obvious irrationality of this activity, the process of making billions in bad loans was comprised of a sequence of individually rational acts.

A home loan often starts with your typical main street mortgage brokers. They get a commission for matching up home buyers or existing home owners with lending institutions (Originators). Their primary mission is to get a deal done. And they know just how to do it. Throughout the housing boom of the early 2000s, if a homeowner's income fell short of lender requirements, they directed them to apply for a no-doc loan, where evidence of income was not required. Or they arranged for the home buyer to take out interest-only or similar teaser-rate mortgage loans that started out with low monthly payments. Of course, these low payments weren't permanent. They increased dramatically, sometimes doubling or more, a few years after the loan was issued. At the time, housing prices were skyrocketing and there seemed to be no end in sight. Home owners could often, and often did, refinance to put off that fateful day of reckoning. As long as interest rates remained low and housing prices rose, these "subprime" loans avoided default.

That way, with commission in hand, the main street mortgage broker faced no risk whatsoever if the homeowner ultimately defaulted on his or her mortgage. That risk now fell to the bank which lent the money. But they too were able to, literally, pass the buck. They did this by bundling their subprime loans and selling them to other financial institutions. The buyers were quite often Fannie Mae and Freddie Mac.

Fannie & Freddie

Fannie Mae, the colloquial term for the Federal National Mortgage Association, and Freddie Mac (Federal Home Loan Mortgage Corporation) are United States Government Sponsored Enterprises (GSEs). This GSE designation means that, although when they were founded the two firms were not officially owned or backed by the U.S. government, they were

---

[104] Elliot Blair Smith, "Bringing Down Wall Street as Ratings Let Loose Subprime Scourge," *Bloomberg* (September 24, 2008).

sponsored by the government in order to help create a liquid secondary mortgage market. They did this primarily by purchasing mortgage loans from originators such as commercial banks. This freed up the banks' capital, enabling them to make additional loans to homebuyers.

Fannie and Freddie, in turn, would finance their purchases by securitizing their acquired mortgages into mortgage-backed securities (MBSs). A securitization occurs when Fannie or Freddie buys mortgage loans from originators and then bundles them into MBSs. Those MBSs, in turn, are sold to banks and other institutions looking for high-yielding securities with the implicit backing of the U.S. government. The term "implicit" is important, for neither the GSEs nor the MBSs they issue, are government guaranteed. It was generally perceived that the U.S. government would stand behind both Fannie and Freddie. In a 2001 congressional testimony, Dan L. Crippen, the director of the Congressional Budget Office, corroborated this perception when he stated that the "debt and mortgage-backed securities of GSEs are more valuable to investors than similar private securities because of the perception of a government guarantee."[105]

That implicit backing became explicit in 2007 when the U.S. government began to infuse billions directly into both GSEs[106], and the U.S. Federal Reserve purchased trillions of dollars of MBSs in order to prevent what they believed would be a total collapse of the global economy.[107]

But Fannie and Freddie were unable, due to their underwriting standards, to purchase many of the riskier subprime loans that were being provided to homeowners during the housing boom of 2002 - 2007. As Daniel Mudd, then president and CEO of Fannie Mae, testified in 2007, "Unfortunately...safe loans in the subprime market did not become the standard, and the lending market moved away from us. Borrowers were offered a range of loans that layered teaser rates, interest-only, negative amortization and payment options and low-documentation requirements on top of floating-rate loans."[108]

So while many subprime loans were purchased by Fannie and Freddie, an increasing percentage were classified as non-conforming, meaning they did not

---

[105] Dan L. Crippen, "Federal Subsidies for the Housing GSEs" (CBO Testimony as provided by Dan L. Crippen before the Subcommittee on Capital Markets, Insurance, and Government Sponsored Enterprises Committee on Financial Services, U.S. House of Representatives," May 23, 2001).

[106] "Fact Sheet: Government Sponsored Enterprise Credit Facility", U.S. Treasury Department Office of Public Affairs (September 7, 2008).

[107] "Agency Mortgage-Backed Securities Purchase program," Federal Reserve Bank of New York. Retrieved February 14, 2011.

[108] Daniel H. Mudd, "Opening Statement" (testimony before the U.S. House Committee on Financial Services," April 17, 2007).

meet the requirements that enabled them to be sold to Fannie and Freddie. This increased the need for a market that enabled the securitization and sale of these loans.

Firms like Bear Stearns and Lehman Brothers stepped into the breach. But there was little demand from their clients for low-rated subprime securities. By consulting with the "experts," the ratings agencies, the investment firms were able to determine how to structure the worst of the subprime mortgages into securities that would receive investment-grade ratings, often triple-A. This securitization process enabled those firms to not only find buyers for the securities, but to sell the securities for prices beyond any they would have received as subprime debt.

So...we had main street mortgage brokers who had more than enough motivation to get their clients' loans approved, while avoiding any associated responsibility from the moment they received their commission checks. Their sole incentive was to get each loan approved, not to ensure it was ever repaid. We had the banks and other originators who loaned the money to the homeowners, but then resold the majority of those loans to Fannie and Freddie and securitizers such as Bear Stearns and Lehman Brothers. Their incentive was to collect fees upon issuance of the loan, and to make sure its structure fell within guidelines that allowed it to be resold, thereby eliminating any risk to themselves in the event of homeowner default. Fannie, Freddie and the securitizers then bundled the loans and sold them to the end investor, such as pension funds and, interestingly, banks. Those firms were able to purchase the securities for one reason – they were rated by the NRSROs as investment grade. This begs the ultimate question. If the loans were subprime, with many likely to default in the event of a housing market collapse, why did the credit agencies stamp them as investment grade? The answer requires us to circle back to expose the flaw in the structure of the ratings agency business.

Profiting from conflicts of interest

We passed with blinding speed and an inflated confidence over President Clinton's "bridge to the next century." The early 2000s saw credit rating agencies earn an ever-increasing percentage of their revenues from, as stated by then-SEC Chairman Christopher Cox in 2007, the "lucrative business of consulting with issuers on exactly how to go about getting"[109] top ratings.

---

[109] Smith, "Bringing Down Wall Street as Ratings Let Loose Subprime Scourge."

So now they had two substantial revenue sources, one from charging issuers to rate their securities, and a second one from consulting with those issuers on how to structure those securities to receive the highest rating. This system resulted in obvious conflicts of interest. If your company was looking for a strong rating on a new bond issue, who would you call?...A rating agency that's been super tough on you in the past, taking a hard line and likely to give you a low rating based on your perceived potential risk?...Or an agency that has been "kind" in the past and made things happen? Of course, firms will seek out the rating that reflects most favorably on their business. This results in a "race to the bottom" in the quality of credit ratings, where each rating agency is financially motivated to appease their clients (or potential clients).

The total disregard for ethical business standards and the widespread greed that fueled this overt conflict of interest came into the spotlight in the credit crisis of 2008. The rating agencies had been competing with each other to consult on and rate the debt of derivative instruments such as collateralized mortgage obligations (CMOs). A CMO is simply a collection of mortgages separated into different tranches representing the relative risk of default. Investment banks such as Lehman Brothers and Goldman

> A "tranche" is one of a number of related securities offered as part of the same transaction. The word tranche is French for slice, section, series, or portion.

Sachs consulted with the rating agencies to ensure that they maximized the value of the pools of mortgages they converted into CMOs. They did this by allocating enough higher-rated mortgages to create AAA-rated tranches, even if those tranches contained risky mortgages. Because the rating agencies not only collected fees for rating bonds and derivatives such as CMOs, but also earned fees by telling issuers how to structure their products to receive the highest ratings, they were piling conflict on top of conflict. The result was that the agencies were not motivated to rate the long-term prospects of repayment of the CMOs they had rated, but rather, in their own words, provide advice that constituted a "point in time" analysis.

This financial alchemy worked wonders. According to *Inside Mortgage Finance*, the annual volume of mortgage securities sold to private investors tripled to $1.2 trillion between 2002 and 2005. The subprime portion of the CMOs rose fourfold, to $456.1 billion.[110] In the opening remarks at a hearing in 2010 by Phil Angelides, the Chairman of the Financial Crisis Inquiry Commission, he stated that:

---

[110] Smith, "Bringing Down Wall Street as Ratings Let Loose Subprime Scourge."

From 2000 through 2007, Moody's slapped its coveted Triple-A rating on 42,625 residential mortgage backed securities. Moody's was a Triple-A factory. In 2006 alone, Moody's gave 9,029 mortgage-backed securities a Triple-A rating. That means they put the Triple-A label on more than 30 mortgage securities each and every working day that year. To put that in perspective, Moody's currently bestows its Triple-A rating on just four American corporations. Even Berkshire Hathaway, with its more than $20 billion cash on hand, doesn't make that grade.

We know what happened to all those Triple-A securities In 2006, $869 billion worth of mortgage securities were Triple-A rated by Moody's. 83% went on to be downgraded.[111]

The experts at identifying default risk, the rating agencies, failed to see the runaway train barreling down the track. Even inside information doesn't ensure more accurate predictions. Ben Bernanke, the U.S. Federal Reserve Chairman, is clearly a brilliant man. He was selected by *Time* magazine as their Person of the Year for 2009[112] for his actions in combating the financial crisis and averting a global depression. But in a March 2007 testimony before the U.S. Congress, Mr. Bernanke stated that "the problems in the subprime market seem likely to be contained."[113]

When CMOs became wildly overvalued, many astute traders shorted them or engaged in other trades that benefited when their prices collapsed. An example is John Paulson of the hedge fund Paulson & Co., who made billions of dollars for both himself and his investors by betting against the housing and mortgage bubble.[114]

The examples given here are just a few of the thousands available. The point is that you absolutely cannot rely on experts to guide your money decisions. You must develop your own systematic plan for managing your money.

Experts do provide tremendous value, however. They and their followers push the markets out of line with the reality of their true value, presenting you with trading opportunities.

[111] Phil Angelides, "Opening Remarks" (statement before the Financial Crisis Inquiry Commission Hearing on the Credibility of Credit Ratings, the Investment Decisions Made Based on Those Ratings, and the Financial Crisis At The New School, New York City" June 2, 2010).

[112] Michael Grunwald, "Person of the Year 2009," *Time* (December 16, 2009).

[113] Ben S. Bernanke, "The Economic Outlook" (testimony before the Joint Economic Committee, U.S. Congress," March 28, 2007).

[114] Daniel Gross, "The Greatest Trade Ever," *Newsweek* (November 10, 2009).

Why experts are so wrong

A truly telling study conducted by Philip Tetlock, a research psychologist at Stanford University, helps to answer this question. The study looked at 82,361 predictions made by 284 experts (pundits).[115]

Tetlock asked the pundits to rate the probability of three potential outcomes for each prediction they felt qualified to make. In the case of an economic expert, he may ask, for example, whether the economy was likely to:

1. remain at the same level of growth
2. grow faster
3. grow slower

What he found was that the experts could literally have been beaten by dart-throwing monkeys. The experts' predictions were worse than if they had randomly selected the outcome.

And it gets worse. Tetlock asked similar questions to those who were not experts. The experts scored no better than did this non-expert group. Their massive level of knowledge relative to the non-experts did nothing to improve their predictive capabilities. Tetlock wasn't the first to discover this. In one earlier study from the 1960s, researchers asked college counselors to predict the grades high school students would achieve as college freshman. The counselors were provided with test scores, grades and the results of personality tests. They were also permitted to interview the students. Their results were compared to those derived from a formula based solely on test scores and grades. The outcome was that the counselors were beat by the formula.

An even earlier study from the 1950s involved the results of tests used to diagnose brain damage in patients. This data was presented to a group of clinical psychologists and their secretaries. The result of the study revealed that the psychologists' diagnoses were no better than the secretaries.'[116]

The fact is that people over-think and quickly form biases based on limited information. Once that bias is formed, substantial effort is employed in supporting it, regardless of whether it is right or wrong. People really hate to be wrong.

---

[115] Philip Tetlock, *Expert Political Judgment: How Good Is It? How Can We Know?* (Princeton: Princeton University Press, 2005).
[116] L.R. Goldberg, "The effectiveness of clinicians' judgments: The diagnosis of organic brain damage from the Bender-Gestalt test," *Journal of Consulting Psychology, Vol. 23* (1959): 25-33.

Rats!

Right before Christmas, in 2009, my wife was searching for the perfect surprise gift for our three boys. She ended up buying three "Dumbo" rats from the local pet store. (The name "Dumbo" refers to the rats' big ears, not their intelligence.) While we were told by the salesperson that the rats were smart and could be trained, no one on earth would ever assume that a rat could outsmart a human in any given situation. But in the basic understanding of probability, without-a-doubt a mandatory skill for achieving any measure of success in money management, rats seem to be able to outperform people. Here's an example that Tetlock witnessed at Yale University 30 years before he published the results from his pundits study.

In this particular Yale study, a rat was placed in a T-shaped maze. The researchers placed food in the left part of the "T" 60% of the time and in the right part 40% of the time. Students were asked to predict on which side of the "T" the food would appear each time. The rat, of course, was left to find the food on his own. The students weren't told that there would be a bias to one side. But it was the rat who eventually figured out that the food was more likely to appear on the left side than the right and, as a result, almost always went to the left first, scoring roughly 60%. In contrast, the students scored only 52%![117] In trying to outsmart the placement of the food, the students seemed to be looking for patterns that clearly didn't exist and, as a result, were outsmarted by the rat.

This is a common human behavior. We try to outsmart the system (or the market) looking for patterns that don't exist – desperate to "beat the system." When that desire is combined with our need to be "'right" and our easily established biases, we can become dumber than a rodent. Experts – pundits and advisors – surprisingly enough, are (in most cases) humans too.

This leads us to a third significant discovery made by Tetlock: the more often an expert appears on TV or other media, the worse his or her batting average. Think about that.

The experts who are most often touted, and who reach the most disciples, are shown to be the most often wrong.

This is not surprising. Experts exist to provide the media with a steady flow of content and, more importantly, entertainment. Their purpose is not to provide you with useful, profit-making information. Furthermore, if an expert has staked his reputation on a prediction announced to millions of fans repeatedly on television,

---

[117] Tetlock, "Expert Political Judgment: How Good Is It? How Can We Know?:" 40.

across the Internet, over the radio, and in print, it will be very difficult for him to have a change of mind – even if the evidence overwhelmingly indicates he is wrong. At that point he is locked in to his bias.

If there was ever a reason to avoid expert opinions, this is it.

"One small step for a man.
One giant leap for mankind."

July 20, 1969 was a huge day for me. As a young boy on a family vacation, I remember sitting in my grandparents' living room in Ohio watching the grainy, small-screen television images of the first humans walking on the Moon. I had always been a space buff. I still vividly recall being totally enamored with the Mercury missions and the hero/astronauts who were selected to fly them, Alan Sheppard, John Glenn, Scott Carpenter, Gus Grissom, Wally Schirra, Gordon Cooper, and Deke Slayton. Starting with the Apollo program, I had made scrap books for all the flights and my brother and I even rigged up a tape recorder to the television to record virtually every telecast of every flight. I still have the tapes today.

The Apollo flights were dramatic from the start. Tragedy struck the U.S. space program for the first time when, in January 1967, the Apollo 1 fire killed Gus Grissom, Ed White and Roger Chaffee during a training accident on the pad at Kennedy Space Center. But the resilience of the U.S. space program was impressive. Less than two years later, Frank Borman, James Lovell and Bill Anders orbited the Moon in Apollo 8. Their Christmas Eve telecast, where they read the first 10 verses from the book of Genesis, was the most watched television program ever up to that time.

NASA had worked hard to earn their newly acclaimed success. The U.S. space program was an endeavor of immense proportion. More than 400,000 people had been working on the program over a 10-year period leading up to the lunar landings.[118] Finally, after this decade of patient, steady advancement in space flight technology, punctuated by triumphs and catastrophe, Neil Armstrong and Buzz Aldrin climbed down the ladder of the lunar module to stamp the first human footprints on the moon. ...Or did they?

---

[118] "NASA Langley research Center's Contributions to the Apollo Program," NASA.gov. Retrieved February 14, 2011.

I've made up my mind – don't confuse me with the facts

An otherwise rational guy I know is absolutely convinced that the Apollo moon landings were fake. He's positive that NASA never reached the Moon. He's not alone. Depending on where you live, between 6% and 28% of your neighbors side with him. These are the results of polls taken over the past 20 years in places ranging from the U.S.A. to Russia. In a 2009 poll conducted by the British *Engineering & Technology* magazine, 25% of Britons stated they did not believe humans had ever walked on the Moon.[119]

These people cite numerous pieces of evidence in support of their claim that the Moon landings were a hoax. All of these have been refuted numerous times by qualified experts, but the "hoax" proponents continue to thrive. And it doesn't take much to gain new converts to their cause. In 2001, public skepticism of the validity of the Moon landings increased from 6% to 20% after Fox Television aired a TV show titled *Conspiracy Theory: Did We Land on the Moon?* In 2000, 28% of Russians polled stated that they did not believe that Americans walked on the Moon [120].

Despite the solid evidence refuting these hoax charges, despite the significant weight of evidence supporting the validity of the Moon landings, despite the enormous implausibility that the 400,000 people who worked in the U.S. space program and the 24 astronauts who went to the Moon, including 12 who walked on its surface, could join together in an elaborate conspiracy to defraud the rest of the world's population – and keep it quiet – millions of people still believe the Moon landings were a hoax.

People have an enormous capability for ignoring the facts and believing what they have already made up their minds to believe. This capability seems to also hold true with their choices of how to manage their money.

---

[119] "Apollo 11 hoax: one in four people do not believe in moon landing," *The Telegraph* (July 17, 2009).
[120] A. Petrova, "Have Americans Walked on the Moon," *The Public Opinion Foundation* (April 19, 2000).

Compounding the problem

Everyone has a bias, which is formed through a combination of research, learned reasoning and intuition. Each bias will be reinforced when you seek out experts, as you will welcome new information that supports your bias and dismiss information that conflicts with your view.

A major problem with following expert advice is that it compounds an individual's bias.

People form their biases and then only welcome the views of those experts who hold the same biases. And those experts in turn dismiss new information that doesn't fit in with what they already believe. As a result, people quickly reach a tipping point where their minds are set and they are locked in to their view.

Another friend of mine is a gold bug. She devours any information that supports her view that gold is going up in price. The fact that gold has risen in price for much of the past 10 years only supports her belief in the truth behind this information and the experts who are presenting it to her. But that doesn't make the information correct. And it certainly doesn't mean that the result of that information will be higher gold prices going forward. But it does provide her comfort in pursuing her goal of owning a significant amount of gold.

When people get locked in to a view and only consume information that supports their view, they are no longer engaged in the pursuit of profits, but the pursuit of entertainment. All of the studies described above indicate that my friend's fascination with gold and her acceptance of expert opinion that supports her view will lead to a loss of money. But following "expert" advice becomes a drug. It's hard to stop. The best advice is not to start.

SUMMARY
MYTH 13

- Studies have shown that "experts" could literally have been beaten by dart-throwing monkeys. Experts' predictions are often worse than if they had randomly selected the outcome.

- The experts who are most often touted, and who reach the most followers, are shown to be the most often wrong.

- Experts do provide tremendous value, however. They and their followers push the markets out of line with the reality of their true values, presenting you with trading opportunities.

- A major problem with following expert advice is that it compounds an individual's bias.

Government Regulations
Protect Investors

In 2005, a money manager by the name of Harry Markopolos wrote a 19-page letter to the U.S. Securities and Exchange Commission, listing 29 reasons that he thought one of his competitors was a fraud and running "one of the world's biggest Ponzi schemes."[121] The SEC, which had both the right and the obligation to audit the firm, didn't. Their cursory audits of several of the firm's affiliates (in the normal course of its oversight duties) only resulted in light-weight citations for a few minor technical infractions. Consequently, the firm in question maintained a rock-solid reputation and attracted billions of dollars in people's money. Three years later, the head of that firm, Bernie Madoff, shocked the world when he told an FBI agent that he was, in fact, running the world's biggest Ponzi scheme.[122]

Bernie Madoff's company was SEC registered. He was the very definition of

---

[121] Harry Markopolos, "The World's Largest Hedge Fund is a Fraud," *Submission to the SEC* (November 7, 2005).
[122] "SEC Charges Bernard L. Madoff for Multi-Billion Dollar Ponzi Scheme," *U.S. Securities and Exchange Commission press release* (December 11, 2008).

"high profile;" at one time he was the chairman of the NASDAQ stock market. His brokerage firm was a member of the National Association of Securities Dealers, or NASD (which merged with the member regulation, enforcement and arbitration functions of the New York Stock Exchange in July 2007 to form the Financial Industry Regulatory Authority or FINRA). Despite his super-legitimate résumé and imagery, he committed the largest fraud the investment industry has ever seen, stealing tens of billions of dollars of people's money. You need no further evidence than this to know that it is a myth to think that regulators will protect you from bad investments.

You must protect yourself from bad investments. Regulators will not do it for you.

A short form of regulation

David Einhorn is the president and co-founder of the hedge fund Greenlight Capital. Mr. Einhorn has done a spectacular job for Greenlight's investors. The basis for his excellent performance is his sound research and straight-up stock picking. He intentionally picks stocks that aren't all winners. Why? ... Greenlight Capital is just as interested in making its money from shorting the stocks of bad companies as it is from buying the stocks of good companies. Famously, and publicly, Einhorn shorted both Bear Stearns prior to its collapse in early 2008, as well as Lehman Brothers stock in time for its collapse into bankruptcy in September 2008.[123] (Lehman Brothers is discussed briefly in *Myth #10 – Short Selling is Destabilizing and Risky*.)

The process Einhorn followed in categorizing those firms as "good shorts" was both systematic and thoughtful. He delved deep into their books, analyzing their balance sheets closely. What he saw convinced him that the firms were under-capitalized and over-leveraged, meaning that their debts greatly exceeded their assets. In the case of Lehman Brothers, he was also concerned that the company was using dubious accounting practices in their financial filings.

As one indication of something amiss, Einhorn noticed that Lehman's numbers seemed to jump around a lot. Over just a couple of weeks in the spring of 2008, Lehman reported earnings that jumped from a loss of $875 million to a gain of $230 million.[124] That discrepancy raised his suspicions.

---

[123] Hugo Lindgren, "The Confidence Man," *New York* (June 15, 2008).
[124] David Einhorn, "Accounting Ingenuity," (presentation at the Ira W. Sohn Investment Research Conference May 21, 2008): 7.

Of even more concern was Lehman's use of a twist in accounting rules that allowed it to profit from its own demise. Because Lehman's financial health was in decline during early 2008, it was perceived as being less likely to pay back the money it had borrowed. Therefore, the value of its debts held by other firms was also in decline. Since the value of what it owed those other firms was now worth less to those other firms, Lehman could write down the cost of those debts, booking a gain as a result. This mechanism was permitted by the regulations. As Einhorn stated in an article in *New York Magazine* in June 2008, "This is crazy accounting. I don't know why they (the regulators) put it in. It means that the day before you go bankrupt is the most profitable day in the history of your company because you'll say all the debt was worthless. You get to call it revenue. And literally, they pay bonuses off this, which drives me nuts."[125]

It is nuts, as many regulations are.

The real fraud

What's even more nuts, and what Einhorn didn't know during the time he was expediting his "shorting" strategy, was that Lehman was engaging in "materially misleading" accounting gimmicks to hide its true financial condition. This only came to light publicly in March 2010, when a bankruptcy report by the firms' examiner revealed transactions entered into by Lehman Brothers in late 2007 and 2008 that were, yes, "materially misleading"[126] and that intentionally deceived people about the firm's ability to withstand losses.

According to the report, Lehman shuffled $50 billion of assets off, and then back on, its books in order to make it appear that it was less dependent on leverage than was truly the case. Lehman reported these transfers as sales when clearly they were not. They simply sold assets prior to quarter end, as they reported their positions, and then bought them back at the beginning of the next quarter. [127]

This illicit activity was completely premeditated on Lehman's part. In a series of e-mail messages cited by the examiner, one Lehman executive writes of the transfers: "It's basically window-dressing." Another responds: "I see ... so it's legally

---

125 Lindgren, "The Confidence Man."
126 Anton R. Valukas, Examiner for United States Bankruptcy Court, Southern District of New York, "In re Lehman Brothers Holdings Inc., et al., Debtors,"(March 11, 2010): 1017.
127 Grace Wong, "What killed Lehman," CNNmoney.com (March 15, 2010), Retrieved February 14, 2011.

doable but doesn't look good when we actually do it? Does the rest of the street do it? Also is that why we have so much BS [balance sheet] to Rates Europe?" The first executive replies: "Yes, No and yes. :)."[128]

The regulators were never aware of these transactions. Neither was Einhorn. But he was aware that *something* was wrong.

Mr. Einhorn expressed his negative view of Lehman at a conference in April 2008.[129] Lehman called Greenlight and asked for a copy of his speech. That led to a call between Einhorn and Lehman's CFO, Erin Callan. After that call, Einhorn became even more convinced something was amiss. According to Einhorn in the *New York Magazine* article, "We had our questions, we were organized, but she (Ms. Callan) was evasive, dishonest. Their explanations didn't make any sense."[130]

Mr. Einhorn is a rational investor. He is simply out to make money for his clients. He does not short the stocks of companies that he thinks are well run. He indentifies companies that he believes are poorly run or engaging in financial wrongdoing and then shorts their stock. He does not destroy value by shorting stocks. It is the actions of each company's management that destroys value and produces the returns for Greenlight and other short sellers.

The regulators didn't foresee the problems at Lehman. In fact, rather than investigate Bear Stearns and Lehman at that time, their perverse, knee-jerk reaction was to investigate the short sellers! They were attempting to find evidence that the short sellers had instigated a run on the investment banks – not whether the investment banks had brought it on themselves through high leverage and deceptive and materially misleading accounting.

While you can't rely on regulators to protect you from fraud, you can count on capitalism.

> *Short sellers serve as regulators and uncover fraud and*
> *dishonest practices precisely because they benefit from doing so.*

Richard Fuld, the CEO of Lehman Brothers, wasn't exactly shy when he went public with his call to arms, "I will hurt the shorts, and that is my goal," while unwittingly overseeing the destruction of his firm. Bernie Madoff seemed to be unabashed about his activities and his internationally high-profile image. He had no qualms about registering with the regulators and exposing himself and his firm to regular audits by the regulators. He served as the president of the NASDAQ stock market and made major charitable

[128] Valukas, "In Lehman Brothers Holdings Inc., et al."
[129] Einhorn, "Accounting Ingenuity."
[130] Lindgren, "The Confidence Man."

contributions. However, Bernie Madoff had a style of operation that is the extreme exception. Most scam artists operate unregistered firms that exist and operate under the radar and receive no public scrutiny. If the regulators can't detect fraud or "materially misleading" accounting practices in registered firms that operate right under their noses, we certainly can't expect them to uncover frauds occurring outside their normal regulatory domain.

Here's one that was brought to me.

15% risk-free

John, a long-time friend of our family, called to say that his wife was considering making an "investment" in a "bank deposit" structure that returned 15% per year. At the time interest rates on bank deposits were in the range of 6%, so that naturally triggered my suspicions right out of the gate. His wife was put in touch with the investment group by her aunt, who had handed over money to this company a few years prior.

John asked if I could look into the investment for him. He was concerned about the legitimacy of the opportunity. I started my research by calling the contact they had for the investment, a salesperson in Canada, and initially asked him a couple of simple questions, "How are the returns produced and where is the money domiciled?"

The answers raised my immediate concern and triggered a new set of questions. First, the money was being held in a Cayman Islands account. There's nothing wrong with that; plenty of legitimate investments require offshore accounts (my company has managed Cayman-domiciled funds), but his reasoning for the Cayman-domicile was that it was also used as the source of the returns. The salesperson said that because the money was in the Caymans, they weren't restricted by U.S. regulations and could therefore pay out more of their earnings to their investors at a higher interest rate. Also, he claimed they could make better investments, again because of the lack of restrictions, than they could if they were in the U.S.

Talk about red flags! This was such a pile of BS that it alone was reason enough not to entrust the firm with my friend's money. But I felt compelled to ask one final question: "Was he registered and was the investment registered to be sold in the U.S.?" No, he replied, because he was in Canada and the investment was in the Cayman Islands, they were not required to be registered.

This was total bunk. An investment offered to U.S. residents must be registered with U.S. regulators unless it meets specific exemption requirements. This one did not. On top of the preposterous claim for why they were able to provide such an unnatural return, they had an illegal explanation for why they weren't registered. I called John and gave him a firm, "Stay away!" warning. And, he did.

There are several distinct warning signs for fraud. In the Action section for this myth, I provide a checklist of mandatory questions that need to be to asked and answered before you hand the first dollar over for investment.

Unfortunately, John's wife's aunt didn't ask these questions. More distressing was the fact that she just didn't want to ask those questions. A week or so after I called John with my assessment, my wife received a call from him. His wife's aunt was not only not thankful for me having uncovered this scam, she actually called John's wife irate that I had potentially disrupted this great investment opportunity with which she had been so fortuitously blessed. In the back of my head I hear a raging Jack Nicholson shouting, "You can't handle the truth!"

Regulators gone wild!

Not being able to red flag frauds - those occurring right under the regulators' noses and those hidden from view - are not the only ways regulations fail to provide real protection. Millions of people lost hundreds of billions of dollars on their long positions in the stocks of financial services companies during late 2008 and early 2009. Citigroup stock dropped from $50 per share in 2007 to less than $1 at its low in March 2008, evaporating hundreds of billions of dollars in wealth. Bank of America's stock dropped from $50 to under $5. Bad as it was, people with money in these companies' stocks were fortunate compared to those with money in Lehman Brothers and dozens of other banks, who lost everything.

What caused this massive value destruction of some of the world's top brands in financial services? The perfect storm was caused by their conscious decisions to engage in bad lending practices, gambling their capital on exotic financial instruments that had nothing to do with "banking," and their persistent use of excessive leverage. The management teams of these firms were all incented to do so. Their bonuses were based on the level of profits earned by their companies. The more leverage they employed, the more profits. But they weren't required to repay those bonuses if there were subsequent losses (or the total failure of their firm). And in seeking their outsized bonuses they were aided and abetted in their failure by U.S. regulators.

In 2004 big investment bankers such as Henry Paulson, CEO of Goldman Sachs, petitioned the U.S. SEC to remove the rules that capped their ability to leverage their capital.[131] Prior to their request, investment banks were limited to leverage of 15 to 1. This meant that if they had one billion dollars in capital, they could lend out or invest in deals of up to $15 billion. But that ratio wasn't steep enough for the bankers, whose bonuses, as we've learned, were generally based on a percentage of the profits they earned. The bankers argued that their risk management procedures enabled them to limit risk even while engaging in higher leverage. The SEC bought their story and removed the rule, letting the investment banks run wild with leverage. Because greater leverage could produce greater profits, and greater profits lead to greater bonuses, leverage exploded. Right before it was sold in a shotgun marriage to prevent its bankruptcy, Bear Stearns leverage had topped out at 32:1. Lehman peaked at 30:1 before it collapsed into bankruptcy and Morgan Stanley also hit the 30:1 mark. Even the historically conservative commercial banks jumped on the bandwagon to boost their leverage. Citigroup increased its ratio about 50% to 15:1.[132] [133]

People lost hundreds of billions of dollars as banking stocks crashed. Ironically, it was Henry Paulson, who just a few years earlier was a major proponent of higher leverage (when his bonus depended on it), who, after being appointed by President George W. Bush as Treasury Secretary, was the one given the task of bailing out those same firms.

To add insult to injury, in August 2010 the SEC determined that Citigroup should be penalized for its failure to inform shareholders of the more than $40 billion of subprime mortgage loans that it held and that contributed to its near collapse. The company was fined $75 million.[134] On the face of it, this appeared to show that the SEC was finally holding Wall Street responsible for its misleading actions...until you realize who is paying that fine – Citigroup's shareholders. At best, these are the same people who were harmed by the collapse in the stock price that resulted from Citigroup management's failure to inform them. At worst, it's the new shareholders who put their money into Citigroup's stock after the failure took place. So the regulators saw to it that shareholders paid twice for the failures of Citigroup's management.

If you can't rely on regulators to protect you from outright fraud, aggressive accounting or excess leverage, you certainly can't rely on them to protect you from making bad decisions regarding the legitimate opportunities. In fact, as I'll show in

---

[131] Labaton, "Agency's '04 Rule Let Banks Pile Up New Debt."

[132] Michael J. de la Merced, Vikas Bajaj and Andrew Ross Sorkin, "As Goldman and Morgan Shift, a Wall St. Era Ends," *Dealbook* (September 21, 2008).

[133] Ira Machefsky, "It Was Leverage Killed the Beast," *thenumbersguru.com* (September 22, 2008). Retrieved February 14, 2011.

[134] Ken Sweet, "Citi Pays $75 Million in Fines Over Subprime Disclosure," www.foxbusiness.com (July 29, 2010). Retrieved February 14, 2011.

the next section, many regulations exist that actually prevent people from "doing the right thing" – employing the types of strategies that result in increased portfolio diversification and that lower the risk in their portfolios.

Regulating gambling

Bank trust departments are subject to state banking laws that restrict their investment choices. Public pension plans face similar restrictions. In fact, for years certain states actually placed limits, called a "legal list," on the investments that could be made by their pension funds. While those have been mostly eliminated, there are still restrictions. New York's Common Retirement System for example, limits its "alternative investments" to 25% of the fund.[135] This means that the fund's performance is dominated by the performance of the stock and bond markets, which comprise the bulk of its portfolio. Because of this, these entities cannot properly diversify their portfolios in the manner I discuss in this book. This also means that it's not the professional investment manager for the fund who is calling the shots. It is the politicians who wrote the rules. Fortunately most of these restrictions do not directly affect *your* ability to make portfolio decisions with your own money. There are, however, regulations that do.

Government regulations contain restrictions which can negatively affect people's investment choices. Certain investments are allowed while, in many cases, specific types of investments are completely outlawed. These restrictions are hurriedly put into place with the intentions of fixing legalities that have been exploited by unscrupulous financial professionals and/or outright scammers. But, in the process, an investor's ability to make the best, most rational investment decision is ultimately hampered.

The rich are different

As the smoke was still settling from the financial crises/implosion of 2008, most people saw the value of their mutual funds sliced in half due to the dramatic drop in stock prices. Some funds dropped far less, and a select group of funds actually profited handsomely. Most people however, were unable to put their money into these funds that had weathered the storm. Federal regulations prohibited them from

---

[135] John Akasic, "It Isn't All Bad," *Institutional Investor's Alpha* (December 2008/January 2009): pg 10.

doing so. That's right; some of the best opportunities available for their money were off limits. That is because most countries have regulations that prohibit "Regular Joes" from putting their money into entire classes of financial products. Those products are historically reserved only for "rich" people.

Like many laws and regulations, the regulations that restrict regular people from putting their money into these funds were based on a benevolent instinct – to protect people from harm. In 1934, in the midst of the Great Depression, the U.S. Congress passed the Securities Exchange Act (the "1934 Act") and in 1940 they passed the Investment Company Act (the "1940 Act"). The 1934 Act created the SEC and the 1940 Act created and regulated the formation and operation of mutual funds. While these Acts were instrumental in helping to reduce abuses in the U.S. financial markets, over time they produced unintended consequences.

The birth of hedge funds

In April 1966, Carol Loomis, a reporter at *Fortune* magazine, wrote an article titled "The Jones Nobody Keeps Up With."[136] The article was about Alfred Winslow Jones and his unique method of trading stocks. Loomis described Jones's trading style as being inherently different from a person who would simply invest $100,000 in stocks: "Jones would use the $100,000 to borrow perhaps another $50,000. Of the $150,000 total, he might put $110,000 into stocks he likes and sell short $40,000 worth of stocks he thinks are overvalued. Thus he ends up with $40,000 of his long position hedged – i.e., offset by a short position – and the remaining $70,000 fully exposed."

Thus was born the term "hedge fund" and as a major unintended consequence of the 1934 Act and 1940 Act, the creation of the hedge fund industry. This industry materialized to take advantage of trading opportunities that were off limits to mutual funds. When the 1940 Act was created, its authors had no way of anticipating the full array of new financial products and investment opportunities that would appear on the scene in the later half of the 20th century. Naturally, at the time, these Acts focused on regulating what was known and popular at that time. Because short selling of stocks was commonly seen as a major contributor to the stock market crash and resulting depression, the 1940 Act severely limited the ability of mutual funds to engage in the practice. Leverage was also restricted.

As a result, when Alfred Winslow Jones sought to limit his risk exposure to stocks

---

[136] Carol J. Loomis "The Jones Nobody Keeps Up With," *Fortune* (April 1966): 237,240,242,247.

by borrowing money and selling short a portion of his portfolio to "hedge" his long exposure, he didn't set up a mutual fund; he set up a hedge fund. For the majority of people, however, hedge funds were off limits. The 1940 Act placed severe restrictions on how a hedge fund could promote itself and to whom it could sell. It became a game of "Accredited Investors Only." To qualify in this bracket you have to have $1,000,000 in net worth or an income in excess of $200,000 per year. In addition, there are only 100 of those so-endowed permitted to invest in any single fund. The law prohibits any public sale of the fund, meaning that people can only find out about the fund through direct contact with the fund's manager. As a result, only well-connected, rich people are able to put their money into hedge funds.

The logic behind these investment prohibitions is perverse. It assumes that people who have more money are more capable of evaluating their money options. This is incredibly patronizing. Of course, while that premise may not be true, it is true that by limiting access only to rich people, these regulations discriminate against regular folks. Unfortunately, it's only getting worse. The Dodd-Frank Wall Street Reform and Consumer Protection Act, signed by President Obama in July 2010, further restricts the ability of smaller investors to properly diversify their portfolios by putting their money into hedge funds. That Act no longer allows the value of people's primary residences to count towards their net worth.[137] There are some mutual funds, however, that have been launched that mimic hedge fund strategies. I introduce several of these in the Action section at www.JackassInvesting.com/actions.

Mandated irregularities in mutual fund accounting

While hedge fund investments are off limits for many people, mutual funds aren't. In fact, mutual funds and similar products, such as ETFs, serve as the cornerstone of most people's portfolios. The governance structure required to get a fund approved as a mutual fund has resulted in there being very little outright fraudulent activity. But there are "gotchas" that exist as a result of mandated accounting rules. A great example is what greeted people with money in the PIMCO Total Return Fund at the close of trading on December 8, 2010 (Figure 41).

------

[137] Matt Storms, "Final 2010 changes to accredited investor definition," WTN News (July 23, 2010). Retrieved February 14, 2011.

Performance of PIMCO Total Return Fund in 2010

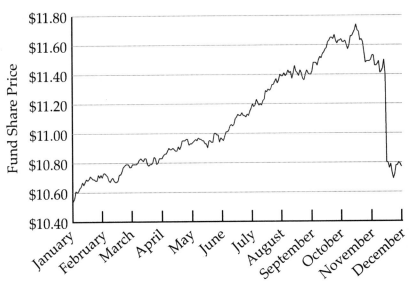

Figure 41

The PIMCO Total Return Fund is the world's largest mutual fund.[138] It gained this distinction by successfully riding the great bond bull market that ran from the early 1980s through 2010. As its returns grew so did its assets, as more and more people bought its shares. As a result, by December 2010 there was more than a quarter trillion dollars invested in the fund. But on December 8th, despite a relatively quiet bond market that day, the value of the PIMCO Total Return Fund dropped a sizable 5%. The drop, however, was not a result of trading losses, but almost exclusively due to the distribution of taxable gains made that day to its shareholders. When mutual funds sell securities, they realize gains or losses. If gains exceed losses, funds are required by law to distribute substantially all of their net gains to their shareholders before the end of the calendar year. These distributions are paid out to all shareholders in the fund on what is called the "record date" and distributed to shareholders on what is called the "payment" or "ex-dividend date." For the PIMCO fund the record date was December 7 and the payment date was the following day. The problem with this mandated accounting is that it didn't matter when the people bought their shares in the fund. If they were a shareholder as of December 7th, they were allocated taxes that accrued throughout the entire year.

At least the taxable gain approximated the fund's return for the year. It doesn't always work out that way. There are years when a fund's share price may drop in

138 "PIMCO Total Return Fund," *U.S. News and World Report*. Retrieved February 14, 2011.

value yet the fund still allocates taxable gains to its investors. That's because the fund's shareholders are required to pay tax on the gain from the sale of individual securities bought and sold by the fund. If the value of the fund's holdings drops during a year, but the fund sells securities at a gain that were previously purchased, the result is a taxable gain at the same time there is a drop in the share price. The shareholders lose twice. Many technology fund investors found this out the hard way in 2000. Their funds lost value as the market declined, but they still had to pay taxes on capital gains earned that year when their fund sold stocks that had soared in previous years.

There is a way to take advantage of the tax laws related to mutual funds, however. Look for the losers. Specifically, buy funds that have solid growth prospects but that have suffered significant losses and redemptions. Those funds serve as tax shelters. They have accrued past losses that can offset gains into the future. You can also avoid the tax by waiting until after the record date to buy into the fund. Don't be a hero. Let the existing shareholders carry that burden. Third, look for funds that have a low, or even negative, potential capital gains exposure. This is a measure tracked by Morningstar, one of the leading providers of independent investment research. Fourth, look for ETFs that you can substitute for, or add to, the mutual funds in your portfolio. Because of the way they are structured, most ETFs do not force taxable distributions onto their investors in the same way that mutual funds do.

There is another irregularity in mutual fund accounting that you can exploit. This is the policy of mutual funds to price the securities in their portfolios as of the close of trading on their primary stock exchange, but to accept new money into the fund until 4 p.m. Eastern time. The result is that many funds with stock holdings concentrated in stocks traded on Asian exchanges, which close in the early morning hours in the United States, or European exchanges, which close around noon Eastern Standard Time, let people buy into those funds as long as 12 hours after those exchanges have closed. This is the equivalent of having tomorrow's *Wall Street Journal* today. If any market-moving events occurred after the close of those Asian or European markets, those closing prices do not reflect the true value of the portfolio. This is an easy irregularity to exploit. Simply buy mutual funds that are heavily concentrated in Asian or European stocks if U.S. markets trade substantially higher after the close of the Asian or European markets. Rather than fixing the root of the problem, which would be to adjust the fund value to reflect the information in the marketplace following the close of trading in Asia or Europe, mutual fund families have instead put a Band-aid on the wound. They restrict people from frequent trading in their funds and require people to hold positions for a minimum period of time. But most funds still allow multiple transactions per year and mandate holding periods of as little as a week, providing savvy investors the opportunity to take advantage of this improper accounting.

Additional unintended consequences– regulated conflicts of interest

Regulations not only discriminate against investors who are classified as unaccredited, but they also segregate the financial professionals who recommend and sell those products to the public into specific classifications. These classifications, such as securities broker, commodity broker and investment advisor, limit each person to sell or promote certain types of products to their potential clients.

Also, the U.S. regulatory structure distinguishes between "securities" (such as stocks and bonds) and "commodities" (primarily futures contracts). Because of this, "securities" professionals – with only limited exceptions – are unable to provide their clients with opportunities to diversify their money across trading strategies that utilize commodity futures. To operate, they need to be registered with the Commodity Futures Trading Commission (CFTC) and most are not. As a result of this division of specialties, those professionals who are not registered with the CFTC will never recommend commodity futures trading strategies to their clients, regardless of the proven value of those strategies to diversify their portfolios.

For example, a typical securities broker will sell mutual funds, stocks and bonds to his or her clientele, but without additional registrations he or she would be unable to serve as a commodity futures broker. And, conversely, a commodity futures broker will not sell a mutual fund to a client, precisely because, without the additional registration, that broker is prohibited from doing so by federal regulations. Investment advisors are associated with broker-dealers who provide them with the products they can sell to clients. While they will generally have available a broad array of mutual funds they can sell to their clients, they usually have a limited selection of other products available. There is no single unified, rational regulatory structure that governs how you can invest your money and how financial professionals can advise you to do so. Furthermore, regulations are cobbled together, often in response to market crises. This creates limitations on your ability to properly invest your money and sizable conflicts of interest among the financial professionals you may engage to assist you.

To paraphrase a popular cliché, the road to a poor-folio is paved with good intentions.

You certainly want your investment professional to have proven knowledge, a requirement of his or her authorized registration, before making recommendations to you. But by having multiple governmental entities responsible for each product classification, the process becomes unduly cumbersome and costly for most investment professionals to expedite. As a result, this "registration segregation" restricts their ability to provide a diversified selection of financial products to their clients.

The end result is that conflicts of interest abound. Despite the best intentions of the financial professional you select to help you manage your money, he or she is faced with severe limitations and will be patently unable to provide you with truly unbiased recommendations. Even if they are aware of a product that is beneficial to you, if their firm does not offer that product, they cannot recommend it to you. That would be considered "selling away," a prohibited action for which they can be fined and censured.

Protect yourself

During a roundtable discussion with investors in October 2007 (prior to his announcement that he had been running a $50 billion Ponzi scheme), now-convicted fraudster Bernie Madoff said, "In today's regulatory environment it's virtually impossible to violate rules and it's impossible for a violation to go undetected, certainly not for a considerable period of time."[139] He knew quite well then that his statement wasn't true. Now so do we all.

This myth reminds me of the classic song of self-empowerment, "Respect Yourself," that was a crossover hit in 1971 for the R&B group The Staple Singers. The song was meant as an anthem for African-Americans following a decade focused on civil-rights issues. Following the decade of the 2000s, a remake of the song could be titled "Protect Yourself." You certainly can't count on the regulators to do it for you.

-----

[139] Bernard Madoff, speaking to a group of senior citizens. As reported in "Bernie Madoff: 'In Today's Regulatory Environment, It's Virtually Impossible to Violate Rules'," New York (December 16, 2008). Retrieved February 14, 2011.

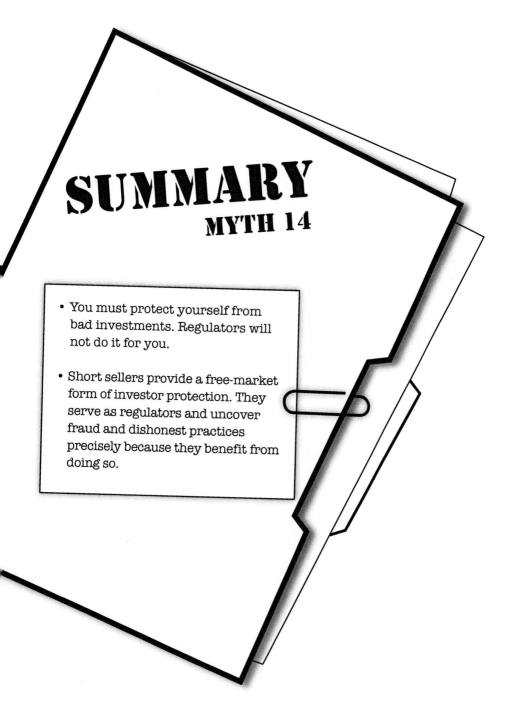

SUMMARY
MYTH 14

- You must protect yourself from bad investments. Regulators will not do it for you.

- Short sellers provide a free-market form of investor protection. They serve as regulators and uncover fraud and dishonest practices precisely because they benefit from doing so.

The Largest Investors
Hold All the Cards

A friend of mine, "Fast" Eddie Chambers, is a heavyweight boxing champion. The nickname "Fast" came from his lightning hand speed. It's that speed that's allowed him to take on far larger opponents and win. His strategy has always been to fight his fight, not theirs. A great example of Eddie's modus operandi is his fight in July 2009 in Germany, against Ukrainian, Alexander Dimitrenko.[140]

Eddie Chambers stands 6 feet, 1 inch tall and, at the time he fought Dimitrenko, he was weighing in at 208 pounds. In contrast Dimitrenko stood 6 foot 7 inches tall and weighed a whopping 254 pounds. Plus, Dimitrenko had Eddie in the reach department by nearly 6 inches.

Their fight in Hamburg, Germany resembled Rocky IV, with Fast Eddie as Rocky and Dimitrenko as the Russian Drago. (This part is a stretch. There's no way Dimitrenko is as whacked-out as Drago was in Rocky, but otherwise

---

[140] Dan Rafael, "Chambers dominates Dimitrenko," *ESPN Boxing* (July 6, 2009). Retrieved February 14, 2011.

the parallels are similar). Dimitrenko owned the crowd, and just like in the original Rocky, the fight took place on July 4th, Independence Day...a perfect example of life impersonating art.

Against the far larger Dimitrenko, Eddie fought his fight, using his fast footwork to attack and retreat and his even faster hands to land flurries of sniper-accurate punches on his lumbering opponent. He avoided getting caught up in Dimitrenko's fight, which would have been to keep Eddie at a distance and purposely slow the pace. Eddie's style paid off. In the words of Eddie's trainer, Rob Murray, "Eddie rocked Dimitrenko with a body shot, and then dropped him with a hook that knocked his mouthpiece over the top rope and into the second row."[141]

Eddie won the fight while gaining the new-found respect of the German crowd, perfectly duplicating the Rocky storyline. Eddie knew exactly what he needed to do to win the fight. He fought his fight. Not the far larger Dimitrenko's.

The same concept holds true with investing. You must take advantage of your own strengths and follow the example of Eddie. Fight (trade) your own fight (portfolio). The biggest advantage you have is your size. You're not a billion-dollar institutional investor. Your smaller size gives you opportunities that are simply unavailable to those larger investors.

Size matters

Cagle's is a second and third generation family-run business. Since the company's founding in Atlanta in 1945 its sales have grown to more than $300 million. Not IBM-sized numbers, but not chicken feed either. Well, actually it kind of is. For Cagle's is in the poultry business, producing and selling chicken products to supermarkets, fast-food chains, schools and restaurants.[142]

Cagle's was also one of the stocks selected to be purchased during 2010 by the Piotroski trading strategy described in the Action section for Myth #1. The Piotroski trading strategy was one of the top-performing strategies tracked by the American Association of Individual Investors in 2010, and a long position in Cagle's contributed to that performance. In the nine months through September

[141] Lem Satterfield, "Eddie Chambers to Face Wladimir Klitschko March 20," *Fanhouse* (January 25, 2010). Retrieved February 14, 2011.

[142] "Cagle's," *Yahoo Finance*, Retrieved February 14, 2011.

2010, Cagle's appreciated 85%. But no mutual fund investors or institutions benefited from this near doubling in price. Only individuals owned the stock. The reason? Cagle's is a microcap stock. At the start of 2010, the market capitalization of the entire company was just $17 million. The daily dollar trading volume was measured in tens of thousands of dollars. The company just wasn't big enough for anyone but individual investors to trade its stock.

But individuals could buy the stock of Cagle's, and those that did in 2009 and 2010 were solidly rewarded. All the larger investors could do was look on with envy at the returns earned by the smaller individuals.

Cagle's is hardly an exception. Most stocks are out of reach of the large institutional investors. Those institutions are constrained to investing primarily in stocks with at least a billion dollars in market capitalization, and those stocks make up less than one-third of all stocks traded on U.S. exchanges. Most institutional investors, with billions of dollars to invest, look to commit at least a few tens of millions of dollars to the stock of any single company. The smaller companies simply do not have enough stock trading each day for those institutions to buy enough to build a position. Unfortunately for those larger institutions, over the past thirty years, study after study showed that those small stocks outperform the larger stocks. An early study of this "small-cap effect" was published in 1983 by Marc Reinganum in The Journal of Portfolio Management titled "Portfolio Strategies Based on Market Capitalization." In the study he showed that from 1963 through 1980, the stocks of the smallest 10% of all companies on the New York and American stock exchanges at the beginning of each year appreciated 32.8% over the course of that year while the largest 10% rose just 9.5%.[143] Subsequent studies continued to confirm a divergence in performance.

> "Capitalization" is the total value of a company's stock that has been issued and is available to be traded.

But just as the small-cap effect became conventional wisdom in support of the advantages of being "small," new research was presented to show that the small-cap effect is really not everything it appears to be. In fact, the primary driver of returns has less to do with market capitalization than with the (in)ability of people to actually trade each stock. As we'll see, this doesn't change the fact that smaller investors have an advantage, but it does change how those smaller investors must act in order to capture that benefit.

---

[143] Marc R. Reinganum, "Portfolio strategies based on market capitalization," *Journal of Portfolio Management*, Vol. 9, No. 2 (Winter 1983): 29-36.

Illiquidity rules

Roger Ibbotson is a finance professor at Yale University and co-founder of Zebra Capital Management. Zebra was founded on the belief that there is an exploitable return driver for selecting stocks to buy that is based on "seeking out fundamentally strong, but overlooked, less demanded, and undervalued securities."[144] The results of a study supporting this belief were published by Mr. Ibbotson and co-author Zhiwu Chen in a working paper titled "Liquidity as an Investment Style"[145] in June 2007. In the paper they show that regardless of market capitalization, the least liquid stocks outperform the most liquid stocks. They define liquidity as total annual trading volume divided by total shares outstanding. Simply put, the stocks that trade less, perform best.

Could something this simple really work? And if so, why? Let's take a look at the results.

Figure 42 shows the performance summary of 3,500 U.S. stocks, differentiated by both market capitalization and liquidity. For all levels of market capitalization, the less liquid stocks outperformed the most liquid stocks over the 38 year period 1972 through 2009. In fact, the least-liquid small capitalization stocks appreciated at 17.87% per year over that period, compared to just 5.92% per year for the most-liquid small cap stocks!

Ibbotson posits three explanations for this illiquidity premium. First, investors like liquidity and dislike illiquidity. Because of this they are willing to pay more for liquid stocks than for illiquid stocks, making them overpriced. Second, as the supply of capital grows, all stocks will have rising liquidity. However, the least liquid stocks receive the greatest relative benefit from this and as a result stocks that were illiquid in the past become more liquid and higher valued today. Finally, it is the most popular stocks that, by definition, attract the most interest. The fact that a stock is popular means that more people are buying that stock, making it more expensive and less likely to score outsized future price gains. Each of these three reasons continues to support the illiquidity return driver today and indicates that this trading strategy is likely to continue to perform in the future. In the Action section for this myth at www.JackassInvesting.com I will show you a way to incorporate this return driver in your portfolio.

---

[144] "Firm Overview," *Zebra Capital Management*. Retrieved February 14, 2011.
[145] Chen Zhiwu, Roger G. Ibbotson and Wendy Y. Hu, "Liquidity as an Investment Style," (June 2007, updated September 10, 2010).

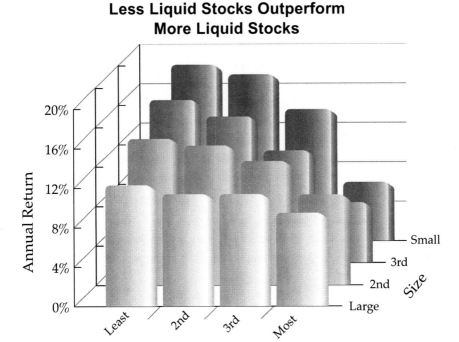

Figure 42

The illiquidity effect in stocks is just one way that small investors hold the cards in a deck stacked against the large investors. Just as two-thirds of U.S. stocks are off-limits from the large investors because they are too illiquid for them to trade, many commodity markets are also illiquid. For example, the orange juice trade I described in Myth #9 could not have been implemented by large institutional investors simply because the orange juice futures market is too small for them to trade in an adequate size. In fact, many of the commodity markets are too small for them to trade actively. As a result, the large investors are forced to diversify into only the largest commodity markets, such as gold and crude oil, limiting their ability to properly diversify their portfolios.

But the ability to place money into less liquid markets isn't the only advantage small investors have over larger investors. You also have the ability to read this book and immediately start incorporating the trading strategies described in the Action section. Imagine instead needing to wait months, or even years, to get approval to do that, if that approval comes at all. That is the process that must be followed by virtually every large pension plan. The investment team reports to a board that sets the investment policy. Almost without exception, that policy follows a framework that is constrained by conventional wisdom. The board specifies which "asset classes" can be used and the percentage of the portfolio that can be allocated to each. (I present my view of asset classes, which I consider archaic, in *Myth # 17 – Lower Risk by Diversifying Across Asset Classes*.) The concept of trading strategies based on return drivers isn't even in their lexicon. If they can't classify a trading strategy into an asset class, it can't even be considered for inclusion in the portfolio. Most institutional investors face these constraints. You don't.

When it comes to investment flexibility, big is most definitely not better. Trust me, most large investors look at your small size with envy. Take advantage of your size and flexibility. Create and manage a truly diversified portfolio. Be Eddie Chambers and knock out performance that beats that of the largest investors.

SUMMARY
MYTH 15

- Take advantage of your own strengths. The biggest advantage you have is your size. You're not a billion-dollar institutional investor. Your smaller size gives you opportunities that are simply unavailable to those larger investors.

- The illiquidity effect in stocks is just one way that small investors hold the cards in a deck stacked against the large investors.

Allocate a Small Amount to Foreign Stocks

The Philadelphia Eagles vs. the New York Giants is one of the NFL's classic rivalries. It was Sunday, December 19, 2010, and the Eagles and Giants entered the game with an equal nine wins and four losses on the season. With just three games left in the NFL regular season, this was shaping up to be a critical game for each team. The winner of the Sunday game would become the division leader.

The Giants dominated the opening half, with Eli Manning passing for three touchdowns and the Giants defense sacking Eagles quarterback Michael Vick twice. The Eagles went into the locker room at half-time trailing the Giants by 21 points. The second half began with more of the same as Vick was under pressure on every play and the Eagles offense struggled to pick up yards. Finally, with four minutes to go in the third quarter, the Eagles scored a touchdown on a pass from Vick to wide receiver Jeremy Maclin, narrowing the gap to 14 points. Hopes for a comeback were short-lived however, as an Eagles fumble in the fourth quarter led to another Eli Manning touchdown on a pass to Kevin Boss. With just eight minutes left in the game, the Giants were once again ahead of the Eagles by 21 points. But that's when what is now called "The Miracle at the New Meadowlands" began.

On the Eagles second play following the Giants touchdown, Michael Vick passed to tight end Brent Celek for a 65 yard touchdown. On the ensuing kickoff, Eagles kicker David Akers shocked the Giants with a perfectly executed onside kick. The Eagles recovered and five plays later Michael Vick ran the ball in to narrow the Giants' lead to just one touchdown. Less than three minutes later, after forcing the Giants to punt, the Eagles got the ball back and with just 1:24 left in the game Michael Vick again passed to Jeremy Maclin for another touchdown. Game tied. After failing to get a first down, and with just fourteen seconds left in the game, the Giants were forced to punt. At this point it was almost certain that the game would be decided in overtime. But the best was yet to come (for Eagles fans at least). The punt was fielded, actually fumbled, on the Eagles own 35 yard line by Eagles' speedster DeSean Jackson. But he picked up the ball and ran the 65 yards into the end zone for another – and the winning – Eagles touchdown just as the clock ran out. Game over! The Eagles beat the Giants in one of the most improbable finishes in the history of the NFL.[146]

Cliff-hanger punt returns, refuted referee calls, and the heart-stopping touchdowns all made for an historic game. But for me, it was the curious and emotional fan behavior, leading up to the kickoff, which held my interest. Prior to the game, I teamed up with Freewire Fan Channels to conduct a study. Freewire manages fan communities (called "Fan Channels") for professional athletes and celebrities. By joining a specific Fan Channel, each fan clearly indicates the players and teams of which they are a fan. We asked these fans two simple questions, "Which is your favorite team?", and "Who do you think will win the game?" The results were quite revealing.

During the NFL season, each team plays 16 regular season games. Because games go into overtime when there is a tie at the end of regular play, ties are rare (although they do occasionally occur, as it is possible to end overtime play in a tie[147]). As a result on average there is just under a 50% probability that any given team will win any given game. Yet in the Eagles – Giants game an overwhelming 74% of the Giants fans picked the Giants to win and a truly astounding 93% of the Eagles fans picked the Eagles to win.

---

[146] Play-by-play from AOL.SportingNews.com. Retrieved March 13, 2011.
[147] *2010 NFL Record & Fact Book* (New York: Time Inc Home Entertainment, 2010): 548.

Obviously, both sets of fans can't be right. Clearly, fans overwhelmingly picked the team they *wanted* to win, not the team *most likely* to win.

This behavior wasn't limited to Philadelphia Eagles and New York Giants fans. I expanded the study to include fans across the NFL. Once again, all else being equal, we would expect that the results would approximate 50% correct answers. After all, that would be the result of a random selection. Yet only 23% of the fans selected the winning team (my boys' rats could do better!). Once again, the fans would consistently pick the team they *wanted* to win. Figure 43 displays the summary of their picks.

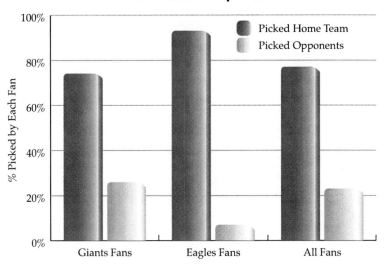

Figure 43

As the table clearly illustrates, the fans once again overwhelmingly favored their favorite team, to the detriment of their success in picking the winning team. I refer to this as the "Home Team Bias." In the Home Team Bias the fans disproportionately root for:

    a. the familiar, and

    b. the team they "hope" will win

People exhibit the same behavior when "investing" their money.

The home team bias in investing

MSCI Barra is a global investment research organization that provides support to traders around the world. In early 2010 they published a report titled "A Fresh Look at the Strategic Equity Allocation of European Institutional Investors."[148] According to their findings, it's not only sports fans who exhibit an overwhelming penchant for home team bias; institutional investors seem to possess the same illogical leanings.

For example, while the U.S equity markets account for just over 30% of the total capitalization of all of the world's equity markets, U.S. institutional investors allocate more than 50% of their money to U.S.-listed companies. This over-allocation to U.S. equities by U.S. institutions, although significant, pales dramatically in comparison with the over-allocation to the home country exhibited by other countries' institutional investors. Japanese institutions hold more than 80% of their money in Japanese companies, despite Japanese markets accounting for less than 9% of the world's capitalization. The figures for the European countries are equally disproportionate, with many of those countries' institutional investors over-allocating to the home country by factors of ten times or more! Figure 44 illustrates this home bias among institutions.

Home Bias by Institutional Investors[149]

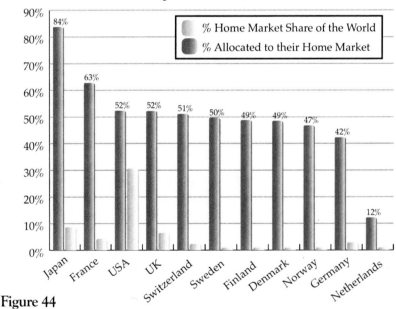

Figure 44

[148] Xiaowei Kang and Dimitris Melas, "A Fresh Look at the Strategic Equity Allocation of European Institutional Investors," MSCI Barra Research Insights (January 2010).
[149] Xiaowei Kang and Dimitris Melas, Page 3.

If the objective of every institutional investor is to make the most money possible for any targeted level of risk, then all institutional investors, regardless of their geographic location, should be making similar allocations. For example, if it makes investment sense for Japanese institutions to place 83.7% of their money in Japanese-listed stocks, then it should make sense for U.S. institutions to place 83.7% of their money in Japanese stocks as well. Obviously, that's ridiculous. U.S. institutions would be crazy to do that. But that's my point. It's just as crazy for Japanese investors to do so.

This is a clear case of the Home Team Bias expanded to the global stage. It is also a clear example of the irrationality and emotional component of what passes for investing. The decision to invest should be based on a rational evaluation of the return drivers. It is no more rational to think that one stock will outperform another simply because that first stock is traded on an exchange located near you than it is to think that a football team will have an exceptional win/loss record because it regularly plays in a stadium that's a short drive from your house.

Individuals make irrational "investment" decisions all the time. Institutional investors are run by people who just happen to have more money to manage. The end result:

Virtually all "investors" behave as irrationally as if they were betting on a football game – they overwhelmingly favor the home team.

Location of a company's headquarters or stock exchange is not a dominant return driver

Coca-Cola is an American icon. The company has been headquartered in Atlanta, Georgia, USA since the first Coke was served in Jacob's Pharmacy on May 8, 1886[150] and its stock is listed on the venerable New York Stock Exchange. But Coke is not a U.S. company. Fully 80% of Coke's profits come

---

[150] "Heritage Timeline," theCoca-ColaCompany.com, Retrieved March 13, 2011.

from outside the United States.[151] Coke is not a U.S. stock, it is an international stock. Its performance is based on the global demand for its products; not the condition of the economy in New York City, where it is traded, or Atlanta, Georgia, where its headquarters is based. To allocate to stocks based on the location of the exchange on which they are traded is a quaint artifact of a pre-globalized economy. This myth is wrong not because it is wrong to allocate to stocks that earn their profits from a range of countries, but because the way the myth is preached is to allocate money to stocks traded on exchanges located in different countries. The decision to allocate money or diversify a portfolio should be based solely on an evaluation of the return drivers that dominate stock performances. And as the Coke example hints at, and Figure 45 shows,

the location of a company's headquarters or stock exchange upon which it is listed is not a dominant differentiating return driver.

To see the significance of a company's location on its stock price returns, let's repeat the simple study we conducted in *Myth #8 – Trading is Gambling. Investing is Safer.* Instead of looking at the correlation among stock sectors in the U.S., however, I'll look at the correlations among stock markets of different countries.

Country diversification and correlations

Figure 45 shows the correlation of returns among the stock markets of various countries during the bull market period 2003 through 2007. I have selected a diverse group of countries; including one from each continent except Antarctica (give it time!).

As with the sector correlation tables I presented in Myth #8, the lighter shaded cells illustrate the lowest correlations and the darker shades highlight the higher correlations. What is apparent is that even during this "favorable" market environment, the various country relationships were highly correlated with each other. Most cells are darkly shaded. Only the Asian markets showed lighter correlation to other markets.

----

[151] Deutsche Bank analyst report referenced in "Earnings Preview: Coca Cola," *Seeking Alpha* (February 11, 2009). Retrieved February 14, 2011.

Monthly Correlations among Countries' Stock Markets During the Bull Market of Oct. 2002 – Oct. 2007

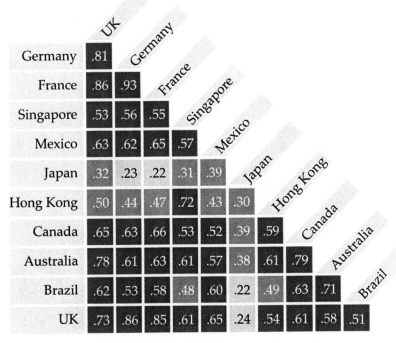

Figure 45. *Stock markets were highly correlated to each other even during the bull market.*

The situation did not improve when conditions worsened. During the financial crisis of 2008, the correlation between stock markets worldwide became even more pronounced. All stock markets fell sharply during the period (Figure 46). This is exactly the opposite of any pattern you'd want to see. When the benefits of diversification were needed most, global stock diversification provided it the least.

Monthly Correlations among Countries' Stock Markets
During the Bear Market of Nov. 2007 – Feb. 2009

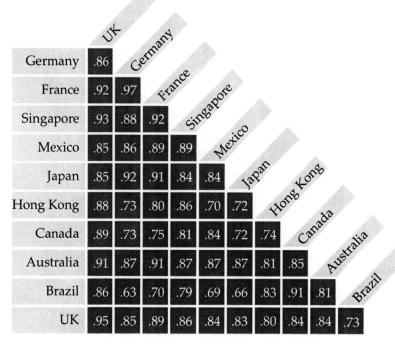

Figure 46. *Stock markets show that EVERY stock market in the study became highly correlated to each other as country-specific fundamentals are swamped by overall negative investor sentiment.*

Figure 47 shows the performances of each market. There was very little difference in both the timing and extent of the losses suffered by each country's stock market.

Performance of Global Stock Markets
During the Bear Market of 2007 - 2009

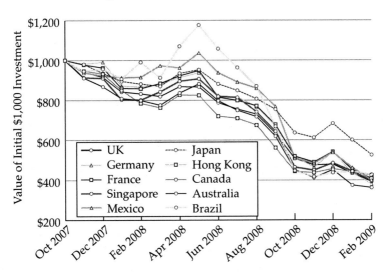

Figure 47. *The performances for each country reflect the performance of the iShares ETF applicable to each country.*

Geographic diversification should follow the same rules as those that apply to portfolio diversification in general. Simply spreading money across different countries does not necessarily spread risk. Often, the same baseline conditions exist across a large number of countries, subjecting a person with money in the stocks of companies based in those countries to the same risks. Furthermore, many companies' stocks are dependent on the same return drivers regardless of their base of operations. Home Team Bias is real and should be taken into consideration as a component of existing investment patterns. Because Home Team Bias is solely based on the emotionally-driven elements of "familiarity" and "hope," it must not serve as a basis for investment decision. The mere fact that different companies' headquarters are located in different countries does not mean that allocating money to each of them produces significant portfolio diversification. Diversification value can only be determined by understanding the return drivers and baseline conditions that drive the performance of each trading strategy.

Any positive or negative perception derived solely from a company's location should never influence the decision as to whether that stock is worthy of inclusion in your portfolio.

SUMMARY
MYTH 16

- Virtually all "investors" behave as irrationally as if they were betting on a football game – they overwhelmingly favor the home team and allocate disproportionately to stocks of companies domiciled in their home country.

- The location of a company's headquarters or stock exchange upon which it is listed is not a dominant differentiating return driver.

Lower Risk by Diversifying
Across Asset Classes

I n 1956 James Lorie, a marketing professor at the Chicago Business School, was
promoted to the position of Associate Dean. His first order of business upon
settling in to his new office was to put every effort into building the school's image
and national ratings to better compete with Harvard, Carnegie Tech (now Carnegie-
Mellon) and MIT, the nation's name-brands in higher education. Four years later,
after succeeding in taking the school to a new position of prominence, Lorie received
a phone call from Chicago alumnus Louis Engel. Engel was head of advertising and
marketing for Merrill Lynch and wanted to run an ad in various financial publications
introducing the notion that stocks were an appropriate investment for individual
investors.[152] This was a rather radical proposition for 1960. At that time only 17%
of households held stocks in their portfolios.[153] As a result, the SEC told Engel that
unless he could back up the claim he couldn't run the ad.

---

[152] "About CRSP – History," *Center for Research in Security Prices*, Retrieved February 14,
2011.

[153] Dorothy S. Projector, "Survey of Changes in Family Finances," *Board of Governors of the
Federal Reserve System* (November 1968): 321.

Lorie's conversation with Engel prompted him to initiate a long-term, detailed study of stock returns. With Merrill Lynch's support, he established the Center for Research on Security Prices, which is better known by its acronym, CRSP (pronounced "crisp").[154] Together with Lawrence Fisher, an assistant finance professor with a Chicago economics degree, he began compiling thirty-five years of price and dividend data on all stocks traded on the New York Stock Exchange. Fisher had to track down, hand enter into a database, and error-check all of the data. It took three years for him to complete the task.

This story is significant, not because of the results it produced (showing annualized returns of 9% per year throughout the study period), but because of the incredible amount of time it took to complete the study. Three years! Today the same research could be conducted in minutes on an inexpensive PC using cheap, accurate, and readily available data.

Around the same time that Engel was hitting Lorie with his stock return study proposal, William Sharpe, an economics doctoral student at the University of California at Los Angeles, was searching for a new topic for his dissertation.[155] Sharpe also worked at RAND, a think tank set up by the air force after World War II to study war and diplomacy.[156] RAND employed mathematicians, physicists, economists and computer programmers. RAND also employed Harry Markowitz, who in 1959 published an expanded version of his Ph.D. dissertation, entitled *Portfolio Selection*.[157] [158] In it, Markowitz developed a method for creating efficient portfolios that, on back-tested data, created the maximum return at each given level of risk. Risk he defined as being the variance (a measure of volatility) in the returns of the portfolio. (I've already expressed my views of why volatility is a poor measure of risk in *Myth #9 – Risk Can Be Measured Statistically*.) Markowitz immediately found himself facing a funding brick wall in the form of the over-the-top costs in the computer time he would require. His formula for portfolio efficiency required him to calculate the covariances of every stock or other instrument in his portfolio. The covariance measures how each stock had moved in relation to every other stock in the potential portfolio. Calculating a single portfolio could cost tens of thousands of dollars in computer time.

In 1960, Sharpe, through an introduction by a UCLA professor, presented himself to Markowitz. They became friends and soon Markowitz suggested a research project that became the first part of Sharpe's doctoral thesis. Markowitz suggested that

---

[154] "About CRSP – History."
[155] William Sharpe, "Autobiography," *Nobelprize.org*. Retrieved February 14, 2011.
[156] "A Brief History of RAND," *Rand.org*, Retrieved February 14, 2011.
[157] Harry Markowitz, "Autobiography," *Nobelprize.org*, Retrieved February 14, 2011.
[158] Harry Markowitz, "Portfolio Selection," *The Journal of Finance*, Vol. 7, No. 1. (March 1952): 77-91.

Sharpe develop a simplified system for calculating the covariances of the components of a portfolio. Rather than comparing each stock to every other stock in the potential portfolio, Sharpe introduced the idea of comparing each stock to the market as a whole. Where it took more than one-half an hour to calculate the optimal portfolio using Markowitz's method (on a one-hundred stock portfolio using an IBM 7090), it took just thirty seconds using Sharpe's method.[159]

This story exemplifies the work that was required to make allocation decisions in the 1960s. So some very brilliant people invented asset classes in order to simplify the process. Today, no one would be overly impressed by anyone conducting simple historical market research. And computing shortcuts of the type required by Markowitz and Sharpe are now passé. But in 1964 the results of the CRSP study were themselves historic. And Sharpe's clever simplification of Markowitz's portfolio selection model enabled calculations for optimal portfolios when the computing power necessary for complete computation was unavailable. This is the environment under which the concept of asset classes was constructed.

What are "asset classes?"

An "asset class" is defined as a specific category of related financial instruments, such as stocks, bonds or cash. These three categories are often considered the primary asset classes, although people often include real estate and private equity as well. Within each of these categories are sub-asset classes, such as international stocks and U.S. stocks; and government bonds and corporate bonds. Institutions and other financial professionals espouse the need for portfolios to be properly diversified across multiple asset classes in order to diversify their risk. Decades of academic research supported the view that the selection of each asset class in a portfolio is far more important that the selection of the individual stocks or other positions. Their research showed that any attempt to outperform the asset class itself by selecting individual stocks or bonds within each asset class would be doomed to sub-par performance. However, there's a single and significant flaw in their research findings. It's the same fault inherent in asset classes in general. They are intentionally self-limiting. This self limitation is a result of the constraints of computing power at the time asset classes were "invented." Today, asset classes are a quaint artifact of our investing past. They pose an unnecessary and risky distraction from creating a truly diversified portfolio.

Today's world is far different and allows for a new approach. What required multi-

---

[159] William F. Sharpe, "A Simplified Model for Portfolio Analysis," *Management Science*, Vol 9. No. 2 (January 1963): 277-293.

million dollar mainframe computers in the 1960s can be done on a home PC today. It is unnecessary to limit potential trading strategies to those few that have been previously defined as an "Asset Class." It is no longer necessary or even advisable to limit your portfolio to being long-only, which the concept of "Asset Class" implies.

Trading strategies replace asset classes

In the preface of this book I introduced the concept of a "Trading Strategy," which is comprised of two components: a system that exploits a return driver and a market that is best suited to capture the returns promised by the return driver:

Return Driver (system) + Market = Trading Strategy

Asset Classes are simply a few of the potentially hundreds (or more) of combinations of return drivers and markets available for you to incorporate into your portfolio. When viewed this way you can see that the

traditional asset classes are simply restricted sub-sets of the many available trading strategies.

For example, the U.S. equity asset class is actually the strategy comprised of the *system* of buying into long positions in the *market* "U.S. equities." This is simply one of many available trading strategies. As we established earlier, the return driver for this trading strategy is, in the long-term, corporate profit growth, and in the short-term, the premium (the P/E ratio) people are willing to pay for that performance. It is this fact that likely led to the short-cut of lumping all long equity positions together into an "asset class." In the short-term most stocks appear to move up and down as an undifferentiated group.

Perhaps the 1960s was the "once upon a time" when it made sense to simplify portfolio allocation in this fashion. But even then, it was a fairy tale to believe that simply diversifying across asset classes would provide you with the optimal portfolio diversification.

The diversification value of the traditional asset classes

It's usually taken for granted that diversifying across these asset classes can lower portfolio risk. There are two reasons why a belief in this approach provides only a false sense of security.

- By classifying asset classes as being long-only in related markets, the various asset classes expose people to the same return drivers. As a result, there is risk that the failure of a single return driver will negatively impact multiple asset classes.

- Limiting your diversification opportunities to asset classes eliminates numerous trading strategies that, because they are powered by entirely separate return drivers, can provide tremendous diversification value to your portfolio.

Let's address each of these issues. First, what are the return drivers underlying the returns for each asset class? Let's take a look (Figure 48) at what a "traditional" diversified portfolio (diversified across asset classes) looks like.

Asset Classes: Their Return Drivers And Necessary Baseline Conditions

Asset Class	Return Driver	Necessary Baseline Condition
Long U.S Equities	Investor sentiment and individual corporate earnings growth	Functioning securities markets
Long International Equities	Investor sentiment and individual corporate earnings growth	Functioning securities markets
Long Private Equity	Investor sentiment and individual company prospects	Functioning securities market
Long Corporate Bonds	Interest rates & credit-worthiness of issuing company	Functioning credit markets
Long U.S. Government Bonds	Interest rates & credit-worthiness of USA	Full faith in credit of USA
Long International Government Bonds	Interest rates & credit-worthiness of issuing country	Full faith in credit of issuer
Long Real Estate	Interest Rates & After-tax Rental income	Functioning credit markets & demand for housing
Cash	Credit worthiness of issuer	Full faith in credit of issuer

Figure 48

When looking at a portfolio diversified across asset classes; it is clear that most of those asset classes are dependent on the same return drivers or baseline conditions for producing their returns. This unnecessarily exposes the portfolio to "event" risk, meaning that a single event, if it is the wrong one, can negatively affect the entire portfolio.

How many people felt they were diversified when the economic crisis hit in 2008? A simple analysis of their portfolios would have exposed the enormous risks they were taking, despite their belief they were properly diversified across asset classes.

Another flaw in diversifying across asset classes is the constraint that is implied in the definition of asset class – which is they limit positions to being long-only. It is obvious to everyone that markets go down as well as up. But for some strange reason it has become accepted that being long is "good' while being short is "bad" and to be avoided. This is ridiculous. Making money is good. Losing money is bad. Insisting on going long-only in your portfolio is the very definition of self-limiting. It only serves to make it more difficult to make money. And *that's* the definition of "bad."

Tons of time and energy is eternally wasted by otherwise intelligent financial professionals, determining the best asset class and proper allocation to own. Instead, successful portfolio diversification could actually be achieved if that same effort was directed into developing and incorporating multiple, uncorrelated trading strategies into a truly diversified portfolio.

Trading strategies provide true portfolio diversification

The use of trading strategies in place of asset classes removes the diversification shackles that were put in place when the concept of asset classes was developed a half century ago. Even a single trading strategy can provide more portfolio diversification than an entire asset class. Evidence for this was presented in Myth #7, where I showed that putting money into the single-strategy S&P Diversified Trends Indicator, trading in just 24 markets, added more portfolio value than diversifying across the 500 stocks held in the S&P 500. There are many other trading strategies presented in the Action section for this book that also provide significant portfolio diversification value as a result of their non-correlation to the traditional asset classes. Figure 49 shows the correlations between a conventional diversified portfolio (this portfolio is presented in *Myth #20 – There is No Free Lunch*), and 1) the traditional "asset classes" included in most people's portfolios, and 2) some of the trading strategies which I present in the Action section of this book at www.JackassInvesting.com/actions.

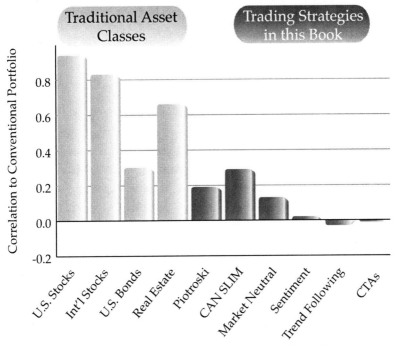

Figure 49. *A description of each of the components of this chart is included in the Table of Figures section at the back of this book.*

While bonds provide some diversification benefit, the low, and even negative, correlations of the trading strategies presented in the Action section show that they provide far greater diversification value than do the traditional asset classes. Even the Piotroski and CAN SLIM trading strategies, which hold long stock positions and because of this might be expected to be highly correlated to the conventional portfolio, are uncorrelated. This is because they employ distinct return drivers. It only stands to reason, then, that limiting portfolio diversification only to the traditional asset classes will result in unnecessary risk. I will explore this further in Myth #20.

Asset classes were originally invented as a means to identify opportunities for portfolio diversification. They were developed at a time when the simplest stock market research took years of research and expensive computers to compile the data. The situation today is far different. It is no longer necessary to simplify the opportunities for portfolio diversification to the primitive level of asset classes. Today's computing power and research opportunities support the ability to create and diversify portfolios across multiple trading strategies.

The fact that many people (including many financial professionals managing billions of dollars) consider the use of asset classes to be the pinnacle of portfolio diversification presents an opportunity for you to create a better portfolio.

They are ignoring portfolio diversification opportunities that remain available for you to use. Your portfolio can include trading strategies that are powered by unique return drivers and that can potentially produce profits across a wide variety of market conditions; even in market environments that others consider to be unsuitable for profits. In the next myth, I address one such market environment opportunity, the 2008 global financial crisis.

SUMMARY
MYTH 17

- Asset Classes are intentionally self-limiting. This self limitation is a result of the constraints of computing power at the time asset classes were "invented." Today, asset classes are a quaint artifact of our investing past. They pose an unnecessary and risky distraction from creating a truly diversified portfolio.

- Today, "trading strategies," each based on a sound "return driver," are able to replace the traditional, and restrictive, asset classes.

- Asset classes are simply restricted sub-sets of the many available trading strategies.

Diversification Failed
in the '08 Financial Crisis

I n late 2008 and into 2009 articles began appearing in major publications with titles such as "Diversification Failed this Year" (The New York Times November 7, 2008)[160] and numerous academics and financial professionals began to question the value of portfolio diversification in reducing portfolio risk (and losses). But an even larger number of articles, white papers and books were published in support of portfolio diversification. They stated that although all asset classes fell during the financial crisis, over the long term diversification works. I disagree with all of them for one simple fact. What they are discussing is not true portfolio diversification.

Portfolio diversification didn't fail during the financial crisis of 2008. Conventional wisdom failed. The conventional wisdom that investment diversification consisted of allocating portions of a portfolio across stocks, bonds, cash and possibly real estate. That certain "risky" "investments"

---

160 Natsuko Waki, "Diversification failed this year," The New York Times (November 7, 2008).

had no place in a "safe" or "conservative" portfolio. That buy-and-hold and dependence on a single dominant return driver was the best strategy for long-term investors to employ. That government regulations would protect investors. That these, and any of the other myths exposed in this book were the proper ways to guide your investing.

The result was that the vast majority of people had their money allocated to trading strategies, such as being long stocks, corporate and municipal bonds and real estate that were based on return drivers that were unified in their dependence on global economic growth and leverage. All strategies required markets to rise in price in order to profit. Because these were the primary strategies promoted by the traditional financial advisors and press, these were the strategies employed by the vast majority of people. Unknowingly, and despite their best intentions, *people were instructed to create poor-folios – not diversified portfolios – and gamble all their money on a single set of return drivers and baseline conditions. People failed to diversify.*

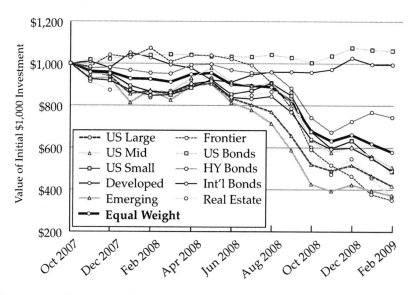

Performance of Conventional Wisdom During the Bear Market of 2007-2009

Figure 50. *Key to portfolio components listed in the Table of Figures at the back of this book.*

Figure 50 supports the cliché that a picture is worth a thousand words. It displays the performance of the components of a portfolio that followed conventional wisdom regarding portfolio diversification. The portfolio includes ten asset classes "diversified" across stocks, bonds and real estate, in both the U.S. and internationally. This would have been considered a *highly* diversified portfolio for the average person. But out of the ten asset classes, only U.S. and International bonds avoided losses. All others declined sharply. A portfolio allocated equally to each asset class declined by more than 40% over the 16 month period. What is obvious is that the conventional wisdom regarding portfolio diversification failed.

As laid out throughout this book, bountiful opportunities exist that allow you to achieve true portfolio diversification. It requires the use of multiple trading strategies that are based on disparate return drivers. In *Myth #20 – There is No Free Lunch*, I show you exactly how you can combine multiple trading strategies to create a truly diversified portfolio. So I won't go into those details in this chapter. But in Figure 51 I compare the performance of some of the trading strategies described in the Action Section at www.JackassInvesting.com/actions with the performance of the "Conventional Wisdom" portfolio during the 2008 financial crisis.

Figure 51. *Key to portfolio components listed in the Table of Figures section at the back of this book.*

While the Conventional Wisdom portfolio, which is spread across ten traditional asset classes comprised of long-only positions in stocks, bonds and real estate, collapsed more than 40% in value, many of the trading strategies produced profits. And one, the trend portfolio described in the Action section for Myth #7, capitalized on the strong trends that took place in many markets to gain more than 70%.

Looking at the performance of the Conventional Wisdom portfolio is what gives rise to the myth that diversification failed in the '08 crisis. Looking at the performance of the other trading strategies is the basis for refuting the same myth and for creating a truly diversified portfolio that can produce more consistent returns across a variety of market and economic conditions.

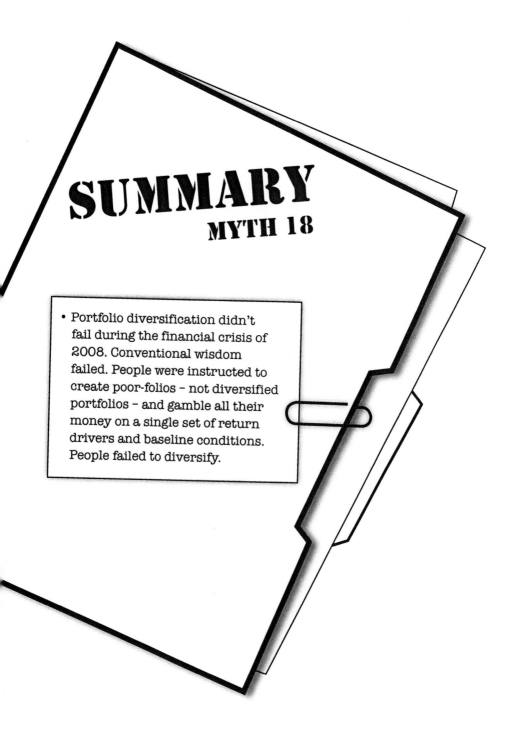

SUMMARY
MYTH 18

- Portfolio diversification didn't fail during the financial crisis of 2008. Conventional wisdom failed. People were instructed to create poor-folios – not diversified portfolios – and gamble all their money on a single set of return drivers and baseline conditions. People failed to diversify.

Too Much Diversification
Lowers Returns

A friend and fellow trader, Kelly Angle, published a book in 1989 entitled "100 Million Dollars in Profits."[161] The book told the story of his father's very first futures trade, which initially consisted of buying 20 gold futures contracts in 1978. With a contract consisting of 100 troy ounces of gold, and with gold prices hovering at $200 per ounce, this represented about $400,000 in face value investment. Because he purchased his contracts on margin, he only had to post $20,000 in cash to secure the position. As the price of gold rose he continued to use his profits and additional cash to buy more gold, ending his entry year with a total of 560 futures contracts representing $11 million dollars worth of gold! The entire position required a margin deposit of just $560,000.

Over the next two months the price of gold continued to rise virtually unabated, and Kelly's father continued to buy. By the end of February 1979, with the price of gold at more than $250, he had accumulated 1,285

---

[161] Kelly Angle, *100 Million Dollars in Profits* (New York: Windsor Books, 1991).

contracts worth a combined $33 million. The profits on his position were nearing $3 million; but the accompanying risk was great. A mere $40 sell-off in the price of gold would destroy every bit of his profit, along with the value of a business he had spent 30 years of his life to build from the ground up. But he was convinced that the price of gold would keep climbing and he stubbornly held on to his position. In March of 1979 his million dollar march hit a brick wall.

After peaking at over $250 in early March 1979, the gold price fell to under $230 by mid-April. That may not sound like a big price move. But at that point, his entire profit was obliterated. He was on the verge of closing out his position just to save his business when the gold decline came to a screeching halt and, miraculously, the market started a comeback. By the end of May the price of gold had rebounded to $270!

Despite his too-close-for-comfort brush with financial disaster, Kelly's father kept buying. By the fall of 1979 he was holding 2,000 gold futures contracts, with a total value of $80 million. At this point even a $10 move in the price of gold would result in a $2 million change in his account's value. Luck was still on his side and gold prices continued to rise, peaking at over $800 per ounce in January 1980. It was that final dramatic spike in prices that prompted Kelly's father to finally climb off his investment thoroughbred and sell out his position, netting over $50 million in profits (Figure 52). The title of Kelly's book underscores the enormous risk that his father took. His account value actually peaked at more than $100 million prior to getting cut in half before he completely exited his position.

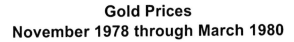

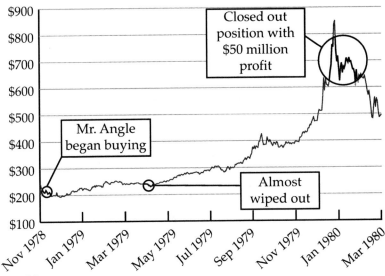

Figure 52

Mr. Angle's wild ride is an extreme example of non-diversification. Not only did he put all his eggs (in his case – gold) in one basket, but he leveraged the size of that basket many times relative to the actual cash he had available.

It is easy to see how people could use stories like this as support for the myth that too much diversification lowers returns. Suppose, instead of posting his $20,000 as margin for what ultimately became a humongous gold position, Mr. Angle had committed his $20,000 to trading a diversified portfolio. There's no question; he would *never* have become the Fifty Million Dollar Man. Even today after thirty years of compounding at 10% annually, his $20,000 would just now be exceeding $350,000, assuming no taxes were ever deducted.

But this cursive evaluation misses one key point. The expected return doesn't just include the potential magnitude of the outcome (the size of the profit) but also the probability of achieving that profit. Despite this story's happy-ever-after ending, the odds of success were never in Mr. Angle's favor, and, in fact, his risk of complete financial ruin could hardly have been higher. As is the case with any gambler, his only chance at beating the table was to score quickly, immediately walk away from the table, and cash out. The odds on suffering a complete loss were skyrocketing with every minute he stayed in the game.

Risk of ruin

In the late 1980s I was in search of a mathematical formula that would guide me to correctly determine the allocations I should make to the various positions in my managed futures portfolio. My search led me to a book written by Fred Gehm titled "Commodity Market Money Management."[162] (Mr. Gehm's work was based on a formula written about in an article in 1980 for *Gambling Times* by Ed Thorp, titled "The Kelly Money Management System."[163] Thorp had an interesting background/skill set. A hedge fund manager himself, he was also a blackjack expert, while holding down a professorship at the University of California.) The formulas developed and used by Fred Gehm and Ed Thorp take into account the probability and size of each winning and losing trade in order to calculate what they define as the "risk of ruin." This is the probability of your account dropping to a point at which, due to insufficient funds, you can no longer trade. What becomes apparent is how even a small amount of risk, over time, can increase the probability of a substantial, or even complete loss of money. One other conclusion can be made from the results:

If you require extreme profits in the short-term there is only one way to achieve this. That is to gamble. But gambling, by definition, never has a positive expected outcome. The odds are you will lose your money – and the longer you gamble the higher this probability of financial ruin.

In the case of Mr. Angle, because he "maxed out" the leverage in his account while he was accumulating his gold position, just a small 12% drop in the price of gold would have wiped him out. The chart that follows illustrates this risk. Based on Monte Carlo simulations that incorporate the price activity in the gold market for the 10 year period centered on his trading, it shows that there was a 99% probability of Mr. Angle losing everything within his first year of trading.

Clearly, time was not on his side. The longer he traded, employing the excessive leverage that was required for him to have gambled his initial 20 contracts into a $50 million profit, the greater was the probability that he would suffer a complete loss, as illustrated in Figure 53.

---

[162] Fred Gehm, *Commodity Market Money Management* (New York: Wiley, 1983).
[163] Edward O. Thorp, "The Kelly money management system, *Gambling Times*, (1980): 91-92.

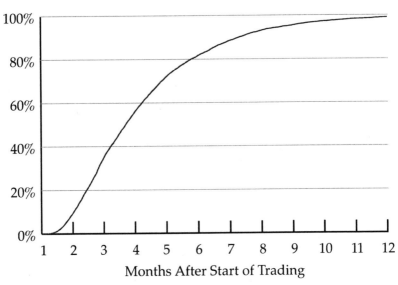

Figure 53

So while it's true that in the short-term concentrating a portfolio on a few select trading strategies may produce outsized returns, it is also far more than likely to produce outsized losses – and it is a near-certainty in the longer-term. Many of the statistics presented in this book, such as those articulated in the DALBAR studies, show the low probability of consistently achieving positive results with this gambling approach, let alone outperforming a properly diversified portfolio. But it's exactly that gambling mentality – in others – which gives us the opportunity to be "the house" and take money from them, resulting in more consistent profits over time.

In contrast, the math is clear:

True portfolio diversification provides the highest returns over time.

To maximize profits over longer periods you must create a portfolio that is truly diversified across a variety of trading strategies and markets. Let's look at a simple example that clearly demonstrates the value of portfolio diversification.

The investment version
of the tortoise and the hare

You're likely to be familiar with the story of the tortoise and the hare, taken from the children's classic, *Aesop's Fables*.[164] The plot is based on how the hare, despite being substantially faster, loses a race against the slow-motion tortoise. The investment analogy is the comparison of the performance of a portfolio with potentially high returns, to that of a steadier performing portfolio with consistent, but lower, returns.

Figure 54 shows the return streams of two unrelated trading strategies over a ten year period. Both averaged returns of 1.2% each year. But at the end of the ten-year period the second portfolio had a total return of 12.8%, while the first portfolio actually suffered a loss of -9.1%.

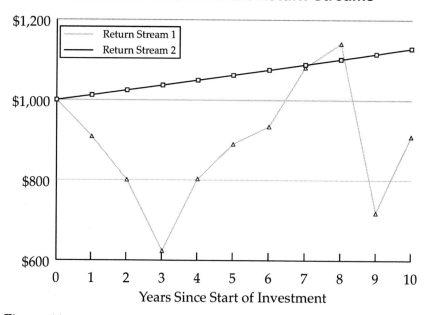

Growth of Hypothetical $1,000 Investment Pursuant to Two Different Return Streams

Figure 54

---

[164] Aesop, *The Hare and the Tortoise* (500ish BC).

The reason for the disparity in performance lies in simple arithmetic and the power of compound returns, which Albert Einstein referred to as "The most powerful force in the universe." It also lies in the greatest enemy of compound returns, "portfolio drawdowns."

The graph showcases the destructive energy contained in portfolio drawdowns. The losses suffered by Return Stream 1 in years one through three required strong returns in years four through seven merely to recover from those losses. And at that point the total return of Return Stream 1 was still below the total return earned by the consistent 1.21% per year return produced by Return Stream 2. So despite the fact that Return Stream 1 had the top six yearly returns produced by either return stream, the benefit of those strong returns was dwarfed by the four annual losses of -9%, -12%, -22% and -37% in years one, two, three and nine.

Summary Performance of the Two Return Streams

	Avg. per year	Total Return
Return Stream 1	1.2%	-9.1%
Return Stream 2	1.2%	12.8%

Figure 55

As Figure 55 shows, despite both return streams having averaged annual returns of 1.2%, the first ended with a loss while the second produced a profit over the ten year period. This points out the true cost of the losses incurred. Despite the first return stream averaging a positive return each year, it ended with a loss because of the fact that a 20% loss requires a 25% gain just to break even, and the first return stream had numerous years with sizable losses. If you think there's something familiar about the Return Stream 1, you're right. They are those of the S&P 500 Total Return Index for the 10-year period 2000 through 2009. Return Stream 2 represents the returns from an investment policy that guarantees 1.2% per year.

The magic of diversification

Criss Angel is an illusionist and magician who starred in Criss Angel Mindfreak, a television show he created and launched on A&E Network in 2005. During season two, in the July 16, 2006 episode, he performed a metamorphosis that utterly wowed the crowd.[165] Criss showed a random gentleman from the audience a number of photographs of beautiful women and asked him to select one. The man picked a photo of Mary, a dynamite

---

[165] Criss Angel, "Metamorphosis," *Mindfreak Season 2, Episode 10* (July 19, 2006).

blond wearing a string bikini. Criss proceeds to shoot what looks like shaving cream out of a can onto the vertical glass front of a store display case. As he smears the cream with his hand, the image of a woman appears. Of course, to the crowd's amazement, it's Mary. But the best is yet to come.

A woman in the audience then walks up to Criss to present him with a table cloth she's made for him as a gift. Following Criss' instructions together with the man who selected Mary, they held up the tablecloth, hiding Criss behind it. After a few seconds pass, Criss asks them to drop the table cloth, and sure enough, there is Mary, standing in front of Criss. The metamorphosis was complete. A picture was transformed into a person.

Even if you're unable to perform the same magic as Criss Angel, you can create your own metamorphosis with your portfolio. But it's not a trick. It involves the process of combining riskier individual positions into a safer diversified portfolio. The benefits of portfolio diversification are real and provide serious tangible and beneficial results. While the next chapter, *Myth #20 – There is No Free Lunch*, is devoted entirely to the benefits of true portfolio diversification, I'll demonstrate a little diversification magic here first. (Think of this as the warm-up act!). I'll start the show by creating a simple portfolio out of two return streams. What we'll see is:

Portfolio diversification is the financial equivalent of magic

---

Beautiful losers

We have already seen how, despite average annual returns of the S&P 500 Total Return Index being a positive 1.21%, the overall return from investing in that Index was negative over the ten year period shown (2000 – 2009). Now let's add another loser to the mix and see what happens.

Figure 56 and Figure 57 compare the S&P 500 Total Return Index with the inverse of that Index. The inverse index is weighted to produce an average annual return of -1.21%, which is the exact opposite of the S&P 500 Total Return Index. Over the entire ten year period the inverse index lost a total of -10.77%. Remember that the S&P 500 Total Return Index also produced a net loss of -9.10% over the ten year period. So the two return streams averaged a loss of -9.94% over the ten year period.

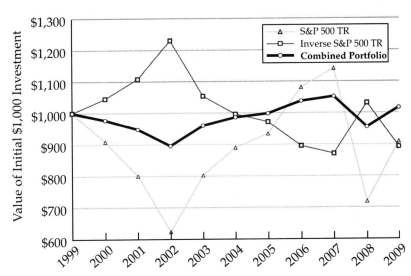

Results of Combining S&P 500
Total Return Index with its Inverse

Figure 56

But combining the two losers results in a portfolio that actually produced a profit of 1.65% over the period. Adding a loser to a loser produced a winner! So even in this extreme example, portfolio diversification worked, and worked dramatically.

What this shows is the magic of portfolio diversification. Because the two portfolios are highly negatively correlated with each other, when one is losing the other is profiting. As a result, the combination never suffers more than an 11% drawdown and the combined two-strategy portfolio becomes profitable with a much smaller recovery. This shows that proper diversification is so powerful that even the combination of two losing return streams can create a positive return. This also shows the importance of controlling losses, rather than seeking large gains, as this results in the desired outcome of *both* lessor losses and larger gains.

Two Losers Produce a Winner

	Avg. per year	Total Return
S&P 500 Total Return	1.2%	-9.1%
Inverse S&P 500 TR	-1.2%	-10.8%
Combined Portfolio	0.6%	1.7%

Figure 57

Concentrated portfolios seldom outperform more broadly diversified portfolios for one simple reason—nobody is always right. And with a concentrated portfolio, when you're wrong, the recovery from those losses requires super-human performance to merely recover the portfolio to the level it would have achieved anyway, had it been properly diversified. You don't have to be Albert Einstein to understand the magic of using true portfolio diversification to limit portfolio drawdowns and increase returns. In the final myth I'll lay out the blueprint for building a diversified portfolio that will produce greater returns with minimal risk.

SUMMARY
MYTH 19

- Extreme short-term profits can only be achieved by gambling; but gambling, by definition, never has a positive expected outcome. The odds are you will lose your money. And the longer you gamble the higher this probability of financial ruin.

- True portfolio diversification provides the highest returns over time.

- True portfolio diversification is the financial equivalent of magic. It can produce both higher returns and lower risk.

There is No Free Lunch

This myth pervades the financial press and has been repeated so often that it is now common knowledge. But its rote repetition doesn't make it right. What is meant by this myth is that if you desire to earn a higher return on your money, you must be willing to accept higher risk.

That's wrong. But it's easy to see why people believe it to be right. If you believe in and follow the conventional wisdom – the myths that have been exposed throughout this book – then you are gambling your money in a poor-folio that is heavily dependent on just a few return drivers and baseline conditions. You are long stocks that are heavily concentrated in your home country and whose price moves are highly correlated with each other. You may be long international stocks; but these, as we have seen, will provide no downside protection when your "home team" stocks drop. You are long bonds that are issued by corporations based in your home country or by your country's national and local governments. You are long real estate, through ownership of your own home and potentially other rental properties or stocks of REITS or real estate-related companies. The value of this real estate is heavily dependent on the same return drivers that affect your bond positions, such as the level of interest rates and availability of credit. So if you start by self-limiting your investment choices to those preached by the conventional wisdom, a single shock will send your poor-folio reeling. When financial conditions deteriorate and asset values drop, you will lose money across all of your positions.

The situation is no better if you wish to earn a higher return on your poor-folio, as there is only one way to do so – apply leverage. This leverage can be obtained outright, by borrowing money and using it to add to your positions; or implicitly, by concentrating your money in higher risk positions such as corporate bonds or stocks of companies that themselves are highly leveraged, either financially or as a result of a concentrated business model. Even in today's financial climate it is easy to obtain outright leverage. You can either borrow on margin to buy your stocks and bonds, or put your money into leveraged ETFs that mimic the market but provide you with up to three times the profit or loss each day. Either way, your risk increases along with your leverage. In fact, because of the negative compounding effect of losses that was demonstrated in the previous myth, your risk increases at a faster rate than does your expected return.

This damaging effect of leverage is illustrated in Figure 58. This chart compares the performance of the double leveraged ProShares Ultra S&P 500 ETF, which is structured to produce twice the returns each day of the S&P 500, with that of the S&P 500 Total Return Index. Both suffered dramatic losses during the 2008 financial crisis. But while the S&P 500 TR Index had recovered to its June 2006 level at the end of April 2010, the ProShares Ultra S&P 500 ETF remained more than 33% below its initial level.

This dramatic underperformance is due to the destructive power of portfolio drawdowns. When the S&P 500 TR Index dropped 50% from October 2007 to February 2009, it required a 100% return to get back to even. As bad as that sounds, it pales in comparison to the additional destruction caused by leverage. The ProShares Ultra S&P 500, because of its additional leverage, fell a truly frightening 80% during the same period. This means that every $1,000 invested dropped in value to just $200. A recovery to breakeven requires a 400% total return on that remaining $200. Four times that of the unleveraged position in the S&P 500 TR Index. Statistics make it clear: it is far easier to lose money than it is to recover from those losses. Any recipe for a free lunch must steer clear of the indigestion caused by excessive drawdowns.

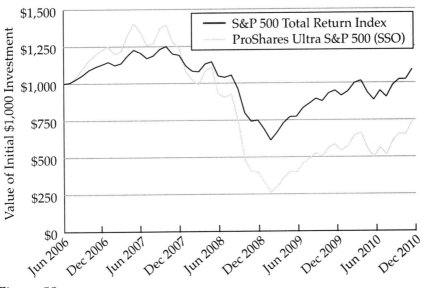

Performance of S&P 500 Total Return Index vs. ProShares Ultra S&P 500 2x (SSO)

Figure 58

Ride 'em cowboy!

Drawdowns are the greatest impediment to high returns and the true measure of risk

To recover from an 80% drawdown requires four times the effort than does a 50% drawdown. But this fact is virtually never discussed by those preaching conventional financial wisdom. In fact, conventional wisdom preaches exactly the opposite: ignore drawdowns. There's nothing you can do about them. So just buy-and-hold and ride-em out. But the ride-em cowboy mentality is not investing. It's just another form of gambling. The conventional approach to control this gambling risk has been to instruct people to diversify their portfolios across stocks, bonds and other "asset classes" such as real estate. Unfortunately, there is no mention of return drivers and the absolute importance of diversifying a portfolio across multiple, unrelated return drivers, which is the only way of obtaining true portfolio diversification. As a result, the limited diversification provided by the conventional approach to portfolio diversification results in limited diversification value.

The conventional approach to portfolio diversification

Figure 59 displays the performance of a conventional portfolio that includes positions in nine "asset classes." (The specific composition of this portfolio is detailed in the Table of Figures section at the back of this book.) In total, more than 3,000 stocks, 8,000 bonds[166] and thousands of real estate properties from more than 40 countries are represented in this performance history. Conventional wisdom considers this to be a broadly diversified portfolio.

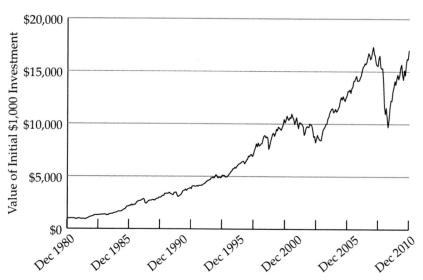

Performance of a Conventional Diversified Portfolio for the Period 1981 - 2010

Figure 59

But conventional wisdom is wrong. Despite holding more than 10,000 positions, this portfolio is not truly diversified. Its performance during the period displayed was driven by only three primary return drivers; corporate earnings growth, a doubling in the P/E ratio that powered stock returns, and a dramatic decline in interest rates that powered bonds and real estate returns.

---

[166] "iShares Barclay Aggregate Bond Fund," *iShares.com*. Retrieved February 14, 2011.

*A dependence on just three return drivers not only results
in unnecessary risk, but also ensures that past performance is
not indicative of future performance, regardless of the length
of that past performance record.*

Without a reasonable level of performance predictability, people are unable to estimate what they need to invest in order to meet their life needs, such as tuition expenses or retirement income. This became clearly evident to millions of people following the great bull market of 1981-1999. They were persuaded by the financial press and their advisors to put money into stocks, bonds and real estate based solely on this past performance. Worse yet, they based their future expectations on this unrealistic past performance.

If these people had been aware of the importance of return drivers in 1999, they would have made a different decision. They would have seen that one of those three primary return drivers, the P/E ratio (which is a measure of the enthusiasm people have for owning stocks), had provided a significant, unsustainable tail wind that accounted for half the stock market's performance over the prior 19 years. The P/E ratio of the S&P 500 had expanded from 9 to 44, increasing stock prices by the same ratio. If the P/E ratio subsequently fell to its long-term average of 16, stocks prices would also fall, unless this drop was offset by a corresponding increase in earnings. This is exactly what happened during the first decade of the 2000s. The P/E ratio reverted to its long-term average of 16, resulting in a stock market that, despite strong earnings growth, ended 2010 at a level just a few percent above where it was at the end of 1999 (including the reinvestment of dividends).

But the expansion of the P/E ratio wasn't the only return driver that produced an unsustainable tail wind for the Conventional portfolio. A dramatic drop in interest rates powered an historic bull market in bonds (as bond prices rise when interest rates fall) from 1981 through 2010. Not only did this contribute to the Conventional portfolio's strong returns from 1981 through 1999, but the bond rally, together with rising real estate prices, accounts for virtually all of the Conventional portfolio's return from 1999 through 2010. But the bond market at the end of 2010 was in a similar position as stock prices were at the end of 1999. In January 1981, the interest rate on the 5-year government bond was 13.25%. At year-end 2010 that rate was 1.93%. This single return driver powered an almost 9% annualized rate of return for the Barclay Aggregate Bond Index over the thirty-year period ending in 2010. Unless interest rates fall further over the next 30 years, bonds will produce returns that approximate that of the 1.93% yield on the 5-year bond. So we can see quite clearly today that the past performance of the bond market over the past 30 years is almost certainly *not* indicative of the performance we can expect over the next 30 years. It is both unreasonable and unrealistic to expect the limited diversification of the Conventional portfolio to produce consistent returns over time.

But there is a way to simultaneously maximize returns, minimize portfolio drawdowns, and improve the predictability of future performance. It is the primary ingredient essential to cooking up a free lunch. That is to expand the number of diverse return drivers employed in the portfolio.

Serving the Free Lunch

I present a variety of trading strategies throughout this book and in the Action section at www.JackassInvesting.com/actions.Because collectively these trading strategies incorporate dozens of independent return drivers, they can be combined to create a truly diversified investment portfolio that trades in the global equity, currency, interest rate, real estate, metals, energy and agricultural commodity markets. This portfolio will serve as your free lunch. It will provide you with greater returns and less risk - and with a greater predictability that future performance will approximate past performance - than has been delivered up to now by the Conventional portfolio. The trading strategies that I include in the portfolio are just some of the ones that I am most familiar with or have traded with my own and my clients' money over the past 30 years. They represent only a small subset of the many potential trading strategies that can be included in a diversified portfolio. There are many more trading strategies that are not covered in this book. In addition, the portfolio intentionally contains only strategies that are easy for the majority of people to employ, such as through mutual funds, ETFs or managed accounts. Because of this, the portfolio I present is far from being the "final word" regarding portfolio diversification. But it is a great improvement over the Conventional portfolio and serves as an excellent example of the benefits of true portfolio diversification.

In creating this "Free Lunch" portfolio I will allocate to each of the trading strategies based on the diversification value they add to the portfolio, which is based on a combination of the uniqueness of their return drivers and the resultant correlations of their returns. This will ensure that there is a reasonable balance among return drivers and that, unlike in the Conventional portfolio, no single return driver will dominate the Free Lunch portfolio's performance. Another benefit of creating the portfolio in this fashion is that we will avoid the "anchoring" bias that is prevalent among those espousing conventional financial wisdom. Anchoring is what causes people to invest a majority of their money in "core" positions such as a stock index or bonds, or believe in and follow any of the other myths in this book, primarily because that is what is accepted as "normal." The Free Lunch portfolio is not bound by these irrational constraints. The performance of the Free Lunch portfolio, overlaid on the performance of the Conventional portfolio, is displayed in Figure 60.

Performance of Free Lunch Portfolio Compared with Conventional Portfolio

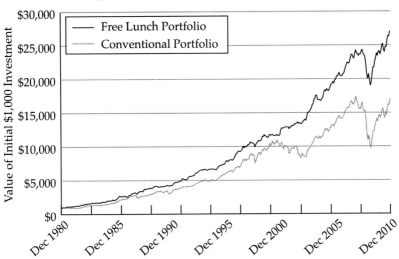

Figure 60. *The specific indexes and funds used to create these portfolios are detailed in the Table of Figures section at the back of this book. More details on how you can create your own Free Lunch portfolio are provided in the Action section for this Myth.*

Throughout the 30 year period, the Free Lunch portfolio outperformed the Conventional portfolio but with less risk exposure. Most importantly, because it is more broadly diversified than the Conventional portfolio, the Free Lunch portfolio also sailed through the financial crisis with much less damage. After a brief drawdown of just 22% – half that of the 44% drawdown suffered by the Conventional portfolio – the Free Lunch portfolio quickly resumed its long-term performance trend. The result is that the Free Lunch portfolio earned higher returns (11.6% vs. 9.9% for the Conventional portfolio) but with substantially less risk. Higher returns and lower risk. This is a free lunch. But it doesn't stop there.

Because of the dramatic difference in the risk levels of the Conventional and Free Lunch portfolios, when you invest pursuant to the Free Lunch portfolio you have an option. You can accept the slightly higher expected returns and substantially lower risk that the Free Lunch portfolio offers over the Conventional portfolio; or you can position the Free Lunch portfolio to earn higher returns while still being exposed to substantially lower risk (as measured by the maximum drawdown) than in the Conventional portfolio. In the following example I will increase the "leverage" of the Free Lunch portfolio to the level where the volatility of the portfolio's returns equals that of the Conventional portfolio. I do this by increasing the portfolio's allocation to the single-most diversified constituent of the Free Lunch portfolio, as described in the Action section for this myth. This is the Global Trading component as represented by the CTA composite compiled by Barclay Hedge (which was discussed in Myth #12). Since most CTAs offer the ability for investors to customize the risk exposure in their accounts, it is possible to increase exposure to the CTA composite without reducing exposure to any of the other constituents of the portfolio. (This is explained in detail in the Action section for this myth.) Increasing exposure produces the following "leveraged" performance for what I will now refer to as the Free Lunch MR (Moderate Risk) portfolio.

What is obvious from Figure 61 is that performance improves dramatically. A $1,000 investment in the Free Lunch MR portfolio grows to more than twice the value as $1,000 placed in the Conventional portfolio. What is less obvious, and counter-intuitive to those who have not yet read this book, is that it did so with lower risk. While the Conventional portfolio dropped 44% in value during the financial crisis, requiring a person to have serious fortitude to maintain their positions, the Free Lunch MR portfolio fell just 21%. This is a testament to its true diversification across a broad range of return drivers, many of which powered profits during the financial crisis. These helped to offset the massive stock market and real estate losses.

Performance of Free Lunch Moderate Risk Portfolio Compared with Free Lunch Portfolio & Conventional Portfolio

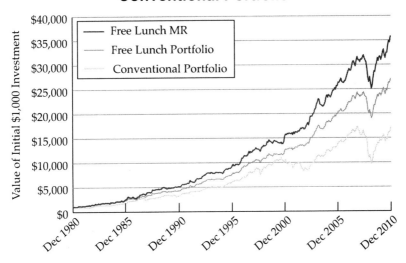

Figure 61. *The specific indexes and funds used to create these portfolios are detailed in the Table of Figures section at the back of this book. Specific actions you can take to create your own Free Lunch portfolio are provided in the Action section for this Myth.*

The Free Lunch MR portfolio, because of its increased exposure to trading strategies that performed well during the crisis, suffered an even smaller drawdown than did the standard Free Lunch portfolio, despite its additional leverage. An improvement in other performance and risk measures, such as the percentage of profitable years, also makes it much easier for investors to maintain their positions in the Free Lunch portfolios compared with the Conventional portfolio.

As a final exercise, let's look at the performance we could achieve if we were to accept the same level of volatility in the Free Lunch portfolio as people are willing to accept by putting money into an S&P 500 Index fund. I refer to this as Free Lunch AR (for "Aggressive Risk") portfolio. Despite its name, because of the broad diversity of return drivers powering the returns of the Free Lunch AR portfolio, its maximum draw-down, and indication of its exposure to Event Risk, is still well under half that of the S&P 500 (Figure 62).

Performance Comparison of Free Lunch Portfolios to Conventional Portfolio and S&P 500 TR Index

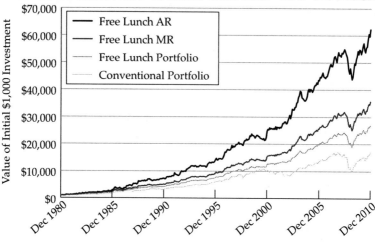

Figure 62

The results are truly spectacular. For less risk than people are willing to accept by putting money into an S&P 500 index fund, the Free Lunch AR portfolio produces a 14.8% annualized return, 40% greater than that of the S&P 500 TR Index. The final result is that the Free Lunch AR portfolio grows to more than three times the size of the Conventional portfolio, while suffering just a 20% maximum drawdown (compared with more than 50% for the S&P 500 and 44% for the Conventional portfolio). This dramatic improvement in performance and significantly reduced drawdown is the measure of the value of true portfolio diversification.

Performance Comparison:
Free Lunch Portfolios & Conventional Portfolio

	S&P 500 TR Index	Conven- tional Portfolio	Free Lunch Portfolio	Free Lunch MR Portfolio	Free Lunch AR Portfolio
Years	30	30	30	30	30
Avg. Annual Return	10.54%	9.91%	11.62%	12.66%	14.77%
Annualized Volatility	15.48%	11.49%	9.07%	11.49%	15.48%
Maximum Drawdown	-51%	-44%	-22%	-21%	-20%
Profitable Months	62%	66%	65%	60%	57%
Prof. Rolling 12-Mos.	78%	80%	96%	93%	92%
Profitable Years	80%	77%	93%	93%	93%

Figure 63

This beneficial performance and risk profile of the Free Lunch portfolios compared to the Conventional portfolio and the S&P 500 Total Return Index are shown in Figure 63.

Another way to view the benefits of the true portfolio diversification of the Free Lunch portfolios is displayed in Figure 64. This chart shows the ratio of the annualized returns to the maximum drawdowns for the S&P 500, the Conventional portfolio and the three Free Lunch portfolios. All of the Free Lunch portfolios provide risk-adjusted returns that are up to four times better than the S&P 500 Total Return Index alone and more than three times better than the Conventional portfolio. This is the natural result of the true portfolio diversification inherent in the Free Lunch portfolios.

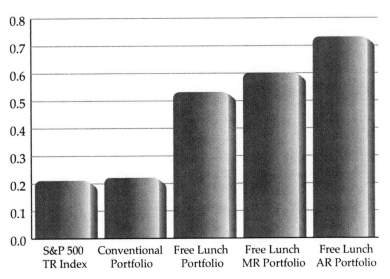

Ratio of Annual Return to Maximum Drawdown For the S&P 500 TR Index & Conventional Portfolio vs. the Free Lunch Portfolios

Figure 64. *The specific indexes and funds used to create these portfolios are detailed in the Table of Figures section at the back of this book. Specific actions you can take to create your own Free Lunch portfolio are provided in the Action section for this Myth.*

There is a free lunch and it is available for you to enjoy. In the Action section for this myth I will describe in detail the composition of the Free Lunch portfolios and provide you with specific actions you can take to create your own Free Lunch portfolio.

Bon appétit.

SUMMARY
MYTH 20

- Drawdowns are the greatest impediment to high returns and are the true measure of risk.

- True portfolio diversification provides the highest returns over time.

- The predictability of future performance can be increased by expanding the number of diverse return drivers employed in a portfolio.

- There is a Free Lunch in investing. It is possible to earn higher returns with less risk. A Free Lunch is obtained by creating a portfolio that is truly diversified across multiple return drivers.

EPILOGUE

I conceived of this book at the peak of the last great U.S. stock market bubble – in 1999. Paradoxically, if I had written it then, when it would have proven extremely valuable to investors over the ensuing decade, it would not have been accepted. In fact, I am certain it would have been derisively ridiculed. People believed that strongly in the myths. They were entranced by the siren call of buying and holding stocks, despite the unnecessary risk that imposed on their portfolios.

After a hiatus, I began writing *Jackass Investing* in 2003. Even then the prevailing wisdom was that those who hadn't panicked and sold their stocks during the great bear of the early 2000s were soon to be rewarded for their virtuous behavior. This book would have been ridiculed then as well. Like many ambitious projects, this book took a back seat to other more pressing business and personal needs and lay unfinished until the financial crisis of 2008 demanded its completion.

As many of the financial abuses of the past were exposed to the light of truth in late 2008 and early 2009, I realized that exposing the myths of investing was more than just that. The book was also a way of awakening people to a safer method of managing their portfolios. I also realized that the working title for the book, *Exploiting the Myths,* didn't have the impact that was required to reach the broadest possible audience. Jackass Investing has that impact and also serves as the definition of taking unnecessary financial risks. As a result, this book has been dually released under both titles.

I'd like to believe that the events of the first decade of the 21st century, such as the Enron fraud, credit rating agencies' conflicts-of-interest and Lehman Brothers risk exposures, would remind people of the need for them to take better control of their portfolios and to diversify them in order to reduce risks. Unfortunately, the loudest chorus I hear continues to come from those who led them to their losses in the first place. The financial industry publications and professionals that, perhaps because of their failure to protect their readers and clients from great financial loss, continue to stress that there was "no place to hide" and that "everything went down" during the financial crisis of 2008. If nothing else, *Jackass Investing* has taught you that is just not true.

That leaves you with two clear choices: continue to do what you've been doing and hope for different results – this is Albert Einstein's definition of insanity – or change your approach. *Jackass Investing* provides you with just such a path to follow to do the latter. There is only one way to achieve consistent returns over time and across a variety of market and economic conditions. That is to diversify the return drivers and trading strategies in your portfolio. Fortunately it is not hard to do. Past performance, if it is based on a single return driver or baseline condition, is absolutely not indicative of future performance. This statement holds true regardless of the length of the track record. That is because conditions will change. When they do the past performance that was recorded under the old conditions is no longer relevant. The only thing that matters going forward is how that trading strategy will perform under the new conditions. Every trading strategy encounters angry environments that are hostile to that strategy. But other return drivers powering the performance of other trading strategies may thrive in that new angry environment – angry for the first trading strategy.

The myths presented in this book expose just a subset of the unnecessary risks – the myths – that permeate conventional wisdom and can cost you money. And the actions presented in the Action section at www. JackassInvesting.com/actions are just some of the potentially hundreds of actions that you can take to exploit the myths for profit. The sample portfolios exhibited in Myth #20 are just a few of the almost unlimited number of diversified portfolios that can be constructed. It's impossible to point to any single action or any single portfolio and say "that's best." But it is easy to point to any of them and say "that's better." Better than the conventional financial wisdom that incites people to place the majority of their hard-earned money on a single bet. Better than the 60-40 asset allocation that has been preached. Certainly better than the myth of "buy-and-hold" that has become the doctrine, or perhaps the excuse, that underlies conventional financial wisdom.

It's always puzzled me why people perpetuate myths rather than uncover the true facts or, better yet, take advantage of the truth. Rather than understanding and capitalizing on the benefits of short selling, or futures trading, or true portfolio diversification, they fight them. If only they'd take the energy they expend on fighting and learn to embrace the benefits, they could turn their poor-folios into truly diversified, profitable portfolios. Perhaps, pursuant to Einstein's definition, they're insane. But you don't have to be.

You don't need to know every myth or to employ every Action in order to avoid a poor-folio and create a diversified portfolio. Every step you take in that direction is a positive improvement. In fact, there is no "final" portfolio – just continual improvements. Make the decision today, right now, to change your behavior. How you got to where you are today financially is irrelevant. The only path that matters is the future path. And that is entirely within your control.

ACKNOWLEDGMENTS

In any project that takes ten years from conception to completion, as did the writing of this book, there are many people to thank for their support. At the top of my list comes **my wife Kim** and **sons Mitchell, Matthew and Charley,** who began to joke whenever I replied to some obscure reference to sports, music, magic or investing they brought up with "that's in the book!" My partner at Brandywine Asset Management, **Rob Proctor, CFA,** who uniquely combines an innovative investment mind with strict investment discipline; and **Michael Luterman,** who developed the technology used to back-test many of the trading strategies presented in this book. Research assistance was provided by **John Phillips, CFA,** a former researcher for Brandywine who is both a passionate and knowledgeable investor, and now a consultant; **Roger Schreiner** of Schreiner Capital Management, a leader in active investment management; **Robb Ross** of White Indian Trading, who has developed more than 1,000 trading strategies during 25 years of trading; **Fred Gehm,** formerly Brandywine's Director of Research, and the author of several books on investing including the forthcoming, *Trust is Not an Option: Evaluating and Selecting Investment Managers*; **Holly Miller,** co-author of the book *The Top Ten Operational Risks: A Survival Guide for Investment Management Firms and Hedge Funds*; **Leslie Masonson,** author of the book *Buy – Don't Hold,* who contributed research on trend following strategies; **Vincent Deluard** of TrimTabs Investment Research, who contributed data for sentiment-based trading strategies; Professor **Chris Geczy, Ph.D.,** Academic Director of the Wharton Wealth Management Initiative at the Aresty Institute of Executive Education of the Wharton School and investment consultant; **Jeff Trewella, Ph.D.,** who assisted with the early drafts of this book and identified many of the myths; and **Doug Bloom,** who helped clarify the most important investment themes and provided editorial assistance. I am extremely grateful to **Matthew Pinto,** who has one of the best minds in the publishing industry, for providing his expertise in editing, marketing and publishing.

The various studies and Actions presented in the book and at the www.JackassInvesting.com web site would not have been possible without accurate data and I would like to gratefully acknowledge the contribution of data providers Barclay Hedge, Pertrac, Zacks Investment Research, the American Association of Individual Investors, Investors Intelligence and TrimTabs Investment Research. Barclay Hedge (www.barclayhedge.com) is a leading provider of performance information for the managed futures and hedge fund industries. Pertrac (www.pertrac. com) provided performance data for many of the indexes referenced throughout the book. Zacks Investment Research (www.zacksdata.com) provided more than 30 years of financial data on over 16,000 active and inactive US and Canadian equities. The American Association of Individual Investors (AAII) (www.aaii.com) provided the descriptions and results of the trading strategies presented in the Action sections for Myth #1 and Myth #6, as well as investor survey data. Additional sentiment data was also provided by Investors Intelligence (www.investorsintelligence.com), a leading provider of research and technical analysis. TrimTabs Investment Research (www.trimtabs.com), provided both fund flow data as well as the basis for the trading strategy presented in the Action section for Myth #3.

GLOSSARY

Accredited Investor is a person with a $1 million net worth, exclusive of their primary residence, or an annual income of $200,000 (or $300,000 if filing jointly with their spouse).

Active mutual funds or ETFs are those that trade more frequently than passive funds (see "passive").

Annualized is a measure of a market's return that accounts for the effect of compounding. This means that (in the case of a positive return) as the initial investment grows, it will earn the same return each year on an increasing investment size. For example, an initial $1,000 investment that earns a 10% annualized return will grow to $1,610 at the end of five years. This is also referred to as the "compound annual return."

Basis point is 1/100 of 1%.

Bear is the term used to describe a falling market.

Bull is the term used to describe a rising market.

Capitalization is the total value of a company's stock that has been issued and is available to be traded.

Cyclical is the term used to define a bull or bear market that lasts for a few years at most. There may be several cyclical bull and bear market trends that occur within one "secular" bull or bear market.

Drawdown is what occurs when the value of any investment falls from a peak price to a lower price and is usually expressed in percentage terms. A drop from $10 to $8 for example is a drawdown of 20%. See "maximum drawdown."

ETF is the acronym for "Exchange Traded Fund." These are similar to mutual funds, in that they track baskets of stocks, bonds, commodities or other assets, but trade like a stock on an exchange throughout the day.

ETN is the acronym for "Exchange Traded Note." This is similar to an ETF, which was defined in Myth #4, in that it tracks baskets of stocks, bonds, commodities or other assets. It differs in that the note is issued by a financial firm and therefore faces the risk that if the issuer goes bankrupt, the ETN may not repay the promised return.

Flat is the term used to describe holding no position in a financial instrument such as a stock or bond. See "long" and "short."

Jackass Investing is the act of taking unnecessary risks when investing your money.

Long is the description used to refer to a person who has bought and owns a financial instrument such as a stock or bond. Being long has nothing to do with how *long* the position is held. You can hold a long position for mere seconds; you are still "long." See also "flat" and "short."

Maximum Drawdown is the largest percentage loss that occurred in a drawdown before the previous peak price is once again exceeded. See "drawdown."

Mean reversion is a type of trading strategy that takes a position in a market when the price of that market diverges significantly from the normal, or "mean," price of that market, or its relationship to other markets, with the expectation that the price will "revert" back to the mean.

Passive mutual funds or ETFs are those that follow a low-turnover approach, meaning they infrequently change the positions in their portfolios. They often track market indexes such as the S&P 500. See "active."

S&P 500 Total Return Index is a measure of the aggregate performance of 500 stocks, including the reinvestment of dividends. A detailed description of the S&P 500 is contained in Myth #4.

Secular is the term used to define a bull or bear market that encompasses the longest trends, often decades in length. There may be multiple "cyclical" bull and bear markets within one secular bull or bear market.

Short is the term used to describe having sold a financial instrument, such as a stock, bond or futures contract, when the previous position was "flat." Selling short is described in more detail in Myth #10. The holder of a short position profits as a stock, bond or futures contract drops in price.

Short squeeze is what occurs when the price of a stock or other financial instrument rises and investors who sold the stock short rush to buy it to cover their short positions. As the price of the stock increases, more short sellers feel driven to cover their positions, thereby pushing the stock price up even further.

Standard deviation See "volatility."

Stock split a company makes the decision to "split" their stock to make it appear more "affordable." A 2-for-1 stock split means that the company issues every shareholder an additional share of stock for each share they already own. This does not create any additional value, as the market price will immediately adjust for this by dropping to half its previous price. A stock split is often effected by a company when its share price rises to a price that is well above that of similar companies.

Tranche is one of a number of related securities offered as part of the same transaction. The word tranche is French for slice, section, series, or portion.

Volatility is a measure of the variability of returns. It can be calculated daily, monthly or annually. The figure represents the range of returns, around the mean return, that can be expected to occur in two out of every three periods. For example, if the annualized return is 10% and the annualized volatility is 8%, then in two out of every three years it can be expected that the annualized return will range from 2% to 18% (10% ± 8%). This is also referred to more precisely as "standard deviation."

TABLE OF FIGURES

Myth #1:

Figure 3: Effect of Earnings Growth and People's Enthusiasm On Stock Prices

This study uses linear regression analysis to determine the degree to which variance in the S&P 500 Total Return Index over various holding periods (1, 2, 5, 10, 20 and 30 years) was explained by the changes in nominal earnings and changes in P/E. A 10 year average was used to represent both the nominal earnings and the "E" in the P/E in order to reduce the impact of economic cycles. The regression analysis included three separate regression calculations for each holding period. The first regression measured the goodness of fit for changes in average earnings versus S&P total returns. The second regression measured the goodness of fit for changes in the P/E versus S&P total return. The third regression includes the two parameters, average earnings and P/E, versus S&P 500 total returns.

Since linear regression assumes orthogonality of the independent variables, that assumption was tested on all of the holding period data. The Percentage change in the nominal earnings versus the P/E ratio had R^2 values ranging from 2% to 6% across all holding periods, suggesting the two regression parameters are mostly independent of each other. Furthermore, the two-parameter regressions were found to explain greater than 93% of the variance in the S&P 500 total return over each holding period. Since nearly all of the variance in the S&P 500 return is captured by the two parameter regression we normalized the R^2 result from each of the single parameter regressions to 100% for use in Figure 3.

The use of the single parameter R^2 to measure the explanatory power of the S&P 500 total return for the two regression variables is an approximation. The subtle (<6%) correlation between the independent variables and the synergy that occurs for the two-variable regression requires cautious interpretation. The results shown in the graph display an estimate of the relative contribution of the change in earnings and the change in P/E towards the change in the S&P 500 returns

Myth #12:

Figure 36: Performance Comparison – S&P 500 TR vs. Trend Following in Five Stock Index Futures for the 20-year Period 1991 – 2010.

The five stock index futures in the trend following portfolio are: S&P 500, DAX 30, FTSE 100, CAC40, Nikkei 225 & Hang Seng indexes. The starting date for the DAX 30 was December 1991. All other contracts are included in the portfolio from the start date of January 1991. Includes interest on cash balance equal to 50% of the 90-day T-bill rate. For comparison purposes, the allocation to the markets in the trend following portfolio were adjusted to equal the same return earned by the S&P 500 TR Index over the same period.

Myth #17:

Figure 49: Correlation Comparison: Traditional Asset Classes vs. Trading Strategies in this Book.

The "Asset Classes" and trading strategies and the first month each was used in correlation calculation (the last month used in the correlation calculation is December 2010) are as follows: U.S. stocks is the S&P 500 TR (Jan 1981), Int'l Stocks is the MSCI All-World ex-USA (Jan 1981), Real Estate is the NAREIT REIT index (Jan 1981), U.S. Bonds is the Barclay Aggregate Bond Index (Jan 1981), Int'l Bonds is the Barclays Capital Int'l Treasury Bond ETF (BWX)(Oct 2007), CAN SLIM as described in Action section for Myth #6 (Jan 1998), Piotroski as described in Action section for Myth #1 (Jan 1998), MN Fund is the JP Morgan Research Market Neutral Fund (JMNAX)(Jun 2002), BTOP 50 is the Barclay Hedge index as described in Myth #12 (Jan 1987), Trend Follow is the trend following trading strategy as described in the Action section for Myth #7 (Jan 1991). See the Table of Figures note for Myth #20, Figure 59 for a description of the composition of the Conventional Portfolio.

Myth #18:

Figure 50: Performance of Conventional Wisdom During the Bear Market of 2007-2009.

US Large is the S&P500TR; US Mid is the S&P400TR; US Small is the S&P600TR; Developed is the MSCI All-World ex US; Emerging is the MSCI Emerging Market Index; Frontier is the MSCI Frontier Country Index; US Bonds is the Barclay Aggregate bonds; HY Bonds is the Barclay High Yield Bonds; Int. Bonds is the SPDR BWX (Barclays Capital International Treasury Bonds); Real Estate is the NAREIT All REITs Index; Equal Weight is an equal allocation of 10% of the portfolio made to each component each month.

Figure 51: Performance of Trading Strategies vs. Conventional Wisdom During the Bear Market of 2007-2009.

Piotroski as described in Action section for Myth #1; CAN SLIM as described in Action section for Myth #6; BTOP 50 as described in Myth #12; Trend portfolio as described in Action section for Myth #7.

Myth #19:

Figure 56: Results of Combining S&P 500 Total Return Index with its Inverse.

The weighting of the inverse of the S&P 500 Total Return Index used in this graph is 50% that of the actual S&P 500 Total Return Index. For example, when the S&P 500 Total Return Index lost 37% in 2008, the Inverse Index produced a return of +18.5%, which is 50% of the inverse of the -37% return produced by the S&P 500 Total Return Index.

Myth #20:

Additional details on the composition of the Free Lunch portfolios can be found in the Action section for this book at www.JackassInvesting.com/actions.

Figure 59: Composition of Conventional Diversified Portfolio.

The allocations made to the constituents of the Conventional portfolio that are presented in the following table are based on an examination of the allocations made by various "Target Date" funds. Target Date funds attempt to create "optimally diversified" portfolios by allocating to various investments based on the amount of time remaining until a specific date. Depending on years remaining until the target date, these funds recommend approximately a 60% to 90% allocation to stocks and a 10% to 40% allocation to bonds, REITs and cash. As you know from reading this book, these funds certainly don't provide an optimal allocation, but what they do represent is an average composite of what is considered to be Conventional portfolio diversification. The allocation to each constituent and the index or fund performance used to calculate the historical performance of the Conventional portfolio is based on the approximate allocations used by Target Date funds designed for people with 25 years remaining until retirement.

Composition of the Conventional Portfolio

Constituent	Period Used
U.S. Large Cap Stocks: 1%	
S&P 500 TR index	Jan 1981 – Jan 1993
SPY	Feb 1993 – Dec 2010
U.S. Mid Cap Stocks: 1%	
S&P 400 TR index	Feb 1991 – Aug 1995
MDY	Sept 1995 – Dec 2010
U.S. Small Cap Stocks: 1%	
S&P 600 TR index	Jan 1994 – May 2000
IJR	June 2000 – Dec 2010
Equal-weighted Large Cap: 2%	
RSP	June 2003 - Dec 2010
Individual Corporate Fundamentals: 2%	
PRF	Jan 2006 - Dec 2010
Dividend Increases: 2%	
VIG	June 2006 - Dec 2010
Insider Sentiment: 2%	
Sabrient Insider Sentiment index	Jan 1997 - Sept 2006
NFO	Oct 2006 - Dec 2010
Selective Small Cap Stocks: 1%	
Piotroski Trading Strategy (Action #1)	Jan 1998 – Dec 2010
Selective Growth Stocks: 1%	
CAN SLIM Trading Strategy (Action #6)	Jan 1998 – Dec 2010
Large Cap Liquidity: 3%	
AZLPX	June 2010 – Dec 2010
Small Cap Liquidity: 3%	
AZSPX	June 2010 – Dec 2010
Market Timing - Investor Sentiment:2%	
Trading Strategy (Action #3)	Jan 1981 – Jan 2007
Sector Timing: 3%	
Trading Strategy (Action #8)	Jan 1981 – Jan 2007

Figures 60-64 reference the composition of the Free Lunch portfolios. The allocation to each constituent and the data used to calculate the performance of the Free Lunch portfolios is as follows:

Composition of the Free Lunch Portfolios

Constituent	Period Used
U.S. Large Cap Stocks: 1%	
S&P 500 TR index	Jan 1981 – Jan 1993
SPY	Feb 1993 – Dec 2010
U.S. Mid Cap Stocks: 1%	
S&P 400 TR index	Feb 1991 – Aug 1995
MDY	Sept 1995 – Dec 2010
U.S. Small Cap Stocks: 1%	
S&P 600 TR index	Jan 1994 – May 2000
IJR	June 2000 – Dec 2010
Equal-weighted Large Cap: 2%	
RSP	June 2003 - Dec 2010
Individual Corporate Fundamentals: 2%	
PRF	Jan 2006 - Dec 2010
Dividend Increases: 2%	
VIG	June 2006 - Dec 2010
Insider Sentiment: 2%	
Sabrient Insider Sentiment index	Jan 1997 - Sept 2006
NFO	Oct 2006 - Dec 2010
Selective Small Cap Stocks: 1%	
Piotroski Trading Strategy (Action #1)	Jan 1998 – Dec 2010
Selective Growth Stocks: 1%	
CAN SLIM Trading Strategy (Action #6)	Jan 1998 – Dec 2010
Large Cap Liquidity: 3%	
AZLPX	June 2010 – Dec 2010
Small Cap Liquidity: 3%	
AZSPX	June 2010 – Dec 2010
Market Timing - Investor Sentiment:2%	
Trading Strategy (Action #3)	Jan 1981 – Jan 2007
Sector Timing: 3%	
Trading Strategy (Action #8)	Jan 1981 – Jan 2007

Continued on next page

Composition of the Free Lunch Portfolios (continued)

Constituent	Period Used
Market Neutral U.S. Stocks: 6%	
JMNAX	June 2002 – Dec 2010
Long-Short U.S. Stocks: 6%	
TFSMX	Oct 2004 – Dec 2010
Developed World Stocks: 1%	
MSCI All-World ex USA:	Jan 1981 – Jan 2007
CWI	Feb 2007 – Dec 2010
Emerging Markets Stocks: 3%	
MSCI Emerging Markets index:	Jan 1988 – Mar 2005
VWO	Apr 2005 – Dec 2010
Frontier Markets Stocks: 3%	
MSCI Frontier Markets index:	June 2002 – Jan 2009
FRNMX:	Apr 2005 – Dec 2010
International Market Timing: 3%	
Trading Strategy (Action #16)	Jan 1981 – Jan 2007
Aggregate U.S. Bonds: 4%	
Barclay Aggregate Bond index:	Jan 1981 – Sept 2003
AGG	Oct 2003 – Dec 2010
U.S. High-yield Bonds: 4%	
Barclay High Yield Bond index:	July 1983 – Feb 2008
JNK	Mar 2008 – Dec 2010
International Bonds: 4%	
BWX	Nov 2007 – Dec 2010
U.S. Real Estate: 5%	
FTSE NAREIT US – All REITs:	Jan 1981 – Dec 1994
MSCI US REIT index:	Jan 1995 – Oct 2004
VNQ	Nov 2004 – Dec 2010
Credit & Equity Arbitrage: 6%	
HFRI Fund-weighted Composite index	Jan 1990 - Dec 2008
ADANX	Jan 2009 - Dec 2010
Currency Carry Trade: 3%	
Deutsche Bank Currency Future Harvest	Jan 1994 - Sept 2006
DBV	Oct 2006 – Dec 2010

Continued on next page

Composition of the Free Lunch Portfolios (continued)

Global trading of currencies, interest rates, stock indexes, energy, metals, and agricultural markets can be obtained through allocations to diversified managed futures accounts or funds, as detailed in Action #20. The contributive performance for this portion of the unleveraged Free Lunch portfolio was derived from a combination of two indexes (prior to October 2010) plus, more recently, four funds (as shown below). The allocations indicated for each constituent is an approximation based on the composition of those indexes and mutual funds.

Constituent	Period Used
Global Currency Trading: 6%	
Currencies - Momentum	
Currencies - Fundamentals	
Currencies - Cross-rates	
Global Interest Rate Trading: 6%	
Interest Rates - Momentum	
Interest Rates - Fundamentals	
Interest Rates - Yield Curves	
Global Stock Index Trading: 5%	
Stock Indexes - Momentum	
Stock Indexes - Fundamentals	
Stock Indexes - Relative Value	
Energy Trading: 3%	
Energy - Momentum	
Energy - Fundamentals	
Energy - Relative Value	
Metals Trading: 3%	
Metals - Momentum	
Metals - Fundamentals	
Metals - Relative Value	
Agricultural Trading: 5%	
Agriculturals - Momentum	
Agriculturals - Fundamentals	
Agriculturals - Relative Value	
Barclay CTA index	Jan 1981 - Dec 1986
Barclay BTOP 50 index	Jan 1987 - Sept 2010
4 Funds: MFTAX, MHFAX , AMFAX & RYMFX	Oct 2010 - Dec 2010

Prior to the starting date of any constituent of any of the portfolios, its allocation in the portfolio was distributed on a pro rata basis to each of the other constituents that were already included in the portfolio. The returns displayed in Myth #20 are the composite of the returns earned by each constituent. The performance of each constituent has been adjusted for the costs that would be incurred by a person replicating this portfolio by using mutual funds, ETFs or managed accounts.

INDEX

ABOUT THE AUTHOR

Michael Dever has been on the front line of investment innovation and trading for more than 30 years. After three years of private research and trading he founded Brandywine Asset Management in 1982. For the past three decades, Mr. Dever and Brandywine have been entrusted to manage the money of global banks, major corporations and high net worth individuals who have been attracted to Mr. Dever's innovative investment philosophy. His out-of-the-box thinking and investment success have also made him a featured subject of three books, *Bulls, Bears and Millionaires, Market Beaters* and *The Investor's Guide to Hedge Funds.*

In addition to his investment management background, Mr. Dever is also a technology entrepreneur. He founded spree.com, one of the first ecommerce communities, in 1996. Spree grew to being the 7th most trafficked ecommerce web site by 1998. Following a venture funding round in 1999, Mr. Dever left spree and founded Mind Drivers, a venture development company that has launched and grown Internet-based technology companies such as Internetseer and marine.com.

Today, Mr. Dever devotes his time to running Brandywine Asset Management, which follows Mr. Dever's Return Driver based methodology to trade broadly diversified portfolios in the global currency, interest rate, stock index, metals, energy and agricultural cash, futures and options markets.

Mr. Dever lives near Philadelphia, Pennsylvania with his wife Kim and three sons, Mitchell, Matthew and Charley. He has a bachelor degree in business from West Chester University (1981) and obtained his CERTIFIED FINANCIAL PLANNER™ certification in 1985.

More information can be found at www.brandywine.com.